THE LITERARY HISTORY

OF ENGLAND

THE

LITERARY HISTORY

OF

ENGLAND

IN THE END OF THE EIGHTEENTH AND BEGINNING

OF THE NINETEENTH CENTURY

BY MRS. OLIPHANT

AUTHOR OF 'MAKERS OF FLORENCE,' ETC.

"Reading maketh a full man."—BACON, *On Study.*
"A good book is the precious life-blood of a master spirit embalmed and
treasured up on purpose to a life beyond life."—MILTON, *Areopagitica.*
"Je ne voyage sans livres, ny en paix, ny en guerre. C'est la meilleure munition
que j'aye trouvé à cet humain voyage."—MONTAIGNE, Livre iii. Chap. iii.
"Books are the legacies that a great genius leaves to mankind." — ADDISON,
Spectator.

IN THREE VOLUMES

VOL. III.

New York

MACMILLAN AND CO.

1882

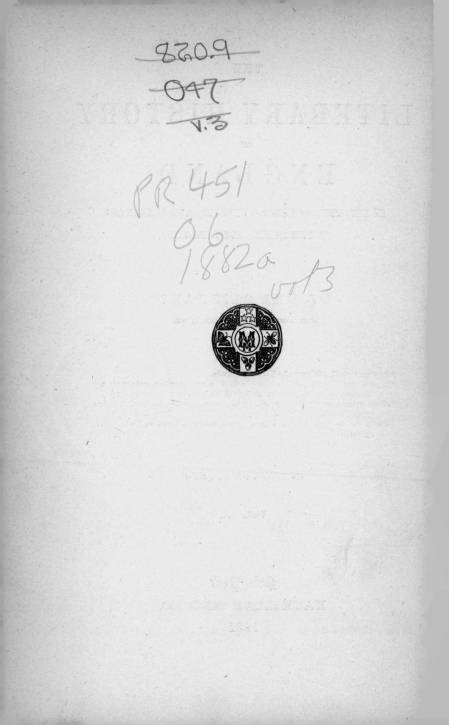

CONTENTS.

CHAPTER I.

CHAPTER II.

CHAPTER III.

CHAPTER IV.

CHAPTER V.

CHAPTER VI.

CHAPTER VII.

CHAPTER VIII.

CHAPTER IX.

THE LITERARY HISTORY OF ENGLAND.

CHAPTER I.

LONDON : THE UPPER CIRCLE : ROGERS—BYRON—MOORE.

IT is Talfourd, we think, in his *Memorials of Charles Lamb,* who compared the cheerful whist parties in those little rooms high up among the housetops of the Temple, where the brother and sister held their homely court, with the much more ambitious home of the muses, in the gorgeous and stately retirement of Holland House. Nothing could more clearly exemplify the difference between London *bourgeois* and literary, and London fashionable, elegant, and lettered. The former is poor and homely, and familiar in all its circumstances—the other, brilliant in external aspect, much farther reaching in its associations, and full of that involuntary consciousness of being the very best and finest development of society, which is only kept from the height of arrogance by being involuntary, and with no possibility of doubt or argument about it. A glimmer of uncertainty as to whether they are really the great people they think themselves to be, will dash the confidence of the most self-sufficing circles on a lower level. The grand distinction of a society which is socially elevated as well as

B

mentally distinguished, is that the mere force of circumstances takes away all doubt upon the matter. However determinedly your man of letters may assert that he is Sir Oracle, the dogs will bark whatever he may say; but when he is a great potentate besides, these vulgar voices are hushed in awe, and nothing contradicts his conviction. It is true that there are audacious persons now-a-days to whom Holland House with all its grandeurs, and the bated breath with which the initiated once spoke of that abode of the gods, and the undisclosed anxiety with which they hoped to please its Juno and Jupiter, have an amusing, half-pathetic side — as showing at once the smallness of the finest shrine, and the pettiness of the most elevated humanity. The poorer and less important sphere, where outside circumstances are nothing, and where men are free to exhibit themselves and their characteristics in their own way, has all the advantage with posterity. We cannot get free of the splendid rooms, fine enough to have an art-history of their own like a mediæval city, nor even in a lesser way can we get free of Rogers's view over the park, his pictures and his luxuries. But there they stand, the other side of this world of literature, mingled with all the flutter of society, the gossip of lords and ladies, the scraps of politics, the secrets of antechambers, all that spray of social life, if we may use such an expression, which fills the air, and confuses the view. Something is gained, indeed, for wherever imperial interests are touched upon there is, at the worst, a *faux air* of enlargement and noble aim, and at the best, a real dignity which mere individualism rarely supplies; but at the same time there is something lost, for it is difficult to make the flattered members of that " best society" aware that the greater part of their enlightenment is merely gossip, and the knowledge of what is going on " behind the scenes," on which they pride themselves, no more than the revelations of the back stairs.

Holland House, however, is unquestionably the most important and brilliant centre of literary society that we have known in England in recent days. It was the headquarters of a band of visitors on whom it conferred distinction, and who gave more distinction than they received. Naturally those who did not receive the flattering compliment of admission indemnified themselves by gibes and satirical assaults : while those who did, occasionally avenged the pricks and scorns to which they were subject under such a despotism, by after-revelations of discontent and rebellion. The master of the house was a man of some literary power and much accomplishment, whose modest hope expressed at the end of his life that, as " nephew of Fox and friend of Grey," he had cast no discredit on his position, conciliates the good opinion of posterity. But he was only a sort of good-natured god in this temple of the muses, often retired altogether from public view, veiled by illness, by gout and invalid habit from contact too close and general ; while the ever active ruler of the community, familiar and imperious, a genial but sharp-tongued despot, exacting much worship, and spreading an atmosphere of awe around her, was Lady Holland, a woman who evidently added to the skill which could collect and manage the different elements of society, a great deal of that witty disregard for other people's feelings which keeps a little community in excitement and amusement, but leaves many a rankling recollection to come forth afterwards in bitter depreciation of the splendid reign and too autocratic rule. The mistress of a *salon*, who exclaims with serious concern, " What a pity ! but couldn't you suppress it ? " when one of her friends informs her he is about to publish a poem ; who told Moore that his *Life of Sheridan* was a dull book, and interrupted Macaulay in his brilliant talk with, " Come, Macaulay, we have had enough of this," must have been a somewhat

alarming person. In most of the records of the society
which she collected round her, a sense of her somewhat
arrogant superiority, her careless treatment of the distinguished guests whose presence alone made her fine house
more remarkable than other fine houses, is quite apparent.
She treated them all with that mingling of admiration and
contempt, condescension and flattery, which is so usual an
attitude of the rich and great towards Art and its professors in general; but in her case, the bold sincerity of
rudeness, the tantalising attractions of a caprice never
to be calculated upon, and the charms of an unusually
splendid and magnificent house, which it was a matter of
pride to be connected with, made the guests endure,
although it was impossible to prevent them from resenting.
Macaulay has left the most graceful and benignant
description of this great coterie, in magnanimous indifference to any of the snubs he received there. He was
always fond of the idea of decadence and hoar antiquity
falling upon the scenes with which he was acquainted;
but Holland House still exists, defying all such gloomy
imaginations.

" The time is coming when perhaps a few old men, the last sur-
vivors of our generation, will in vain seek among new streets and
squares, and railway stations, for the site of that dwelling which
was in their youth the favourite resort of wits and beauties, of
painters and poets, of scholars, philosophers, and statesmen. They
will then remember with strange tenderness many objects once
familiar to them, the avenue and the terrace, the busts and the
paintings, the carving, the grotesque gilding, the enigmatical
mottoes. With peculiar fondness they will recall that venerable
chamber, in which all the antique gravity of a college library was
so singularly blended with all that female grace and wit could
devise to embellish a drawing-room. They will recollect, not
unmoved, those shelves laden with all the varied learning of many
lands and many ages, and those portraits in which were preserved
the features of the best and wisest Englishmen of two generations.
They will recollect how many men who have guided the politics of
Europe who have moved great assemblies by reason and eloquence,

who have put life into bronze and canvas, or who have left to
posterity things so written as it shall not willingly let them die,
were there mixed with all that was loveliest and gayest in the
society of the most splendid of capitals.   They will remember the
peculiar character which belonged to that circle, in which every
talent and accomplishment, every art and science, had its place.
They will remember how the last debate was discussed in one
corner, and the last comedy of Scribe in another ; while Wilkie
gazed with modest admiration at Sir Joshua's Baretti ; while
Mackintosh turned over Thomas Aquinas to verify a quotation ;
while Talleyrand related his conversations with Barras at the
Luxembourg, or his ride with Lannes over the field of Austerlitz :
they will remember above all the grace, the kindness far more
admirable than grace with which the friendly hospitality of that
ancient mansion was dispensed.   They will remember the venerable
and benignant countenance, and the cordial voice of him that bade
them welcome."

This delightful description balances with stately eulo-
gium the revelations of private letters and journals, which
show in many cases a schoolboy sort of anxiety on the
part of the illustrious guests as to whether my lady would
be in a good humour, or Lord Holland's gout not too
severe to permit him to be visible, and a certain sense
that things might possibly turn out badly at any moment,
and those stately rooms and brilliant assemblies be closed
upon them for ever.

Of the names mentioned above, Mackintosh, one of the
most remarkable members of the society, must be left to
another chapter for an outline of his life and works.   He
was one of the foremost of the " Scotchmen" whom Byron
in his ill-tempered verses declared to " feed," and of the
" critics who carouse" at " the banquets spread at Holland
House."   All the members of the belligerent band of the
Edinburgh Review were to be found there by right of their
party, just as, in the same right, they were banished from
so much in their own capital.   There were now resident
of them in London, in the beginning of the century,
Henry Brougham, beginning with characteristic energy

and power his wonderful career, a man never popular, yet
impressing his fellows with a perception of boundless force,
vivacity, and power, such as we scarcely attribute now to
the robust and restless Chancellor, who gained every prize
that his profession and his country could give, and yet
remained in some inexplicable way always an unsuccessful
man; Francis Horner, one whose abilities we have in a
great measure to take on trust from the panegyrics of his
companions—for he did not live to give much proof in
literature of the powers they saw in him: and Allen,
whose post in the household of Lord Holland made him a
sort of vizier of the brilliant despotism. Mackintosh, the
mild and candid, had his balance in Hallam, a historian
of a different mettle, whose judgment cannot be called
mild.   And Sydney Smith, with the "faun-like face,"
which "was a sort of promise of a good thing when he
does but open his lips," lent his lighter wit to dispel the
sometimes oppressive atmosphere, a man able to meet my
lady on her own ground, and laughingly extract the sting
from her impertinences. The coterie would not have been
complete without a certain number of lesser members,
poets of society and amateurs in literature, such as Henry
Luttrell—a brilliant man about town, with the faculty of
writing agreeable verses, of whom Rogers says that "none
of the talkers I meet in London society can slide into a
brilliant thing with such readiness as he does"—a quality
which of itself was recommendation enough.

The representative of poetry in this brilliant company
was, however, Rogers himself, the last, as he is somewhere
called, of the old school, the only wealthy member of the
confraternity living, a patron of literature, as well as
practising the same, at once Mæcenas and poet. He had
a *cortége* and following of his own, not indeed equal to the
sublime and exclusive circle of Holland House, yet important and distingushed, and as the years went on, including

all that was greatest in poetry and letters. It was his ambition to surround himself with beautiful things, fine pictures and gifted people, and the company he collected at his table for nearly half a century was in its way the best in England. His poetry was not of such noble quality : but the *Pleasures of Memory*, which he published in 1792, had more than its meed of praise, and has not yet ceased to hold an active place as a gift-book and prize-book in handsome bindings, while its position as a poem which no library can be without, is permanent. In those days it was read devoutly by all who professed any love for poetry, and exalted by the critics far above the hotly contested productions of Wordsworth and Coleridge. And his other profession of banker, and his beautiful house, and his wealth, gave Rogers such a position as, alas, the greatest genius by itself will never confer. He was the friend, in his early days, of Mrs. Barbauld and Isaac Disraeli, two persons who might almost be taken to represent the opposite poles of literary society. He had little to do with the literary folk who lived at the other end of London and of life, though, when the great poets from the north came to town, there would be meetings in which Lamb, and sometimes even Godwin, were for the moment brought within his range ; but to all writers who belonged ever so little to the great world, or had managed to get themselves introduced there, he gave his notice and hospitality, and sometimes help to the rising and unknown.

How it was that the little Irishman from Dublin, Tom Moore, who came across the Channel in the very end of the century with a few introductions and some translations from Anacreon in his pocket, scrambled into good society, it is somewhat difficult to make out. But he did so, and made himself the fashion, and got admission, he also, though not till some years later, into that heaven of Holland

House which dazzled every candidate for fame. There could not be a greater contrast than between the respectable sentiments, and apparently life, of this lively little candidate for poetical distinction, and the character of his first original publication, the poems by Thomas Little, of which Posterity remembers nothing except that they were of a licentious tendency, and patronised by the Prince Regent, to whom that class of literature was attractive. Whether Moore's poetical improprieties were simply artificial to suit the taste of the moment, or if he himself had gained the premature enlightenment of a *jeunesse orageuse*, it is hard to tell. His little scrap of autobiography, and his innocent home-letters, give no ground whatever for the latter supposition. He began his life apparently with a dutiful love and reverence for his parents, and an honest desire to earn his living and aid his family, which he did steadfastly through some misfortunes and many temptations, notwithstanding the fact that he loved society dearly, and was never so happy as when among the great. Amid so many greater names, to which the higher classes gave little or no recognition, Moore was the only one who found success easy, and was petted and made much of in the most elegant circles. Perhaps he was more amenable to the blandishments of fashion than poets of a larger kind. " In anecdote, small-talk, and especially in singing, he was supreme—for many years he had been the most brilliant man of his company," says Crabb Robinson. "My songs have taken such a rage ! even surpassing what they did in Dublin," he writes to his mother, to whom he reports every pleasant thing that is said of him, with something which the critics call vanity, but which seems to us almost the best point in his character—an unfeigned desire to give her pleasure. None of his contemporaries, names to which it would be laughable now to compare his, had penetrated as he did into the heart of polite society.

They were all on the outskirts, among the undistinguished masses, poor men little noticed by the great. But Moore found his way, in the very beginning of his career, to the society of lords and ladies, and into the class which considered itself as the highest in England. Of the new generation there were but this lively little Irishman and Campbell, who had some small links of connection with the gilded crowd, and shyly appeared from time to time among them—to represent the morning lights of a new poetical age.

There was now, however, to blaze upon the busy world of society, with Mr. Rogers in St. James's Place twinkling a very mild little taper across its darkness, and Canning and Hookham Frere carrying into statesmanship only a pungent recollection of verse which was satire rather than poetry, and Gifford uttering from his corner, in the same breath with the Baviads and Mæviads, a sentimental song which was not much less ornate and feeble than the chirpings of the poor little Della Cruscans whom he slew —a sudden meteor of the first magnitude dazzling the unaccustomed eyes of Town. A child born of two unruly houses, English and Scotch, brought up as badly as ever unfortunate boy was, spoiled alike by good fortune and bad, a lord, a braggart, and a genius, passionately wrong-headed, self-adoring, yet self-disgusted, poor, extravagant, dissipated, and lonely, a kind of young outcast from humanity, yet favourite of fortune, had come through doubtful episodes of •restraint at school and college, and wild license and wandering elsewhere, to man's estate. He had published the first flowers of his youth in an idle volume, and then, stung to the very marrow of his bones by unnecessary severity of criticism thereupon, had revenged himself in a trenchant and fiery satire, a very different kind of stuff from the Baviads, and was now come back after various travels, with a trumpery manu-

script in the same vein, which he called "Hints from
Horace," and was eager to publish, and a neglected bundle
of Spenserian verses of which he thought nothing, but
which turned out to be no less a thing than the first part
of *Childe Harold's Pilgrimage.* This young Lord Byron
was twenty-three, and one of the most forlorn beings
imaginable, though possessed of wonderful gifts of fortune
— without friends or family, or a home, or anything to
make up to him for the precocious and miserable knowledge of "life" in its worst aspect, which he had been so
unfortunate as to acquire. His school and college friends
were dead or estranged; relations he had scarcely any;
his mother, for whom, so long as she lived, he had felt
little affection, died immediately after his return from his
wanderings; and his manner of life, before he set out upon
these wanderings, had been such as to prejudice most of
the people who knew him against him—indeed, this would
seem to have been one of the objects of his uncomfortable,
unlovely, and unenjoyed life, to make so much stir at
least, that everybody should think as badly as possible of the
hapless young reprobate. It was not a great ambition, but
he would seem to have succeeded in it. When he took his
seat in the House of Lords there was not a creature to
stand by him, not another peer—and he loved peers—to
give him the countenance which a young man needs.
Unfortunate young Byron! He was proud, very conscious
of his own rank, and eager for the deference it ought to
have brought him. But the doors of society, which we
are apt to think so very ready to open before such a young
hero, remained obstinately closed in his case. He had
nobody to introduce him, or teach him how to get the
entrée, and he found the homage he loved only among
servants and humble country folk. And being but a boy,
and far from wise, he had made a little flourish of self-
importance about his peerage in the little book that he

had innocently issued to a hard world. Jeffrey's review, after all, was nothing so very dreadful. Any graceful young lordling of the present day who should put forth his "Hours of Idleness" would get as hard or harder from the *Saturday Review*, and would in all likelihood bear it like a man without gratifying his critics by any outcry of pain or vengeance. But criticism was a new art in those days, and though no more ferocious (we think) than now, was much more keenly felt. And the *Edinburgh* had the art of planting wounds so that they should sting and burn. The reader must not suppose, however, that young Byron and his pretty little poems (for they were no more) had the honour of being the subject of such an elaborate article as those we now see in the great Reviews. Such small deer were not exposed to pursuit so lengthened. The *Review* in its earlier stages admitted articles of very varied extent, and that which the young poet so deeply resented was not longer than a literary newspaper would devote to a similar offender now.

But what an outburst of young passion and energy was in the reply ! "English Bards and Scotch Reviewers" is not a great poem. If it were possible to drop it out of Byron's life and works, we believe his lovers would always have been glad to do so, and he himself not the least contented ; but it could not be dropped out of a literary history. Never was there a more remarkable example of "how it strikes a contemporary." It is always a matter of curiosity and interest to get at the opinion of youth, and to form an idea what the tendencies of the time are by the likings of its future masters— especially when these are the most highly endowed and educated of their day. Young Byron, indeed, was not of the latter class ; his education was imperfect, his information desultory and chaotic, and his university had conveyed to him but a small share of those humanising

influences with which we are fondly apt to credit that
seat of learning.   But there was not such another literary
genius in all the ranks of English youth, and he, if any
one, should have seen and appreciated the nobler gifts,
which had come to full development just as he reached
that opening day in which everything that is beautiful in
nature is most beautiful to the young seer.   How strange
is the difference between this high probability and the
real state of affairs !   The young Byron, the new poet, he
who should have recognised by instinct his immortal
brethren, vindicates above all things else the blindness of
human intelligence, the obstinacy of prejudice, the old-
fashionedness and conventionalism of youth.   Nothing so
artificial, so prejudiced, so blindly conservative could be,
as the violent charge he makes in hot exasperation of
vanity and injured *amour propre* against all who were
before him in the lists of honour : all, or almost all, the
exceptions being as edifying as the abuse.   An indiscriminate assault upon all sorts and conditions of poets,
Coleridge and Monk Lewis, Wordsworth and Grahame, all
holding about the same place, apparently, in the young
champion's eyes, is more remarkable than the rush at
Jeffrey which was comprehensible and perhaps not illegiti-
mate.   Scott comes in for the most prolonged abuse of
all, as " Apollo's venal son," as a " hireling bard " with a
" prostituted muse," as one of the poets who " rack their
brains for lucre not for fame."   Then comes " ballad-
mongering Southey," on whom he is scarcely so severe,
though he means to be so, for indeed poor Southey, though
he produced " annual strains " to take the field like armies,
never was lucky enough to get half-a-crown a line.
" Vulgar Wordsworth," whom the young avenger in all
sincerity does not seem to think worth his steel, is described as " the meanest object of the lowly group," and
his " verse of all but childish prattle void :" and Cole-

ridge " to turgid ode and tumid stanza dear," as " the
laureate of the long-ear'd kind ;" while poor Mr. Cottle in
Bristol, the gently garrulous bookseller, to whom we owe
many pleasant reminiscences if we have all forgotten his
poetry, comes in, in the absolute absence of all perspective,
for rather more remark than either of these preceding
poets. " Smug Sydney," " blundering Brougham," " paltry
Pillans," are more naturally, as being Edinburgh reviewers,
the object of this schoolboy vituperation. But at last
the young man in the crowd he has raised about him
falls in with some one whom he can praise. " Neglected
genius ! let me turn to you," he cries.

> " Come forth, oh Campbell ! give thy talents scope ;
>   Who dares aspire if thou must cease to hope ?
> And thou, melodious Rogers ! rise at last.
> Recall the pleasing memory of the past ;
> Arise ! let blest remembrance still inspire,
> And strike to wonted tones thy hallow'd lyre ;
> Restore Apollo to his vacant throne,
> Assert thy country's honour and thine own.
> What ! must deserted Poesy still weep
> Where her last hopes with pious Cowper sleep ?
>
>   .   .   .   .   .
>
> No ! though contempt hath mark'd the spurious brood,
> The race who rhyme from folly, or for food,
> Yet still some genuine sons 'tis hers to boast,
> Who, least affecting, still affect the most :
> Feel as they write, and write but as they feel—
> Bear witness Gifford, Sotheby, Macneil."

These illustrious names were the representatives,
according to the young poet who was so soon to seize the
very crown of rapid fame in England, of the poetry of his
time. The last name will scarcely be known even to the
most well-informed reader. Macneil was the author of
" Scotland's Scaith," and the " Waes of War," of which we
are told " ten thousand copies were sold in one month."
It is about all that history has to say on his account.

The reader will smile to see what the poetic youth, fresh from Cambridge, and touched himself (though his genius was as yet undiscovered, either by himself or others) by the divine fire, thought of the poets of his time.

Curiously enough, however, it was to this assault upon his contemporaries that Byron owed his first introduction to the world of literature, and through it to society. It has been mentioned in a previous chapter that a duel of a somewhat ludicrous description took place between Jeffrey and the young poet Moore on the occasion of a severe review (these were days in which reviews were dangerous for the critics as well as for the authors) of the first volume of dubious verse, which he published under the name of Little. This absurd incident exactly suited Byron's purpose. He brings in with delighted malice

> " That ever glorious, almost fatal fray,
>   When Little's leadless pistol met his eye,
>   And Bow Street myrmidons stood laughing by."

Moore, however, who had published an accurate account of the transaction, exonerating himself from the ridicule of the " leadless pistol," considered Byron's allusion to it as directly giving him the lie, and being as Irish and as warlike as ever, wrote a sort of challenge to the new assailant, which, however, never reached Byron till a year later, when the little Irishman was married and had cooled down. Several letters followed, and Moore was glad to accept the explanation that Byron had never seen his published denial of the more ludicrous part of the circumstances, and not unwilling to meet and make friends with the young man who had proved himself at least a dangerous enemy, and who was a lord and a wonder besides. On receiving Byron's letter proposing a friendly, not a hostile meeting, " I went instantly," he says, " to my friend Mr. Rogers and informed him of the correspondence in which I had been engaged. With his usual readiness

to oblige and serve, he proposed that the meeting between
Lord Byron and myself should take place at his table,
and requested of me to convey to the noble lord his wish."
The invitation was immediately accepted. It was intended
at first that Rogers and Moore alone should form the party,
" but Mr. Thomas Campbell, having called upon our host
that morning, was invited to join it." It is easy to imagine the curiosity and interest with which these three
awaited the altogether unknown and remarkable young
stranger. The two elder men had been specially distinguished by his praises, and little Moore, though laughed
at, had been far more leniently treated than his betters.

> "—Little ; young Catullus of his day,
>   As sweet, but as immoral in his lay !"

was such a shaft as made no very serious wound.   Lords
were familiar to Rogers, and probably not exciting ; but
yet rank adds an attraction the more to all other qualities,
and a noble poet is piquant and picturesque ; whereas the
other two *convives* were of a humble position, and could
scarcely fail to be dazzled by the title of the new brother,
who had it in his power to be so potent a friend or enemy.
And already many stories had been told of this wild and
wandering spirit ; youthful orgies at Newstead exaggerated
into something portentous, and adventures innumerable,
by sea and land, all contributed to rouse the expectations
of the poets, who waited for the opening of the door and
the announcement of the novel, the terrible, the delightful
guest. He came, and Moore, for one, was enchanted
with everything about him—" the nobleness of his air,
his beauty, the gentleness of his voice and manners,
and—what was naturally not the least attraction—his
kindness to myself." " Being in mourning for his mother,
the colour, as well of his dress as of his glossy, curling,
and picturesque hair, gave more effect to the pure, spiritual

paleness of his features, in the expression of which, as he
spoke, there was a perpetual play of lively thought, though
melancholy was their habitual character when in repose."
Altogether, it was a hero of romance who thus burst upon
the vision of the assembled poets—good Campbell, fresh
from his respectable, middle-class, suburban cottage;
Moore, out of his economical retirement; middle-aged
Rogers, who from another point of view could scarcely
fail to be dazzled too by the youth and limitless future
which lay before his young guest. It was a little embarrassing that there was nothing for him to eat, for the
young poet, afraid of getting fat,—a very natural if somewhat absurd fear,—lived upon vegetables; and "biscuits
and soda water," for which he asked, were not to be had.
"He professed, however," says Moore, "to be equally well
pleased with potatoes and vinegar, and of these meagre
materials contrived to make rather a hearty dinner."
Barring this whimsical difficulty, the meeting was very
successful, and Moore continued Byron's devoted liege-
man for the rest of his life.

This is the first glimpse we have of the poet in anything that can be called or imagined the society of his
peers. He had as a boy been received at one or two
houses of his kinsfolk, in one of which he formed a
romantic and premature attachment, which certainly was
the inspiration of several poems, and which is romantic-
ally supposed to have helped to overshadow his life.
The terrible want of that life was, it is evident, something
to fix him in his orbit, some ties of home or duty, some
sense of responsibility, anything that would have freed
him from the restlessness that consumed his soul, and
which no excitement satisfied. The air of hurry and
breathless reposeless movement which is about him
during this early period, when as yet there was no fatal
step taken, or irrecoverable mistake made, is very remark-

able. His letters, which in our opinion are never very attractive, have an air of haste for which there could be no necessity save in his nature. Everything is mentioned in the curtest manner, not a pause, not an indication of interest beyond the most cursory and trifling. His friends, his occupations, the (fine) people he meets, the news of the time, all come in hurriedly to the breathless record. Few glimmers of genius, and not even much that could be called human individuality, the features that mark one man from another, are to be found in these productions. His biographer gives them at full length, and it has again become a fashion in the present renaissance of Byron's fame to applaud those hasty chapters of his experiences : but we cannot find them worthy of any serious remark. They are the kind of letters which any undistinguished young man, with coarsish tastes, and time entirely occupied with the frivolous occurrences of the day, might have written : nor, if he had not turned out to be Byron, would any one have supposed them worth the dignity of print.

He was very lonely, Moore tells us. The humble little poet would come and dine with his noble friend at a tavern when he could escape from the more important people who invited him to their houses. Only Mr. Dallas, who was a connection, and whom Byron trusted with the management of his literary business, and his solicitor, knew him in all that world of London, where a young man of his rank has generally such hosts of friends. Galt, whom he had met on his travels, is the only man of any kind of reputation who speaks of him at this dim portion of his career ; and Galt was nothing more than a half-ruined adventurer in these days. Even the " coffee-house companions," who had given him an undesirable society on his first appearance in town, had dispersed and fallen away, as it is the way of loose company to do.

And it is impossible to imagine a more forlorn figure
than that of this noble, handsome, gifted, young man,
wandering about from one poor tavern to another, now
and then rescuing an evening from the dreary inane
around by the note, " I dine with Rogers to-morrow,"
knowing nobody, caring for nobody, with neither hope to
inspire nor duty to fix him to any spot or any occupation
on earth.   It is extraordinary to realise such a position.
He had done nothing worse than hundreds of other careless young men——nothing that could make a Pariah of
him or shut him out from friendship and kindness at so
early an age.   And there does not indeed seem to have
been any inclination on the part of society to reject him.
He was forgiven with wonderful readiness for his general
abuse of the literary profession.   Lord Holland interposed
his friendly offices to give him information on a subject
on which he meant to speak in the House of Lords, notwithstanding that both his wife and himself had been
visited with the young poet's utmost scorn.. In short,
there seems to have been absolutely no reason for his
entire isolation ; and yet it existed.   When he made that
first speech and appearance in the House of Lords (on
behalf of the poor rioters in his own county——a very good
object), he describes himself with his usual curious osten-
tation as " a person in some degree connected with the
suffering county, though a stranger not only to the House
in general, but to almost every individual whose attention
I presume to solicit."   And yet he had been educated at
Harrow and Cambridge.   The fact is so strange that it
seems impossible to credit it ; poverty, which is sometimes
represented as the cause, scarcely seems a sufficient one ;
and the explanation to which we are driven is the painful
one that the company of his own class was really not
agreeable to Byron.   He had accustomed himself to a
reedom and self-indulgence incompatible with the re-

straints of society.   It is easier for the lawless mind to
" get on" in a tavern than in a drawing-room.   What
other elucidation of the mystery can we find or suggest ?

Perhaps this speech about the Nottingham stocking
weavers was an attempt to find an entrance into a better
sphere.   The applause with which it was received seems
to have given this fortunate-unfortunate the highest
gratification.   His friend, Mr. Dallas, who met him directly
after its delivery, found him " glowing with success and
much agitated."   He had been told that Sheridan thought
he would make a great orator, and Lord Holland and
Lord Granville paid him " high compliments " in their
speeches in the same debate.   " Lord H. tells me I shall
beat them all if I persevere, and Lord G. remarked that
the construction of some of my periods is very like
Burke's," he says in a letter to Hodgson.   It was the
first social success of his life, and soothed and stilled the
uneasy sense he seems always to have had of not really
belonging to the sphere of which, even while seeming to
despise it, he had such an exalted opinion.   But it was
not to be to his oratory that he owed his admission into
society.   Two days after this hopeful speech the young
poet delivered his real credentials to the world.   He had
brought with him from his travels, as has been said, two
manuscripts, one which he looked upon with complacency,
and was hot to publish—a satire after Horace, a reminiscence at once of his previous spites against society and
the critics, and of that youthful classicism which it is the
object of the schools to foster; and another, a miscellaneous bundle of verses, written apparently on the pressure
of the moment, and mingled with fugitive poems of all
descriptions, which he took " from a small trunk," and
felt were not " worth troubling " his friend with.   Mr.
Dallas, fortunately, was a better critic than Lord Byron ;
and he it was whose insistance brought into the world

the poem which was to found a new school of poetry, and
influence the public mind, at least for the time, as no
other poem of the generation did. That he himself had
no sort of notion of this is evident from the very flutter
of delight and gratified vanity with which on the edge of
a success so much greater he speaks of this speech of his
in the House of Lords. Two days after *Childe Harold*
appeared. It is not too much to say that the public
mind was moved by it to a sort of sudden ecstasy of interest such as is almost incredible in our calmer days.
" I awoke one morning and found myself famous," he says.
The first edition was sold out at once, and a universal
ferment of interest about the young author flew through
that society which up to this time had known and cared
nothing about him.

" At his door," his biographer tells us, " most of the leading
names of the day presented themselves,—some of them persons
whom he had much wronged in his Satire, but who now forgot
their resentment in generous admiration. From morning till night
the most flattering testimonies of his success crowded his table—
from the grave tributes of the statesman and the philosopher down
to (what flattered him still more) the romantic billet of some incog-
nita, or the pressing note of invitation from some fair leader of
fashion ; and in place of the desert which London had been to him
but a few weeks before, he now not only saw the whole splendid
interior of high life thrown open to receive him, but found himself
among its illustrious crowds the most distinguished object."

It is seldom that genuine poetical fame, that fame
which is to last, and become an inheritance for the very
land that produced it, arises so suddenly. Scott, with
his easy, fresh, delightful *Lay*, rose almost as soon into
the heaven of popular applause ; but his can scarcely
be called a genuine poetical fame ; and Byron's, rapid
as it was, was also complete and lasting—a fame which,
as yet, though subject to the revisal of two or three
generations, has not been diminished, though it has had

fluctuations like all things human. In many ways this instantaneous leap into the highest places of success was extraordinary. But for the introduction of the traveller in the beginning of the poem, the *Pilgrimage* was almost entirely descriptive of scenes unfamiliar to the English reader, who had not then become the cosmopolitan wanderer he now is, and whom wars and tumults had for long shut out from the Continent. And it was written in elaborate verse, which, however melodious, is always a tax, more or less, on the faculties of the reader. When we open *Childe Harold* now, we turn instinctively to the later cantos,— those which reflect the turning point of the poet's life,—and in which there is all the excitement of real calamity and suffering. But no such catastrophe had befallen the young Byron when he set out upon his travels, and the poem in which he embodied his experiences, and which he did not think " worth the while" even of his indulgent friend and critic, was, in reality, little more than an itinerary, though of the most splendid kind. How it was that the serious sweetness of those long stanzas which celebrated nothing more moving than the praises of " august Athena," or " stern Albania's hills," should have produced so great a commotion at once in society, and among the general world of readers, is difficult to understand. Greater poems have had very much less effect, and yet have been well received ;—this attained in a moment the universal attention, and dazzled all who beheld it,—springing suddenly like a comet out of the vapours.

It is difficult, we have said, to understand this instantaneous fame ; but, indeed, it is evident enough upon what it was founded. The secret of its power was in the hero who traversed vaguely those classic countries, giving a certain mystery and interest even to scenes in which his figure was imagined rather than seen—and in

the revelation of him which occupied the beginning of
the poem : a brief effective sketch, original and captivating to the popular imagination, which never in English
literature had met with anything like this embodiment
of youthful tragedy before.   Réné had preceded him
in France, and Werter in Germany, but *Childe Harolr*
was different from both.   He was the symbol less of
revolt against established laws than of that personal
grievance which is felt so bitterly in youth, when things
do not go as we wish.   Not the loss of a Lotte or a
Mary, but wild despite at his own insignificance, a fierce
disgust with the world which did not do him homage, nor
cared very deeply whither he went or came, was in every
line of the picture.   It is a picture of youth awakening
from its first wild burst of enjoyment and confidence in
itself, to the bitter sense that its pleasures are naught,
and itself of no particular importance in the economy of
the Universe.   The pang with which he gazes wildly
round to see the indifference of gods and men to his weal
or inclination, the calm routine which goes on unmoved,
howsoever the young hero may suffer and even if he sinks
altogether in his struggle to have everything and enjoy
everything, is, in its astonishment, its fury, its pathos of
self-pity, a very real pang ; and the force of tragic superiority to the cruel world and all its ways, even the pretence
of having earned that world's anathema by guilt as mysterious as the suffering, is comprehensible enough to the
heart, a natural refuge for pride deeply wounded and
mortified feeling.   But the image was new to the age,
and affected it in a powerful way.   It was the first time
this young misanthrope, this mysterious cynic, this proud
and scornful rebel, sufferer, and outcast, had been put in
bodily shape before the world.   And its attraction was
increased by the fact that, amid all its truth to nature,
there was a subtle half-conscious fiction running through

every line. No despair could have been so black and
profound that did not conceal a secret consciousness of
unlimited hope behind, and the very grandeur with which
that sublime melodramatic figure averted his eyes from
all delights, made it more certain that, when he chose to
" take a thought and mend," all these delights were yet
well within his reach. Thus the mingling of the fictitious
and the real, the sincerity and good faith of present
passion with all the casuistry and artifice of fictitious
sentiment, gave an additional attraction. The guilt, and
grandeur, and hopeless misery were all alike sham, yet
the feeling was true : and this artificial character, if we
may be permitted to employ a paradox, made the conception more real, and helped, as nothing else could, to
express the strange chaos of wilfulness and waywardness,
of suffering and satisfaction, the complacent masquerading
and genuine misery which are involved in the first tragedy
of youth.

This publication changed life and the world to Byron.
It was in February 1812 that it took place, and all doors
were thrown open to him. In 1815 he married. In
1816, a year after, he left England, separated from his
wife, a broken man, with neither hope nor possibility
left him, so far as appeared, of ever making up with the
world or presenting himself again in society. Thus his
entire career in England was limited to four years, beginning in total obscurity and ending in general reprobation.
As it is almost incredible that a young man of his rank,
not to speak of his genius—for that was at the time
unrevealed—should have been so friendless and forlorn
to start with, so it is hard to understand his entire abandonment afterwards. He was not without partisans to
offer pleas in his favour, and breathe for him all the
commonplace and well-worn excuses which are supposed
to account for the follies of genius. But the general

impression was as entirely against him as ever public
opinion was ; and this brief space of unbounded applause,
and equally boundless disapprobation, represented all his
life in England, the entire cycle of his rising and falling.
A more extraordinary career could not have been imagined.
The violent onslaught which, while still utterly unknown,
he had made upon almost every famous individual of his
contemporaries, had been generously and fully forgiven
to the author of *Childe Harold's Pilgrimage,* with a mag-
nanimity which, so far as we know, is quite unrivalled
in history.   The most royal pardon had been granted to
him with acclamation, and the fairest chance a man could
have, fully accorded.   Society, which had been coldly
unconscious of his existence, opened its doors wide to the
young poet who had so many claims on its consideration.
Without entering in a manner totally inconsistent with
our purpose into the scandalous chronicles of the time,
which was as unlovely a moment as can be found in
social history, we cannot give the reader any account of
the life of Byron in this brief epitome of his existence.
It was a lawless life, bound by no rule of principle, full,
it is to be supposed, of enjoyment, full of remorse, of
pecuniary miseries and wild expenditure, of passions and
separations, all headlong, unregulated, prodigal.   In n
way is the picture of the young poet an attractive one
Moore says everything for him that a counsel retained
for the defence could say, but never is able, evidently, to
divest himself of the sense that his client has a very poor
case, and that in reality there is very little to be said.
His own letters and journals seem to us superficial in
the highest degree, and give little idea of anything but
the froth of a restless nature.   They are a mere record of
events, and full of the hurry-scurry of society, the chatter
of a noisy circle in which there is nothing great but the
names that appear and reappear, but show little of either

thought or feeling above the level of a frivolous young man of fashion. We are unaccustomed in these days to the discretion which casts out everything purely personal, and hides under asterisks every allusion that might wound or grieve, and it is difficult in the face of the damaging revelations which of late have soiled some great memories, to object to the reticence which, by this time, to readers unacquainted with contemporary talk and scribblings, envelops the whole question of Byron's life and relations before his marriage in a mist. It seems doubtful which is best, and whether entire silence would not be better than either indecent candour or tantalising concealments.

This at least we know, that Byron lived a life capable, perhaps, of excuse, but not of justification; that after having dissipated the ordinary prospects of existence on that high level, he had another chance in marriage—and somehow, more dolorously, more shamefully still, failed in that also, and so far as England was concerned in life altogether. There are times in which concealment is the worst injury that can be done a man, as there are also cases in which disclosure is a crime. We are incapable of saying in which category Byron's story is to be placed. His wife is one of the greatest mysteries of recent times. Admired and almost worshipped by an adoring circle for the greater part of her life, she was at the crisis of her story regarded with fierce indignation by her husband's partisans, and at the end of her life sank into something like the contempt, as well as execration, of the greater part of the public. The world will never know the rights —or wrongs—of the question. The woman in the end has had the worst of it, as women generally have in such a conflict. In some particulars there can be no doubt she was brutally treated, but her incapacity for carrying a secret long guarded to the grave with her, has done more harm to her memory than if she had told that secret at

the moment, supposing it to be true ; if it is all an invention, then words cannot express the wickedness of the
deed.   One moral of the whole miserable story would
seem to be that candour about every event, while the
parties are alive to defend themselves, is after all the best,
since it seems beyond the range of human faculties to
keep silence for ever, and some blabber, sooner or later, is
sure to let the most unsavoury revelation out.

During these four years which comprise his life in
England, the young poet, in the midst of all his loves,
his frivolities, and his embarrassments, produced a succession of poems, written with the greatest rapidity, and
with a total absence of the study or retirement hitherto
thought necessary for such composition.   In the heart of
London society and a hundred intrigues, he managed to
pour forth canto after canto and couplet after couplet,
glowing and hot from a heart which he did his best to
represent as worn out, misanthropical, and disgusted with
the world.   The *Giaour*, the *Bride of Abydos*, the *Corsair*, *Lara*, the *Siege of Corinth*, and *Parisina*, were all
the product of this time.   They raised the reputation he
had gained into an overwhelming flood of praise and
admiration.   They are all Eastern in subject, and all
penetrated, more or less, by the same character which had
enchanted the world in the first sketch of *Harold*.   The
Giaour indeed, is too fragmentary to afford any clear
view of character at all ; and the *Bride of Abydos* has
a virtuous and excellent youth for its hero ; but these
are the only exceptions.   The *Corsair* and *Lara* out-
Harolded Harold, and fixed upon the public mind the
lineaments of that mysterious personage, gloomy and
grand, wrapped in his cloak, and self-separated from all
the world, with dark brow and darker shadow, awing
the Universe—a being abstracted from any human connection save one,   So far the *Corsair* improved upon

the *Childe*. He had one love which linked him to humanity. But, whereas Childe Harold was guilty of nothing but dissipation, Conrad was a pirate chief, familiar with blood and crime, and Lara under some still deeper, shameful stigma, which it was worth his while to hush up by murder. These were the heroes whom the new poet introduced to the world; and while one half of the critics were admiringly shocked by his majestic criminals, the other half were delightfully stimulated by this new conception of the sublime. The idea that he himself was the model from whom he drew, increased the feeling on both sides, and between the people who were shocked and those who were pleasingly startled into a new sensation, his fame swelled higher than ever fame had swelled before. He did not himself at all discourage the idea that his subject was himself. "He told me an odd report—that I am the actual Conrad, the veritable Corsair, and that part of my travels are supposed to have passed in piracy. Alas! people sometimes hit near the truth, but never the whole truth," Byron says, with a smile of complacency one can imagine about his mouth—"Wrote to * * the 'Corsair' report," he says, in another place, "she says she don't wonder, since 'Conrad is so *like*.' It is odd that one who knows me so thoroughly should tell me this to my face. However, if she don't know, nobody can." Thus he adopted the popular fancy, not without pleasure, and the identification of poet and hero added indefinitely to the effect, and raised his fame higher and higher. The poems were read eagerly to throw more light upon the man; the man's antecedents, and all the gossip that could be collected about him, were studied and talked of, in order to add a little to the revelations of the poem. The poetry was fine—and it was scandal at the same time : what society could resist two charms so potent, mingled so skilfully and so well?

But to find any special human features now in this
melodramatic type is an achievement beyond our powers.
Harold, upon the deck of his ship, looking back bitterly
upon the land in which he has wasted his youth and his
chances, pretending to scorn, yet in reality keenly affected
by the circumstances of his self-banishment—has a certain
amount of humanity in him, and might very naturally be
supposed to reflect the being of his creator; but the
Corsair, though he may be but the same impersonation
heightened and wrapped in stage clothes and draperies
still more gloomy, has lost all individual features, and is
a mere symbol of the conventional sublime.

> " That man of loneliness and mystery,
>   Scarce seen to smile, and seldom heard to sigh ;
>   Whose name appals the fiercest of his crew,
>   And tints each swarthy cheek with sallower hue ;
>   Still sways their souls with that commanding art
>   That dazzles, leads, yet chills the vulgar heart.
>   .   .   .   .
>
> But who that Chief ? his name on every shore
>   Is famed and fear'd—they ask and know no more.
>   With these he mingles not but to command ;
>   Few are his words, but keen his eye and hand.
>   Ne'er seasons he with mirth their jovial mess,
>   But they forgive his silence for success.
>   Ne'er for his lip the purpling cup they fill,
>   That goblet passes him untasted still—
>   And for his fare—the rudest of his crew
>   Would that, in turn, have pass'd untasted too ;
>   Earth's coarsest bread, the garden's homeliest roots,
>   And scarce the summer luxury of fruits,
>   His short repast in humbleness supply
>   With all a hermit's board would scarce deny.
>   .   .   .   .
>
> Thus prompt his accents and his actions still,
>   And all obey and few inquire his will ;
>   To such, brief answer and contemptuous eye
>   Convey reproof, nor further deign reply."

And here is Lara, who is popularly supposed to be the

Corsair grown older, and returned out of his wild career
into the paternal halls, where his fierce and troublous life
of adventures is unknown :—

> " That brow in furrow'd lines had fix'd at last,
> And spake of passions, but of passion past :
> The pride, but not the fire, of early days,
> Coldness of mien, and carelessness of praise ;
> A high demeanour, and a glance that took
> Their thoughts from others by a single look ;
> And that sarcastic levity of tongue,
> The stinging of a heart the world had stung,
> That darts in seeming playfulness around,
> And makes those feel that will not own the wound ;
> All these seem'd his, and something more beneath
> Than glance could well reveal, or accent breathe.
> Ambition, glory, love, the common aim,
> That some can conquer, and that all would claim,
> Within his breast appear'd no more to strive,
> Yet seem'd as lately they had been alive ;
> And some deep feeling it were vain to trace
> At moments lighten'd o'er his livid face.
>
> .   .   .   .   .   .
>
> Around him some mysterious circle thrown
> Repell'd approach, and show'd him still alone ;
> Upon his eye sat something of reproof,
> That kept at least frivolity aloof ;
> And things more timid that beheld him near,
> In silence gazed, or whisper'd mutual fear."

To assert that any human being, with individual habits
of his own, is " so *like* " this conjunction of abstract qualities is as curious as any other particular of the history.
There was indeed one point in which Byron distinctly
resembled the Corsair, but that was not a point of
character. The poet, like his hero, ate " earth's coarsest
bread, the garden's homeliest roots," and little or nothing
more ; but this was from a most unpoetical reason ; and
could we imagine that Conrad, like Byron, used this
regimen in order that he might not grow fat, the finest
poetry would not save him from that ridicule which is

death to sentiment.   All, or almost all, the enchantment which once surrounded the hero has vanished, and a profaner public smiles at the gloomy grandeur and self-absorbed conscious sublimity of this mysteriously guilty personage, who, under pretence of concealing his remorses and despairs, wears them conspicuously as his livery. But the sincerity of the poet himself in setting forth so theatrical a figure, his genuine admiration of it, and inability to perceive any possibilities of ridicule, is proved by the constant repetition, in tale after tale, of the same wonderful creation, sardonic, mysterious, and grandly superior to the crowd.   Byron, it is evident, was never himself weary of the one type of being which he had evolved.   It satisfied his vanity, which was great, and his imagination, which, notwithstanding his great genius, was not great, but limited and somewhat formal, if we might even dare to say vulgar, delighting in strong effects, and indifferent to the more delicate gradations of nature. The other personages in these early works are entirely vague, indistinguishable, mere names and little more. But his generation received every *replica* with acclamation. They were transported by the sombre charm of those dark looks and tragic gestures.   Not even the critics reproached the poet with the monotony of his central figure.   In the full illumination of the nineteenth century the sham-heroic pirate chief was to them as a revelation from heaven.

This is, perhaps, the most wonderful evidence ever given to the force, and beauty, and intense vitality of a literary medium.   These are not the words we would naturally employ to describe the divine stream of great poetry ; for even the poetry of Byron's tales is not of a divine kind.   It is full of splendour, and strength, and brilliant adaptation to the subject.   The impression of mingled force and smoothness in it is admirable ; but

it is not the highest strain of poetry; it is a fine and
powerful literary vehicle, brilliant, effective, and forcible.
Glancing over these tales, after a long interval, the reader
will be surprised to find how few passages in them have
fallen into universal use. That triumphant criticism of
the simple-minded which pointed out that Hamlet was
nothing but a mass of quotations, could never be applied
to the *Corsair* or his peers. The beautiful passage in
the *Giaour* beginning—

> " He who hath bent him o'er the dead,
>   E'er the first day of death is fled,"

is one of the few exceptions. But though it seldom
reached the point at which verse thus falls into the
popular heart, it was so full of force and harmonious
movement, so living in every line, so rapid in narrative,
so intense in sentiment, that the monotony of the one
oft-repeated impersonation was not only forgiven but
delighted in. In such a case reproduction is either a
weariness or an additional and cumulative charm. In
pure fiction of the higher class, it is one of the greatest
pleasures of the reader to meet again in one story with
the friends he has acquired in another; but poetry has
seldom permitted such a repetition. Here, however, the
license was fully awarded. It gave the world a thrill of
pleasure to re-find the wandering and weary Harold, with
his bitter smile intensified, and his disgust with men and
life accounted for, in the guilty, and gloomy, and mysterious Corsair, the hero of " one virtue and a thousand
crimes;" and then once more to trace him in *Lara*
with gloom ever deepening, and mystery ever increasing,
the dark and proud chieftain, full of secret remorse, yet
unconquerable—confronting gods and men with haughty
defiance. And these were all Byron! and nobody of his
generation had swept onward in such a resistless current

of song. Scott, indeed, had led the way in this fashion
of poetry, but Scott's fresh fountain of verse was greatly
inferior in passion to the fervid strains of his young competitor. There is a comparison made by Byron himself
of a passage of his *Parisina* with a passage in *Marmion,*
which makes this wonderfully clear. " I fear there is
a resemblance," he says, " though I never thought of it
before, and could hardly wish to imitate that which is
inimitable." The passages in question are descriptions of
the guilty heroines of the two tales—Parisina and
Constance—at the crisis of their fate. We give that of
Marmion first :—

> " Her look composed, and steady eye,
> Bespoke a matchless constancy ;
> And there she stood, so calm and pale,
> That, but her breathing did not fail,
> And motion slight of eye and head,
> And of her bosom, warranted
> That neither sense nor pulse she lacks,
> You might have thought a form of wax
> Wrought to the very life was there ;
> So still she was, so pale, so fair."

This is Constance on her trial—the betrayed and
betraying maiden—victim and instrument of wickedness
—on the verge of a doom which destroys her alone.
The other is Parisina, more, yet less, sinful—contemplat-
ing, not her own, but her lover's fate :—

> " She stood, I said, all pale and still,
> The living cause of Hugo's ill ;
> Her eyes unmoved, but full and wide,
> Not once had turn'd to either side—
> Nor once did these sweet eyelids close,
> Or shade the glance o'er which they rose,
> But round their orbs of deepest blue
> The circling white dilated grew—
> And there with glassy gaze she stood,
> As ice were in her curdled blood."

Nothing could better show the range of the two poets. Scott's picture is pathetic, and moves the reader with a sentiment of tenderness and pity, such as the sufferings of innocence, rather than guilt, should call forth. Constance appears to us as a victim—almost a martyr; but in Byron's companion sketch, the half-stupefied yet all-conscious stillness of doom, the awe, the anguish, the horror, affect us with something of the same overwhelming cessation of thought and sense as has befallen the miserable, beautiful creature, standing dumb, in agony ineffable, to see destruction overtake the sharer of her sin. The very background glows with a pale flame of passion behind her head, and those wide-opened, motionless eyes. Constance breathes and moves, but Parisina's whole being is arrested like a frozen stream.

Another characteristic which helped to secure Byron's instantaneous triumph was one which we have already noted in respect to Scott—his intelligibility—the entire absence of the mystic in him. None of those gleams of secret insight into the depths of nature which fill with enthusiasm the sympathetic and understanding, but confuse the crowd, ever flash from the genius of Byron. The mysteries with which he deals are purely material, capable of explanation, and affording an easy exercise to the fancy in making them out. This is one of the greatest and most marked distinctions between one class of poetry and another. When we introduce a simple intelligence, say that of a child or an entirely uneducated person, to the wonders and glories of song, there must always be a great deal at which the untrained intelligence will make momentary pause, perplexed by something which has not occurred in the phraseology and thoughts of every day. Who could explain the *Ancient Mariner ?* The soul divines, and he that hath an ear to hear, hears and understands: but Scott and Byron, the one in a tame, the other in a grander sense, are both cheerfully intelligible, explainable, making no impossible demand on the faculties of the reader.   Nothing could be more mysterious than the *Corsair*, but we can hold our breath and guess at those secrets of his with much of the satisfaction which accompanies our ordinary researches into the secrets of our neighbours.   There is nothing in them which reaches that region beyond sight, that darkness round us and within, which it is the highest function of the poet to divine, the highest exercise of the mind to search into, catching such glimpses as our faculties will allow.   On this, Byron has no communication to make, no light to offer.   He is as profane and ignorant as any one of us.   When he himself risks a wondering question before these dark portals, it is with that despairing levity which is the resource of those who fear and know nothing, not of those who love and ponder and by moments see. There is no kindred with the mystic and unknown in the range of his genius ; he belongs entirely to the solid earth, and his mysteries are those of the theatre and the tale, nothing greater or more.

We need not enter farther into the incidents which caused his departure from London and the entire breaking up of his life.   With these the world would have had little to do at the time had he not taken it into his confidence : but at this distance, when both the chief actors are dead, the story is one which is open to the discussion of all, and cannot be ignored.   Domestic convulsions, even when they reach the height of tragedy, can scarcely be without many petty elements.   Byron's *Farewell* to his wife, which was in everybody's mouth at the time, is a piece of sentimental comedy added on to, and making a pitiful commentary upon, the really tragical crisis which made England and reasonable existence impossible to him thenceforward.   That he should have arrived at so

terrible a turning point, and, ruined in fortune, bankrupt
in reputation, doubted by all and condemned by most of
his contemporaries, should have celebrated the conclusion
of this tragic episode of life in a strain so commonplace
and unreal is as extraordinary as any other of the confusing events of that extraordinary moment. He who
took up the interrupted song of *Childe Harold* with so
much genuine feeling, how did he, how could he, inter-
pose the sentimental and theatrical *romanza* of an offended
primo tenore between himself and human sympathy?
We are told that the manuscript was blurred with his
tears, and that there is every reason to suppose him to
have been in earnest in the superficial pathos of his
appeal to the wife whom he never seems even to have
pretended to love—a fact which makes the confusion all
the greater, since it is difficult to imagine any serious
emotion expressing itself in such verses. But Byron's
imagination was, as we have said, much inferior to his
genius, and he wanted both good taste and that critical
discrimination which has so much to do with personal
dignity as well as with excellence in art. He could not
divine how such an effusion would be regarded by his
contemporaries, and was not even aware of its unreality
until, with an angry illumination afterwards, he discovered
the folly of it and perceived too late, through other
people's eyes, what he had failed to perceive with his
own. But, indeed, the interested reader will hail with a
certain relief this crisis in Byron's career. His after life
was wild and reckless enough, but it was not so miserable
as the forced and fictitious life in London, where ruin
lurked at every corner, and the semblance of prosperity
and happiness was scarcely skin-deep. It ended in an
inevitable explosion, all the elements having worked
towards this since the wedding-day on which he had
called his new-made wife Miss Milbanke with an absence

of mind almost incredible in a young bridegroom. When we read the journal, so full of fictitious liveliness, yet pain, so matter-of-fact, so commonplace, so angry and wretched, with still the same record of trivial things and talk, warped and made miserable by splenetic and reckless sentiment, and the chaos of an unregulated soul, it is with actual satisfaction that we see the end come. When the smoke and ashes clear off, and the passionate pilgrim storms away again over land and sea, leaving the failure and the misery behind him, our minds are eased from a painful burden. The gates of society may be closed against him, but again there seems a chance for him in the wider world.

CHAPTER II.

BYRON——SHELLEY.

WHEN Byron was reaching the stormy climax of his career in London, another poet, younger in years, whose beginning in life had been almost as wayward and unfortunate, though far less guilty, had appeared and disappeared again, not in the brilliant illumination of society, but among the struggling makers of literature in the other end of London. Percy Bysshe Shelley was born, more like a fairy changeling than an ordinary British infant, in a handsome country house in England in 1792, when Byron was but four years old in Aberdeen. The family of the younger child of genius belonged to that rural aristocracy which has produced many men of note and a great deal of respectable stupidity, but few poets ; and from the beginning of his life he seems to have been out of tune with everything about him. His father, his family, and surroundings, were as opposite to him in character, hopes, and prejudices, as it is possible to conceive. Where it was that the respectable squire's son imbibed the ideas which dominated his life there seems no record ; but he was a revolutionary born, a freethinker from his cradle, atheistical and democratical, in everything going contrary to all the traditions of his race, of which he was the heir and representative by a strange irony of fortune, a position which made steady-going

orthodoxy and conservatism almost necessities of existence.
Young Shelley's rebellion against all that was, seems to
have pervaded everything else that is known of him.
By the time he went to Eton, if we may credit his own
record, he had already come to recognise, in the hum of
voices proceeding from the schoolroom, " the harsh and
grating strife of tyrants and of foes," and to find in every
little fret of schoolboy life marks of the chains in which
free-born nature was bound.   The small oppressions of
fagging, the little round of punishment and obligation,
were in his eyes evils large enough to fill the soul with
bitterness :

> " Nothing that my tyrants knew or thought
>   I cared to learn,"

he says, with a sentiment not indeed uncommon with
boyhood, but differing much from the schoolboy's usual
light-hearted perversity.   There was not a laugh in him
throughout his life, nor had his hot young enthusiasm any
conception of the happy calm of ordinary youth.   His
young life is a record of strife and resistance ; but it is so
wildly dreamy and mystical, and the facts all through are
so confused with fictions and heated interpretations of the
real, that it is hard to know what to receive and what to
reject.   He believed himself to have been expelled from
Eton ; but there does not seem the slightest evidence that
such an event took place.   At Oxford, however, it did
occur ; he was sent away from University College on
account of a pamphlet called *The Necessity of Atheism*,
which he considered it his duty not only to publish, but
to send, with serious intentions of instructing them, to the
heads of his College.   One of his biographers speaks of
this as a mere boyish freak ; but another treats it with
much grandeur, declaring that " Percy Shelley had as good
a right to form and expound his opinions on theology as

the Archbishop of Canterbury," an assertion somewhat appalling to all who have the charge of persons of nineteen, an age at which no Archbishop ever promulgated doctrine. Thus one more youth of genius was cast out of her bosom by the University, that *Alma Mater* who has so little kindness for the poets. Young Shelley ran wild after this severance of all legitimate bonds. His father was angry, and made that feint of casting him off in which bewildered and angry fathers so often take refuge, and he was left to his own foolish devices at this momentous moment of his life. His sisters, who were soft-hearted and anxious to help him, sent him aid by the hands of a schoolfellow, a foolish romantic girl, who by a series of accidents was thrown upon Shelley's companionship and into his power. They were both very young, utterly inexperienced ; and he had wild views about the relationships between men and women as well as upon most other subjects, in which she was perfectly willing to follow. In these circumstances it is very much to the credit of the lawless young man that, though somewhat embarrassed and bewildered by the overpowering trust which Harriet showed in him, he married her, and gave the reckless foolish girl all the safeguards which the most carefully guarded bride could have required. He was not twenty when (in the year 1811) this marriage took place, and it completed the wild confusion of his life ; since the poor young pair were equally inexperienced and unwise, though one of them had the lamp of genius, not to guide, but to mislead them on their devious way. They wandered vaguely about after this, in Scotland one time, in Wales the next, meeting with all kinds of tragi-comic adventures, and living a life which was never more than half-real. It was in this phase of his existence that we find him starting up suddenly in the path of Southey, who gives his opinion of the young wanderer as follows :——

"Here is a man at Keswick who acts upon me as my own ghost would do—his name is Shelley. Beginning with romances of ghosts and murder, and with poetry at Eton, he passed at Oxford into metaphysics ; printed half-a-dozen pages which he entitled *The Necessity of Atheism;* sent one anonymously to Copleston, in expectation, I suppose, of converting him ; was expelled in consequence ; married a girl of seventeen, after being turned out of doors by his father ; and here they both are, in lodgings, living upon two hundred which his father allows him. He is come to the fittest physician in the world. At present he has got to the Pantheistic stage of philosophy, and in the course of a week I expect he will be a Berkleyan, for I have put him upon a course of Berkeley. It has surprised him a good deal to meet, for the first time in his life, with a man who perfectly understands him, and does him full justice. I tell him that all the difference between us is that he is nineteen and I am thirty-seven."

Excellent Southey! He did not suspect how absolutely out of all possibility of resemblance were his own well-ordered conservative character and this wild spirit of the clouds and elements, the fantastic delicate Ariel of poetry. How sternly different his opinions became afterwards will be apparent farther on.

Of Shelley's momentary repose amid the quietness of the lake country we know little more than this. Soon he was away again, as changeful as summer lightning, flashing now here, now there, unrestrained and irresponsible. His extreme youth adds a pathetic touch to the record of fitful misadventures, unhappinesses, panics, and quarrels, which in itself could scarcely be other than ridiculous. It was in 1813, a year after Southey formed this opinion of him, that *Queen Mab* was printed—a strange poem which he did not after care to reckon among his works, and which shows traces of something like the influence of Southey in its measure and structure, though so completely unlike in everything else. Mab, a fairy queen most un-Shakspearian, carries off the soul of Ianthe—for no particular reason the poet knows of—to show her the past and present of the earth : that is to say, the horrors that Religion and Government have wrought, with side glimpses into the miseries inflicted by kings, and the supreme tyranny of the God whom Christianity has imagined. It is a rhapsody, an impassioned embodiment of that fervent creed of Atheism which in those days had here and there a prophet, as again in our own. Shelley thought, like other enthusiasts, that the world was to be freed of all its troubles by the recognition of his tenets of faith, or rather, as it was in his case, of no faith—its abrogation of God, and law and rule. He had begun to correspond with Godwin while he was at Keswick, and the doctrines of *Political Justice* had taken hold on his congenial mind. It appears by some authorities that *Queen Mab* was begun at a much earlier period of his career; but the verse with which the poem opens bears very distinct marks of *Thalaba* about it:—

> " How wonderful is Death !
> Death and his brother Sleep—
> One pale as yonder waning moon
> With lips of lurid blue ;
> The other rosy as the morn
> When, throned on ocean's wave,
> It flashes o'er the world :
> Yet both so passing wonderful !"

Out of this Southeyan echo, however, the young poet falls after a while into dignified and melodious blank verse, even in this early and chaotic utterance, which neither in sentiment nor poetry is very much worth any one's while. It is said that Shelley, who printed it for private circulation, sent a copy to Byron with a letter, in which he enumerated all the accusations he had heard against his elder brother in poetry, with a demand to know if they were true ; as, if false, he wished to make Byron's acquaintance. Altogether, it is evident that the young poet, in the elation of his genius, felt himself full of power, and in a position to influence and almost command. Among other enterprises, he went solemnly to Ireland to assist in Catholic emancipation, strong in that unbounded belief in reason, and in himself as the expositor of reason, which a young man may be pardoned for entertaining at nineteen. He was still under twenty when he became a father, his poor little wife being still younger. Their life was one of perpetual difficulties of all kinds, as well as of restless and continual wanderings. Sometimes Shelley got an allowance from his father, sometimes lived precariously on the help afforded by Harriet's family and a sister of hers, who after a while came to live with them, and tyrannised over the pair of foolish wedded children. Leigh Hunt asserts that his position as heir of entail made it possible for him to secure from the Jews an income of a thousand pounds a year, upon the security of his future prospects, which seems feasible, since even a poet cannot subsidise and pension his friends unless he has some money to do it with; but this may have been at a later period. He married his poor young wife a second time in March 1814, at St. George's, Hanover Square, lest there should be any question of the legality of their Scotch marriage and in order, it appears, to secure to her quite certainly in case of his death the portion to which the widow of Sir Timothy Shelley's son would be entitled. This cautious step had scarcely been taken when the pair seem to have separated. It is not necessary to enter here into the much discussed and much questioned dates of these incidents. Shelley had begun to visit Godwin, with whom for some time he had kept up a close correspondence, and for whom he seems to have conceived a reverential attachment, in the beginning of this year; and in Godwin's homely house, in the parlour behind the bookseller's shop, in the midst of the mixed family which consisted of Mary Wollstonecraft's daughter and the existent Mrs.

Godwin's daughter, besides Godwin's own children, the young poet had seen a fair and serious girl of seventeen, full of philosophies and fancies like himself, and with a charm for him which Harriet had never possessed; for Harriet, it is supposed, had loved Shelley more than Shelley ever loved her, and had by this time fully convinced him that happiness with her was impossible. The story is altogether wild and strange, like his own mind. Whether he separated with a certain formality from his wife, whether he went off suddenly, leaving her with her two babies and fourteen shillings in her pocket, no one seems able to decide. The only thing certain is, that meeting with Mary Godwin suddenly "one eventful day in St. Pancras Churchyard by her mother's grave," he declared his love to the enthusiast girl, who had been brought up to believe in no necessary restraints upon such a passion. He told her his story "how he had suffered, how he had been misled, and how, if supported by her love," says the sympathetic historian, Lady Shelley, "he hoped in future years to enrol his name with the wise and good, who had done battle for their fellow-men, and had been true through all adverse storms to the cause of humanity. Unhesitatingly she placed her hand in his and linked her fortune with his own." No doubt the poet had eloquence at his command, and that the girl, so young and come of such a race, believed not only fervently in "the cause of humanity," which he intended to serve, but in her own power to support him by her love. A mother's grave seems a strange place for such a declaration; but not in this case, for no one would have been so ready as Mary Wollstonecraft to acknowledge the claim of love, and to dispense with the sanction of law. To neither of them did marriage seem either sacred or necessary. Harriet did not satisfy the poet; she was not enough for him: he had ceased to love her; what more

was there to say ?   Such was the creed of both.   "Unhesitatingly" they linked their lives together.   The verses
which he addressed to her, probably in the moment of
doubt before the decision was come to, do more to soften
our hearts than any other particular in the tale :—

> " Upon my heart thy accents sweet
>   Of peace and pity fell like dew
> On flowers half-dead ; thy lips did meet
>   Mine tremblingly, thy dark eyes threw ·
> Their soft persuasion on my brain,
> Charming away its dream of pain.
>
> " We are not happy, sweet ! our state
>   Is strange, and full of doubt and fear—
> More need of words that ills abate.
>   Reserve or censure come not near
> Our sacred friendship, lest there be
> No solace left for thee or me.
>
> " Gentle and good and mild thou art,
>   Nor can I live if thou appear
> Aught but thyself, or turn thy heart
>   Away from me, or stoop to wear
> The mask of scorn, although it be
> To hide the love thou feel'st for me."

It is wonderful to think of this young pair, with all
their feelings and impulses warped into a wrong way,
calling good evil, and evil good, and believing that the
indulgence of their inclinations was a sort of duty, setting
out together in defiance of all law and sacred custom and
constancy, without sense of guilt or feeling of shame.
The elopement took place in July 1814, only a few months
after the re-marriage.   Shelley was only twenty-two even
now, and Mary not seventeen.   The deserted wife, left
behind with her two children, came between the other two
in age, and was still under twenty.   They were little
more than children, fantastic, wayward, and self-willed,
playing with the mysteries of life, and not knowing what

they did.   It is half pitiful, half ludicrous, to hear the
account of this wild and criminal journey, which is like
the freak of a couple of truant children running away
from school, if it had not been for the tragical climax that
was to follow.   Godwin believed in marriage as little as
they did, and had both written and spoken against it as
one of the slaveries of the race; but he was a respectable
London citizen, a sort of John Gilpin in his way, notwithstanding all his lofty theories, and that his young visitor
should thus carry off his child did not please him any
more than it would have pleased a much less philosophical
parent.   It is curious to note how indulgently the world
has judged the actors in this wild drama.   Neither then
nor now has any harsh judgment been passed upon Mary
Shelley.   That offence which people are so fond of saying
is always cruelly visited upon the woman, scarcely seems
to have told against her.   When the event occurred which
turned the tale of lawless love into a tragedy, when poor
Harriet, forsaken, took away her own life, no one concerned has any strong feeling in the matter except one of
pity for Shelley and his new companion.   We are almost
required to regard the suicide as an ill-natured act towards
these two innocent people on the part of the third, whose
existence, indeed, was sadly in their way, but whose death
was a reproach to them: so strangely do human partialities colour the events of life.

Before this terrible interruption of the curious irresponsible self-pleasing life of the young poet, there had,
however, been an interval, in which many events occurred.
Shelley was not much less an unsettled wanderer with
Mary than he had been with Harriet; but under the
great trees in Windsor Park, on the edge of which he
lived for some time, and afloat upon the soft-flowing
Thames, the great tide of poetry, which had already moved
within him in broken impulses, rose full in his mind.

The first of his poems, which really was worthy of his powers—*Alastor*—was written in the first year of this union. It is the first real indication of the new voice which had awakened in English literature. It was like nothing else then existing; nor do we know to what to compare it in the past. Shelley had no story to tell, no character to disclose; his was pure poetry, music such as charmed the ear and filled the mouth with sweetness. Never was poet so eager to teach, or with so many wild assertions to make, or so strong a conviction of the possibility of influencing humanity and changing the world; but the soul of his poetry was the same as that of music, not definite, scarcely articulate, only melodious, ineffably sweet. *Alastor* was ushered into the world with a somewhat pompous preface, in which it is described as " allegorical of one of the most interesting situations of the human mind," the search of the poetic spirit, which has exhausted every form of intellectual enjoyment, for something better, for the ideal, which he seeks in vain to find in another human being. " The picture is not barren of instruction to actual men. The poet's self-centred seclusion was avenged by the furies of an irresistible passion pressing him to sudden ruin." But the reader never pays much attention to the directions which prescribe to him what he is to understand and admire; and probably no one now thinks of looking at the preface, or even asks, as he reads, what *Alastor* means; for, indeed, the meaning is wholly lost in the music of the words. " Actual men" have nothing to do with it; and it conveys no lesson, nor anything that is within the reach of the practical. This was not the intention of the writer; to his own thinking, he was nothing if not a teacher.

The simplicity of the primitive moral which Coleridge by poetical caprice chose to affix to his *Ancient Mariner* reappears, in still less feasible connection with anything that has gone before, in the new strain. Probably it was the example of that poem which suggested to Shelley the idea of putting a moral to his rhapsody. "Those who love not their fellow-beings live unnatural lives, and prepare for their old age a miserable grave," he says, from his pulpit as it were : and then plunges into the word-music, the soft fleeting of melodious syllables, descriptions of what never was in earth or air. Here is the first striking of the key-note, more definite than anything that follows :—

> "Earth, ocean, air, belovèd brotherhood !
> If our great Mother has imbued my soul
> With aught of natural piety to feel
> Your love, and recompense the boon with mine ;
> If dewy morn, and odorous noon, and even,
> With sunset and its gorgeous ministers,
> And solemn midnight's tingling silentness ;
> If autumn's hollow sighs in the sere wood,
> And winter robing with pure snow and crowns
> Of starry ice the gray grass and bare boughs ;
> If spring's voluptuous pantings when she breathes
> Her first sweet kisses, have been dear to me ;
> If no bright bird, insect, or gentle beast
> I consciously have injured, but still loved
> And cherished these my kindred ; then forgive
> This boast, belovèd brethren, and withdraw
> No portion of your wonted favour now !
>
> "Mother of this unfathomable world !
> Favour my solemn song, for I have loved
> Thee ever, and thee only ; . . .
>   ·   ·   ·   ·   ·   ·
>   And though ne'er yet
> Thou hast unveiled thy inmost sanctuary,
> Enough from incommunicable dream,
> And twilight phantasms and deep noonday thought,
> Has shone within me, that serenely now
> And moveless, as a long-forgotten lyre
> Suspended in the solitary dome
> Of some mysterious and deserted fane,
> I wait thy breath, Great Parent, that my strain

> May modulate with murmurs of the air,
> And motions of the forests and the sea,
> And voice of living beings, and woven hymns
> Of night and day, and the deep heart of man."

This aspiration was as near fulfilled in Shelley's verse as poetical prayer could be; not his was Wordsworth's lofty religious use of nature and her sacred sights and sounds; not his the mystic revelations which Coleridge found in the unseen : but a voice modulated " with murmurs of the air and motions of the forests," with all the inarticulate harmony of being, with those fragmentary thoughts that give a soul to the musings of the solitary, and those profound sensations which move the heart, all the more deep for being undefined. The old-fashioned harp had come back to the hands that could touch it. The instructors, the prophets, the seers, even the minstrels had a different office. Shelley was song embodied. In vain did he pour forth miles of verses, his *Alastor*, his *Revolt of Islam*, his wild politics and wilder morals upon the world, believing in his inmost soul that this was his mission, to convince men that their God was a Fiend and their laws tyranny, and that Godwin's *Political Justice* was the new gospel. Mankind has instincts which are wiser than genius. We have rejected, some with horror, but more with a smile, his vain teachings; but we have not rejected Shelley. So long as he stands before the world and sings, we will listen though his subjects be to us as folly and his meaning as madness. No matter what he says—even the *Witch of Atlas*, even the *Epipsychidion*, which the multitude can only listen to with a bewildered sense of something melodious but no clearer notion—contain such a soul of harmony as beguiles the sternest critic. It is like that voice which Wordsworth heard in the harvest field. We do not even ask to know what it is about—

" Whate'er the theme the Maiden sang,
    As if her song could have no ending.

    •   •   •   •   •

I listen motionless and still ;
    And as I mounted up the hill,
    The music in my heart I bore
    Long after it was heard no more."

After the composition of *Alastor*, Shelley, with his
Mary and the young woman who had accompanied them
on their first flight, Jane Clairmont, the daughter of
Mary's stepmother, went to Switzerland in the early
summer of 1816 ; and here it was that Byron, setting
out, sick with trouble and discovery, and a disorderly life,
upon the second tragical round of his pilgrimage, encountered the other poet and his belongings in the neighbourhood of Geneva. In opposition to the story that
Shelley had sent *Queen Mab* to Byron with a sort of
indictment against him and desire to know if these things
were true, it is said by some that Shelley now sent to
Byron an account of the sins attributed to himself, and
desired his acquaintance if he thought fit to bestow it on
knowing all that was said against him. However that
might be, the two met at the inn, where they both lived,
and formed instant acquaintance. There is as much in
common among poets as among craftsmen of a humbler
kind. Coleridge and Southey first, Coleridge and Wordsworth afterwards, had come by freemasonry of genius and
youth into instant friendship and mutual communication
to each other of all poetical properties some twenty years
before. What a wonderful difference between that frugal
and poor brotherhood, pure, honourable, and unknown, in
all their flush of youthful ardour and high thought, and
this other two, perhaps more splendidly endowed, richer,
of higher fortunes, and far more unhappy ! The former
held their position against all the pinches of need, in face

of the outcry of the world.   What could the world do to
them ?   Coleridge, indeed, exposed himself to much painful criticism and comment, especially in the latter part of
his career ; but the others lived such upright and simple
lives, as took all possibility of a sting out of every evil
tongue, and vindicated the high office of poetry over all
the world.   They preached the sacredness of love, the
wonder and mystery of life, the nobleness of duty, the
loveliness of self-devotion.   Strange contrast ! The younger
brethren proclaimed a different, an altered code.   Duty
to them had no existence, nor authority, nor the restraints
of nature grave and chaste.   Their principle was that of self-
will, the satisfaction of desire, the destruction of control, the
perfect liberty of doing, not as they ought, but as they would.
To Shelley's fantastic soul, the fact that a certain thing
" ought" to be done made the doing of it an offence against
human freedom.   It was not that he loved evil, for, notwithstanding his desertion of one woman for another, there
is no evidence in him of a nature impure.   But immorality,
as we name it, was to him a matter of principle, and the
wish of the moment a sacred impulse which it was duty to
obey.   Byron, a thousand times less innocent, was without this visionary philosophical preference for the for-
bidden, and while he sinned was ever conscious of a
tremor of conscience ; but with Shelley, all instincts were
good, and that self-will which Christianity insists shall be
subdued, was the only god and potentate he acknowledged.
Byron, so far as appears, had no philosophical code, but
he was a man of unbridled self-regard and what we call
passions—and when he wished for anything secured it
when that proved possible, without proclaiming it right to
do so, yet with a preponderance of fleshly appetite to
which the sectary beside him was a stranger.   To carry
out the contrast, this second group and brotherhood of poets
on the banks of another lake fell into a manner of united

living which controverted not only the laws and customs
of society, but all that the common consent of mankind
has considered necessary for the well-being of the race.
The strange code in which the children of Godwin's house
had been trained, and which the three wilful young souls
who composed Shelley's irregular party, held with combative ardour, saw little harm in the idea that the friend-
sister who had accompanied Mary should become to Byron
what Mary was to Shelley. It is possible even that they
may have believed this connection a possible way of
reclaiming and saving Byron, as Shelley congratulated
himself on having been saved. As for Byron, a soul far
more polluted, he plucked without hesitation a flower where
he could find it, and in the desperation of his soul, after
the catastrophe which had made all pretences at respectability useless to him, was ready to plunge into any and
every such excitement. Thus license reigned in one
company of the poets, to whom, the one philosophically,
the other sensually, inclination and passion were the
powers that swayed existence—a wonderful contrast to
the stainless living and lofty teaching of the elder brotherhood among the colder lakes and mountains of the north.

This joint life lasted for about four months, a whole
wonderful (but wet and stormy) summer. The Shelleys
took a smaller house near to the greater one inhabited by
Byron. They were both poor enough; but it was the
reckless pennilessness of a wealthy class always capable
of procuring luxuries, and not the thrifty and limited
existence of the really poor. Their life was spent in a
succession of refined and delightful amusements, in boat-
ing parties on the lake, in moonlight wanderings, in parties
of poetic conversation prolonged far into the night, which
sometimes made it expedient that one household belated
should encamp under the roof of the other : all was indulgence, pleasure, society, without any of those limits

which ordinary life enforces. Once the two poets set out together round the shores of the lake, going over the scenery of Rousseau's great work with enthusiasm and emotion indescribable. Shelley had never read the *Heloise* before, which was so happy a chance! They lingered about " sweet Clarens, birthplace of deep Love," and strayed through the " bosquet de Julie" silent, moved almost to tears, glad that no vulgar spectator was by to see their emotion : and felt that Rousseau had not chosen for uses of fiction this wonderful landscape, but that it was the very " scene which passion must allot to the mind's purified being." It is to be feared that most of us nowadays find the Lake Leman somewhat prosaic, re-membering little and caring less about Julie and St. Preux, unwholesome lovers ; but to Byron and Shelley they were divine. Off the rocks of Meillerie they were once caught in a storm, and for the moment looked for nothing but destruction. All this may be seen reflected in the third canto of *Childe Harold,* which is little more than a poetical narrative of the musings and wanderings of that summer holiday. Shelley would seem to have been passive for the moment, receiving all these images into his mind without immediate use of them : but Byron was in full tide of creative power, roused by the great storm of his life into restless energy and force. He could not be still or keep silence in that flood-tide of his genius. His passions, his wild impulses, his wrongs, surged high within him and quickened every faculty. " Agitation or contest of any kind," he himself says, " gives a rebound to my spirits, and sets me up for the time." Perhaps, too, though the breaking up of his life contained so much that was miserable, it was a relief to him to get rid of the unreal and wretched existence which he had been leading in London, in forced subjection to rules which he hated, and in companionship with a woman whose inspiration, in every point, was at variance with his own. And Shelley, too, had wrongs and profound grievances, which sometimes burned within him, and somtimes overflowed in expressions of anguish. They were both miserable and injured because the world would not permit them, unchecked, to do as they would, and retained to themselves the privilege of railing, with high indignation and poetic fervour, against that world and its restrictions, even while emancipated from its juris-diction, and following their own pleasures triumphantly as the rule of their life. Strange contrast and pendant to the poetic life of Grassmere and Keswick, with all their pieties and solemnities, the grave simplicity, the laborious calms, the mountain stillness, and voices of the cataract from the steeps ! On Lake Leman the two young pairs talked endless sentiment, shed tears of voluptuous emotion, talked through the warmth of summer nights, floated in their boats on the warm bosom of the luxurious lake ; or were awed by the semi-grand, semi-theatrical artillery of the storm among the mountains, and in the midst of their enjoyments gave themselves up to corresponding storms of injured feeling, of reproach and fiery outcry against earth and heaven. What had earth and heaven done to them ? Objected to let them have their own way—that, and little more.

The third canto of *Childe Harold* has a warmth of individual life in it, an emotion and power which the vaguer miseries and wanderings of the previous portions of that poem share in a much smaller measure. Every-body remembers the address to Ada with which it opens, and which is so much more genuine and real than the theatrical commonplace of Byron's *Farewell*. Nor is the key of real emotion, thus strongly struck, ever altogether lost through all the changes and variations of the strain. Some of his finest rhetorical passages, some of the tenderest touches of musing, of which by times his fiery soul was

capable, are to be found here. The description of the
night before Waterloo is now what people call hackneyed
—the strongest evidence of its splendid force and effect
which could be offered—since no poem is ever hackneyed
which has not gone straight to the popular heart. It
has embodied for us the wonderful excitement of that
historical scene as few historians could do, setting before
us as in a picture, as in a vision, the stern marching
columns, the dark preparations and readiness underneath,
with that light glowing brilliant scene in front of it suddenly arrested, the mirth turned to horror and dismay,
the gay sounds into a silence of tragic suspense and
despair. It is so breathless, so full of movement and
excitement, that the reader has no time to consider its
claims to poetical excellence. He is swept away by the
force of it, as if he had heard it glowing from the lips of
the spectator : it is eloquence of the highest kind. On
the other hand, those pictures of natural scenery which in
Byron's earlier days had been somewhat vague and conventional, have taken a new intensity and reality of life.
The following landscape, the very background of land and
water upon which the life of the two poets was set, we
select almost at random among many. Everything is in
it, sound and sight, and the sentiment of the summer
night with all its exquisite sensations and associations.

> " It is the hush of night, and all between
>   Thy margin and the mountains, dusk, yet clear,
>   Mellowed and mingling, yet distinctly seen,
>   Save darken'd Jura, whose capt heights appear
>   Precipitously steep ; and drawing near,
>   There breathes a living fragrance from the shore
>   Of flowers yet fresh with childhood ; on the ear
>   Drops the light drip of the suspended oar,
> Or chirps the grasshopper one good-night carol more ;
>
> " He is an evening reveller, who makes
>   His life an infancy, and sings his fill ;

At intervals, some bird from out the brakes
Starts into voice a moment, then is still.
There seems a floating whisper on the hill ;
But that is fancy, for the starlight dews
All silently their tears of love instil,
Weeping themselves away, till they infuse
Deep into nature's breast the spirit of her hues.

" Ye stars ! which are the poetry of heaven,
If in your bright leaves we would read the fate
Of men and empires,—'tis to be forgiven,
That in our aspirations to be great,
Our destinies o'erleap their mortal state,
And claim a kindred with you ; for ye are
A beauty, and a mystery, and create
In us such love and reverence from afar,
That fortune, fame, power, life, have named themselves a star.

" All heaven and earth are still—though not in sleep
But breathless as we grow when feeling most ;
And silent, as we stand in thoughts too deep :
All heaven and earth are still :—from the high host
Of stars, to the lulled lake and mountain-coast,
All is concentred in a life intense,
Where not a beam, nor air, nor leaf is lost,
But hath a part of being, and a sense
Of that which is of all Creator and defence."

If it were not that the soft purity and sweetness of
this picture is invaded and disturbed beyond remedy by
the other features of the story, we might be tempted to
forgive all that was included within the framework of
this lovely scene ; and, putting aside the ugly facts of the
story, the intercourse of these two young poets, their
prolonged and endless talk, the mutual stimulation of
minds so extraordinary, has an interest which nothing
can take from it. They were both in the earliest chapter
of manhood, though one of them had already wrecked the
prospects of his life, and the other set himself at variance
with every authority, and transgressed at least one primary
law of nature. Lawless and defiant of all rule, yet hot

and indignant that the society they outraged should have
pronounced against them, they stood beneath the pitying
heavens, the most nobly endowed of all their generation
—two rebel angels, beautiful, fortunate, unhappy ; everything in nature ministering to them, offering of its best ;
with faculties within them rich enough to atone for every
privation, yet enduring none—proud voluntary outcasts,
revolted kings of men.

On one of these wanderings, detained for a couple of
days by rain and stormy weather in little Ouchy by the
waterside, not far from the sober coquetries of Lausanne,
where Gibbon has left his formal memory, Byron wrote
the *Prisoner of Chillon*, one of the most perfect and purest
of his poems, but perhaps the least like his of anything
that ever came from his hand. It is the one grand
tribute which the great rebel of the age paid to Wordsworth, its greatest yet most strongly-resisted influence ;
and why that shadow should have touched and stilled
his spirit just at this tumultuous moment who can tell ?
It is one of the strangest caprices of his genius. Chillon,
where it stands projected into the silent blueness of the
lake, with its oubliettes, its dungeons, and those gloomy
openings into the water that suggest many a nameless
victim, has no doubt a dark and eventful history ; but
this little poem is its record to the world, and nobody,
now at least, asks further. No one of Byron's poems is
so purely narrative, or has such a unity of lofty and
tender interest, uninterrupted by a single distracting
image. But this very perfection makes it tame and cold
among the heat and animation of the rest : it is the only
one in which Byron is left out. No Harold smiles or
strides between the massive pillars. For once the conception of a being, who is not himself, has entered his
mind, an atmosphere of love and reverence and acknowledgment of the sanctities of human affection. We might

be beguiled into a speculation whether some wavering of
the compass towards virtue and truth, some vague comprehension of the secret of a higher happiness had come
to him from that calm of nature ; but there is no record
elsewhere of any such pause in the force of the torrent
which was his life.

Byron was not always in this chastened and purified
mood ; but he was in great intellectual activity during
this period, his mind thrilling with new life and passion.
He composed *The Dream*—that curious picturesque sentimental review of his own life, and insinuation of a remote
and inadequate cause for all its imperfections—at the
same time ; and also the address *To Augusta,* and several
other detached poems, all eloquent, animated, and fine.
On the other hand, it would not be difficult to find
episodes which are full of glittering rhetoric and little
more.   Of these is the well-known description of the
storm among the mountains :—

> " The sky is changed !—and such a change !   Oh night,
> And storm, and darkness, ye are wondrous strong,
> But lovely in your strength, as is the light
> Of a dark eye in woman !   Far along,
> From peak to peak, the rattling crags among,
> Leaps the live thunder !   Not from one lone cloud,
> But every mountain now has found a tongue,
> And Jura answers, through her misty shroud,
> Back to the joyous Alps, who call to her aloud !
>
> " And this is in the night :—Most glorious night !
> Thou wert not made for slumber ! let me be
> A sharer in thy fierce and far delight,—
> A portion of the tempest and of thee !
> How the lit lake shines, a phosphoric sea,
> And the big rain comes dancing to the earth !
> And now again 'tis black,—and now, the glee
> Of the loud hills shakes with its mountain-mirth,
> As if they did rejoice o'er a young earthquake's birth."

Another curious production of the two poetic house-

holds must here be noted. Lewis, popularly known as
Monk Lewis, paid Byron a visit at his villa, and became
one of the little society, which was often confined within
four walls by the rain, and eager after every new excitement, as people imprisoned in a country house so universally are. They told each other ghost stories, and tales
of mystery and wonder under the inspiration of the kind
little inoffensive romancer, who was then master of that
branch of the arts ; and he or some one else suggested that
they should all write for their mutual diversion tales of
this character. The only one who carried out the suggestion was Mary, the youngest of the party, a girl not yet
eighteen, notwithstanding the turmoil of life into which
she had been plunged. That a young creature of this age
should have produced anything at once so horrible and so
original as the hideous romance of *Frankenstein*, is one of
the most extraordinary accidents in literature ; and that
she should never, having made such a beginning, have
done anything more, is almost equally wonderful. Byron
is said to have begun a similar sketch, entitled *The
Vampyre*, which his physician-attendant, Polidori, afterwards added to and printed ; but none of the detailed
records of the time inform us what were the feelings of
excitement and terror with which the little company,
thrilled by the tales of Lewis, listened to the portentous
and extraordinary production with which the fair small
girl, with her big forehead and her sedate aspect, out-
Heroded Herod. Mary Shelley's individual appearances
afterwards are only those of a romantically-desolate
widow, pouring out her grief and fondness in sentimental
gushes, which look somewhat overstrained and ridiculous
in print, whatever they may have done in fact ; but to
hear her read, with her girlish lips, this most extraordinary
and terrible of imaginations, must have been a sensation
unparalleled. It is one of the books adopted into the

universal memory, which everybody alludes to, and thousands who can never have read it understand the main incidents of — which is a wonderful instance of actual fame. That this should be merely stated as a fact in the history, and no one pause to wonder at it, is another odd instance of the insensibility of contemporaries.

Shelley and his companions left Switzerland in the end of August 1816, breaking up this poetical society, and returned to England. Byron stayed longer, until other friends—his always faithful brethren, Sir John Cam Hobhouse and Mr. Scrope Davies—joined him : and went on in October to Italy. There he settled, in Venice, where his life is said to have been such as scandal itself dislikes to dwell upon. His letters are of the same lively and superficial character as before, but, when any evidence of feeling breaks out, there is nothing but disappointment and misery in the record. "My day is over," he says to Moore. "What then ? I have had it. To be sure, I have shortened it"—and he describes the poems he had sent home from Switzerland, especially the third canto of *Childe Harold*, as "a fine indistinct piece of poetical desolation." "I was very mad during the time of its composition," he adds, "between metaphysics, mountains, lakes, love inextinguishable, thoughts unutterable, and the nightmare of my own delinquencies. I should many a day have blown my brains out, but for the recollection that it would have given great pleasure to my mother-in-law." Amid this levity it is hard to understand how much real feeling there was. His "love inextinguishable" was no doubt the passages with Miss Clairmont, which lasted but a little time ; but that there is a kind of madness in the headlong and irregulated life which avoids all pauses for thought, and keeps itself intoxicated with something—mountains and moonlight, or light loves, or

.grosser stimulants—no one will deny. Unfortunately it is not the poet only who applies such opiates to a troubled conscience and a broken life.

The third canto of *Childe Harold* had expressed the more manly moods of Byron's mind, and the more wholesome interests of his life; but all the time, while he floated about the lake and climbed the hills and composed those melodious stanzas, another poem of a different order was shaping itself in his mind. From the often noble musings of *Childe Harold*, and the grave tenderness and dignity of the *Prisoner of Chillon*, he threw himself back upon the old stage-hero, upon that theatrical sufferer of the past, the Conrad, the Lara, of former years, and made him into a shape still more tragic and solitary. It is curious to read all the tranquil extracts from his Swiss diary, which are quoted as notes to *Manfred* by way of showing how much real observation and study of nature was in that poem, and to perceive how carefully all the images that struck him at the moment are saved up for use, and how the scenes of his careless journey, cheerfully recorded and made in the congenial company of friends, are made to serve and heighten the solitary sufferings of the self-tormented hero. *Manfred* has passed, we think, in great measure, from the mind of the reader. The number of students who read an author through, and know everything he has written, is always few. The greater part of the world makes instinctive selection of what is immortal, and leaves the rest, if not to perish, at least to freeze and crystallise, without any living soul of human remembrance to keep it fresh. But at the moment when these works are getting published, nobody can tell which it will be that posterity will choose : and when we read Jeffrey's awe-stricken applause and Wilson's enthusiastic appreciation, and find that even such an authority as Goethe declares *Manfred's* mouthings of mock despair to be an improvement on Hamlet's soliloquy, the extraordinary mistake takes away our breath. The one idea of Byron's limited imagination had been worked hardly enough in the previous tales, which made no such claim upon the reader. Subdued and enshrined in the fine poetry of *Childe Harold*, it has been added to the permanent population of the world; but to place this conventional form among the mighty mountains, and to surround him, in emulation of greater witcheries, with the vapoury visions of an unseen rather more vague and pyrotechnic than himself, was a rash and unfortunate experiment. The subject is one which only the most exceptional merit in the poetry could make tolerable; and the poetry is not exceptional, but below the highest level of Byron's power. To compare his *diablerie* with that of Goethe, or the songs of the spirits whom Manfred evokes, with the melody of Shelley's responses in the *Prometheus*, is to put him at an extraordinary disadvantage. Mr. Matthew Arnold has selected several of these dialogues between the magician and the powerful creatures of the air and elements whom he is supposed to call forth, as instances of Byron's dramatic power; but the dramatic meaning of these passages is surely of the smallest. The following fragment of a scene, after a laboured representation of the court of Ahrimanes, and the turbulent spirit-courtiers who endeavour vainly to make Manfred do homage to their ruler, does for one brief moment thrill the reader. After failing in all his demands upon the aërial potentates, he requires that the dead should be raised, the spirit of his love and victim, that from her he may understand the final mysteries. "Speak to me," he exclaims, when the vision stands silent before him—

> "Yet speak to me ! I have outwatch'd the stars,
> And gazed o'er heaven in vain in search of thee.
> Speak to me ! I have wander'd o'er the earth,

And never found thy likeness—Speak to me !
Look on the fiends around—they feel for me :
I fear them not, and feel for thee alone—
Speak to me ! though it be in wrath ;—but say—
I reck not what—but let me hear thee once—
This once—once more !
 Phantom of Astarte. Manfred !
 Man.   Say on, say on—
I live but in the sound—it is thy voice !
 Phan. Manfred ! To-morrow ends thine earthly ills.
Farewell !
 Man. Yet one word more—am I forgiven ?
 Phan. Farewell !
 Man.   Say, shall we meet again ?
 Phan. Farewell !
 Man. One word for mercy ! Say, thou lovest me.
 Phan. Manfred !"

In this scene there is great force and an almost awful
pathos. The impossibility, even when the highest spells
have been spoken and the most terrible dangers run, to
receive any satisfying token from beyond the grave : and
the anguish of the man's appeal to a being so far beyond
his reach, who has so entirely escaped him, yet was once
his, is very powerful and effective. In a very different
way, and with a sudden rupture of continuity and every
dramatic rule, the description of the moonlight night
and of the Colosseum in Rome may be called fine poetry :
but nothing could be more entirely out of place in the
soliloquy of a racked and tortured spirit on the brink of
destruction. " 'Tis strange that I recall it at this time,"
Manfred himself acknowledges in the very spirit of Mr.
Puff and his critics. And it seems very unnecessary to
create a highly endowed and intellectual spirit for the
purpose of singing a song like this ;—

  " Mont Blanc is the monarch of mountains,
   They crowned him long ago,
  On a throne of rocks, in a robe of clouds,
   With a diadem of snow."

Dr. Watts could have done it quite as well.

Byron lived in Venice for nearly four years. It would be out of place here to enter into the history of his life. He seems to have been delivered from the grosser indulgence of his senses by a real love, as he understood it, for the Countess Guiccioli, to whom he was deeply attached, yet of whom he wrote to his English correspondents with a levity which is little appropriate to a woman adored. In Venice he wrote *Manfred ;* the concluding canto of *Childe Harold ;* various shorter poems, which count for little among his works ; *Mazeppa ;* and at the same time made a beginning in a new order of verse and new kind of subject, in the airy gallop and original gaiety of *Beppo ;* afterwards ripening into the longer and more impassioned strains of *Don Juan,* two cantos of which were written and published during the year 1819, his last in Venice. After this he went to Ravenna, following the lady whose fortunes were henceforward linked with his, and who was faithful and devoted to him, although in a lawless way. It requires no great strain of charity, we think, to pardon Teresa Guiccioli. She was married at sixteen to an old man, according to family arrangement, as was usual ; and had scarcely married when she met the fascinating English poet, about whom all Venice was raving, and who was young and noble and unfortunate, an object of romantic interest everywhere. It was according to the morals of her time and country to permit a lover, the tie between the old husband and young wife in a *mariage de convenance* being so unnatural that permitted license has always been the consequence. This Italian girl had never been taught nor known better, and no hero of romance could have exercised a more powerful spell upon a young creature full of romance and sentiment, yet shut out from all legitimate indulgence of the poetry of youth. All that Italian morality required of her was a discreet audacity in the management of the situation. To English feeling, on the other hand, the rashness of self-devotion is a plea for forgiveness rather than a crime; and the woman who is unable to *ménager* the claims of her husband and her lover has a hold upon our regretful sympathy which a wiser sinner can never claim. We will not be thought to approve an immoral connection in attempting to say a word of tenderness and pity for the sweet and tender Italian girl from whose lips there never falls an unwomanly word, and whose breast was pure of all interested and worldly motives. She deserved far better than to be spoken of with disrespectful levity as la Guiccioli, and discussed by her lover with his publisher and his friends, in tones which probably do little justice to his feeling for her, but are part of the unpleasant garb of levity in which he thought proper to present himself even to those he esteemed most.

During the two years Byron spent in Ravenna he continued at full pressure of work, producing, except *Don Juan*, nothing upon which posterity has laid hands with any passion of approval, but at least one work, which once more set England and the critics by the ears. This was *Cain*, the wild and singular drama in which all the rebellious heroes of Byronic inspiration ascend, so to speak, to their origin and source. The first sceptic, the first doubter, the first rebel, a definite personage in whose difficulties we can at least see reason, attracts more of our sympathies than any weird recluse, or mysterious bandit. It is difficult to understand why, but for the reputation of the author, and a sort of scriptural prejudice against the art which could endeavour to interest us in that first criminal, so great an outcry should have been aroused by this poem, in which there is no real profanity. The sentiments of Lucifer, it is true, are not such as would become a churchwarden, but they are no more than we should expect from the individual in question. We have all been brought up upon Milton's Satan, and taught to consider his gloomy grandeur, not only as a lawful subject of our regard, but an edifying and religious one. Byron's Lucifer is not nearly so splendid, but he is not more opposed to Christian feeling; his assertion of power equal to that of God is more modern and shallow than Satan's nobler claim; but this vague self-assertion, and his failure to promise anything that can be called happiness as the reward of disobedience, and the tragical issue that follows, have a moral rather than an immoral tendency. What is a great deal more unfortunate is that Byron here falls into the temptation to use big words and swelling syllables to an extent unknown in anything else he has produced: and that Cain's sullen instinct of rebellion, his refusal to worship, his churlish assertion of the fact that he has been brought into the world without being consulted upon the subject, and that gratitude to the power which has bestowed such an equivocal favour as life upon him is by no means a necessity—in themselves sufficiently legitimate subjects of study—is couched in language too big and high sounding for poetry. Here is one of his speeches, and not the most grandiloquent :—

> "Oh, thou beautiful
> And unimaginable ether! and
> Ye multiplying masses of increased
> And still increasing lights! what are ye? what
> Is this blue wilderness of interminable
> Air, where ye roll along, as I have seen
> The leaves along the limpid streams of Eden?
> Is your course measured for ye? Or do ye
> Sweep on in your unbounded revelry
> Through an aërial universe of endless
> Expansion—at which my soul aches to think—
> Intoxicated with eternity?"

This is not poetry, whatever it may be; and Byron's philosophy was far from being his strong point. *Cain* is intended for the intensified and primal type of all the *Manfreds* and the *Laras;* but he is inferior to them in language and even dignity. His original attitude of passive rebellion is sulky, and himself churlish and ill-tempered. The primitive rebel and misanthrope wants the draping of the melodramatic cloak and sable plume, the furniture of mystery, in which his predecessors, yet descendants, have the advantage over him.

Of the dramas produced at the same period it is not necessary to say much. They are full of fine passages, and the subjects are worthy the genius of a great poet; but Byron's genius was not dramatic, and political passions, however tragic, do not furnish the individual note which it was in his power to strike. What old Faliero and old Foscari might have been in the hands of Shakspeare, who can say? but even to Shakspeare, who made choice of the "foolish, fond old man," the deceived and mistaken Lear, to produce his highest tragical effect, the intellectual and stoical Venetians would have given a difficult task. Byron acquitted himself creditably of a fine undertaking; but he did not stir the heart of the reader, or add any charm to the enchantments of that city, which has fewer personal associations than any other historical place, and reigns by right of its own beauty solely. The description of Venice given by Lioni in *Marino Faliero*, and which has been quoted to weariness, is perhaps the one passage which has found a place in the popular memory. It would be difficult to find a more beautiful picture, or more true to the scene; but the young noble, leaning over his balcony, and painting for us with so fine a touch the ideal portrait of his beautiful town, is entirely out of place dramatically, and if the interest were stronger, not the most beautiful poetry could

justify such an arrest and hindrance of all the movement
for the sake of anything unconnected with it. *Sardanapalus* is more in the poet's way : the effeminate reveller,
whom the touch of necessity can turn on the moment into
a hero-king, might indeed have afforded a noble subject to
a poet perhaps still capable of the same transformation.
But none of these works have any right to count as
foundations of Byron's fame. If they do not detract from
his greatness, that is all. His real titles to immortality
lie in *Childe Harold* and *Don Juan*, the two great supporters of his poetic skill.

Mr. Matthew Arnold has characterised poetry as " a
criticism of life." It is not, we think, a sufficient definition, but it is just so far as it goes. Poetry has other
and, we think, higher qualities. In its creative aspect
it reveals new chapters of life to our criticism, and new
creatures to run their little round like us, but in a concentrated and perfected circle for our example, not only as
commentators, but chief and splendid actors, more great
than we. But no poetry has ever more clearly carried
out and justified the definition of this writer than that
of Byron. His great poems are both criticisms of life,
investigations within a limited range of its course and
incidents. In *Childe Harold* the poet passes in review all
civilised nations, all the scenes of exceptional beauty which
have been dearest to mankind—the art that has illustrated
and immortalised them, the history which has filled them
with undying associations. Man and nature, and knowledge and beauty, all pass before him ; or rather it is he—
supreme observer, narrator, spectator, of all, heir of time,
and lord of creation—who glides by all that has been and
that is, made for our instruction, like the types and the
prophecies in which even the prophets themselves saw
darkly, a meaning to be unfolded only in after generations.
In *Don Juan* the situation is somewhat different ; the

hero is no longer a spectator, but yet the poet, in him and through him, threading a maze of incidents and innumerable digressions and commentaries, carries on the most lively, profane, unscrupulous criticism of life on which man or poet has ever ventured.   Both these critics are, so to speak, on the outside of the subject, fathoming the heart and its deeper mysteries little, yet penetrating social pretences with scornful levity and indignation, with fierce laughter and contempt.   The life they comprehend is limited, and their insight is limited; but, so far as it goes, keen as the lightning and recklessly unmerciful.   The reader, perhaps, will exclaim against this assertion, taking Byron, as he is so often taken, for the poet of passion, the impersonation of all that is most unbridled and unlimited in human feeling: and we must endeavour as best we can to justify our opinion.   It will be necessary, first, however, to indicate what seems to us the essential division which exists between the two theories of life which all poetry, all fiction, and indeed literature in every sphere, has to illustrate and set forth.

And we cannot better illustrate our meaning than by turning back once more upon our comparison of the Wordsworthian and Byronic group—the two great poetic tribes of the period.   Nothing can be more different than the two aspects of life of which these poets, on one side and the other, are the critics and expositors.   Each has his natural band of sympathisers and disciples.   The distinction between them is regulated to some degree by the influence of external position; those who are exempted from their birth from the vulgar burdens of humanity are more likely to enter into the views of the one, those who have their share of toil and privation into the other.   But no such external influences hold universally, and many a hardworking soul has found a relief in leaping into the freedom and individualism of Byron's heroes; while to some, amid all the softnesses and leisure of life, Wordsworth's revelations of supreme and lowly Duty have been a refreshment and renewal of the soul.   But the distinction is as clear as that between night and day.   He who contemplates life with the eyes of the latter sees men and women bound by a hundred ties, burdened by weights not of their making, under command of duties and of circumstances, and as incapable of extricating themselves from the hands that cling to them, and the exertions that are required of them, as a soldier at his post is incapable of asserting the freedom of a savage to follow his own devices.   And a great part of humankind are of the opinion that the career of a man thus burdened—his vindication of truth and honour amid all trials, his steadfast standing at his post, his subordination of himself and his wishes at all cost of pleasure and comfort, and even of existence, to those for whom he is responsible, and the office he has to fulfil—is the worthiest object of regard, of admiration, and sympathy.   But the others take a different stand.   To them the individual, detached from all other individuals, is the object of supreme interest.   The adventures he passes through, the intrigues in which he is entangled, his pleasures, and the price he pays for them, are considered as means of education for himself, and fulfil their highest object in maturing and completing that separate being whose progress, as he moves across the stage of life, without ever losing himself in the crowd or stopping short in his individual career, has a charm which is never exhausted.   Whether he sweeps recklessly along upon the tide with Byron, or picks his way through the lessons of experience, like Goethe, he maintains always his isolation, his complete independence, taking what he wants or wishes out of the various groups he passes through, but owing no debt or responsibility to them in return.   Life is the study of both schools of poetry, but how different the life !   In

the one case full of all the complications of humanity,
those liens upon natural freedom which most men have to
accept, the burdens that love and pity bind upon the soul,
the noble restraints of duty, the inextricable minglings of
social existence ; in the other an individual career in which
these bonds are either eluded or defied, and which, though
it gains in unity what it loses in breadth, must always
be exceptional—a prodigy and wonder in a world full of
confused and interlacing interests.   How it is that the
progress of such an isolated soul towards perfection, or
towards satisfaction—or towards that exhaustion of hope
and weariness of soul which the first great poet who
handled it has proclaimed with such force in the solemn
sadness of Ecclesiastes—should be rather through vices
than through virtues, it is hard to tell.   But so it is.
When a man has fathomed all things, and finds them
vanity, it is almost invariably the sinful indulgences, the
license and excitement of evil-doing, through which he
makes his essays.   The art which selects for its sphere
this development of individual mind is not necessarily
immoral ; but it is almost bound to deal with the immoral
for the sake of the freedom which is indispensable to its
operations, just as the other, which places its ideal in
the high fulfilment of duty, must be moral by the mere
exigencies of art.

Byron is the chief and greatest British exponent
of this classic independence and individualism.   Childe
Harold and the other more active repetitions of that hero,
are presented to us in the stillness of their gloomy self-
completion, after they have investigated life and found it
nought—like Solomon, a vanity of vanities.   But in *Don
Juan* we are presented with the process itself, according
to the poet's conception of it.   And what an extraordinary
process it is !   This poem, in which Byron has poured
out a force and fulness of life which it is hard to find a

match for, spontaneous as running water, rapid, eloquent, extraordinary, full of the vulgarities and pettinesses of the meanest mind, and of sentiments and perceptions worthy of the highest, is a web of reckless and heartless licentiousness from beginning to end. His hero lacks the charm which other and inferior bearers of the name have possessed in that dauntless gallantry and bold confronting of whatever offers—hell and its mysteries, as well as all lesser penalties of the flesh—which have always given the spectator a thrill of admiration for the daring cynic, the splendid criminal of the original legend, the Juan of Molière, even the Giovanni of the opera. Byron's Juan in himself is a mixture of an amiable and pretty youth with a mischievous and elvish spirit. He is no more at best than a dissolute page, to whom vice is partly fun, a depraved Cherubino, an impudent and shameless boy, too trifling to be guilty. After the tragic death of Haidee, which has roused the poet to a higher art, and moved him for the moment into impassioned and genuine poetry, the hero skulks off like a whipped schoolboy. If he had robbed an orchard or a cupboard he could scarcely have been less dignified in his punishment, or more easily cured of his smarting. The heartless and soulless young scapegrace has nothing whatever to do with any higher penalty or consciousness. His whipping over, he goes forth again an impudent young rover once more. It is possible that it pleased the angry spirit of Byron to put forth to the world which he regarded so bitterly, and which he believed had wronged and injured him, a worthless image like this as the quintessence of youth and romance; but it is just as likely that it was the mere recklessness of composition, and that he put down Juan as printers in their proofs sometimes put a hieroglyphic in the place of a much-used letter, to save him the time and trouble necessary for the creation of a worthier hero. And the hero is fitly set in

the greater part of those moral or immoral reflections in
which the poet, shameless as himself though so much
greater, chooses to frame his rambling story.   Criticism
of life !   Lord Byron is not the first who has dignified the
hackneyed fable of uncleanness with that name ; but it is
strange with what ease it has always been accepted as
such, as if life were limited to one combination and confined to the narrow span of existence in which " passion "
so called, bears sway.

It would be easy, however, if this were all, to dismiss
Don Juan as something like the insult to his language
and his country which, at the first appearance, to judge
by the universal assent of all contemporary writers, it was
felt to be.   But this strange poet, this cynical commentator upon vice, this critic of wives found out and husbands
made ridiculous, of confidential maids and complaisant
duennas, and all the frowsy paraphernalia of debauchery,
would not have been the wonder he is had there been no
admixture in the strain.   But when the reader, disgusted,
turns the leaf, from where the laughing devil on one page
flouts at vice alike and virtue, he finds an angel, all
unabashed by such company, unconscious of it, on the
next.   Imagine the man who, in the midst of his filthy
story, drawing breath for a moment to enable him to
pile the excitement higher, glides unaware into verses
like these :—

> " We'll talk of that anon.——'Tis sweet to hear
>   At midnight on the blue and moonlit deep
> The song and oar of Adria's gondolier,
>   By distance mellow'd, o'er the waters sweep ;
> 'Tis sweet to see the evening star appear ;
>   'Tis sweet to listen as the night-winds creep
> From leaf to leaf ; 'tis sweet to view on high
> The rainbow, based on ocean, span the sky ;
>
> " 'Tis sweet to hear the watch-dog's honest bark
>   Bay deep-mouth'd welcome as we draw near home ;

> 'Tis sweet to know there is an eye will mark
>   Our coming, and look brighter when we come ;
> 'Tis sweet to be awaken'd by the lark,
>   Or lull'd by falling waters ; sweet the hum
> Of bees, the voice of girls, the song of birds,
> The lisp of children, and their earliest words."

Still worse, still more wonderful, is the contrast between the nasty repetition of an oft-told tale in the discovery of Julia's sin by her husband, and the letter of noble and devoted love which, introduced and followed by the most cynical banter, the poet makes his vulgar *intriguante* write to his impudent boy-lover.   Nothing before leads us to expect it, nothing after justifies it.   Genius, grown sick of its own wilful self-desecration, and of all the filth about, flings out into this sudden caprice, and in a moment, and for a moment, vindicates itself.   Was it, one wonders, the appeal of some pure glance, the clearness of some reproachful sky, that shamed his reckless spirit ? Thus for page after page the riotous brilliant stream runs on, full of everything we hate, yet dazzling us with its sparkle and impetuous flood, which here and there changes, is stilled, and reflects no more vile earth and its most debasing passions, but catches through the tangled shadows in their rank growth overhead, a sudden bewildering glance of heaven.

This redeeming touch, if we may call it so, only added to the natural indignation of the better critics of the time, who were revolted by the introduction of refined sentiments in unworthy mouths, and pure and noble feeling, even a fragment of it, amid the steam and fermentation of impurity.   The first two cantos appeared alone in 1819, without the name of either author or publisher, a foolish attempt at mystery which warranted the common reproach that both were ashamed of the production.   Mr. Murray, most respectable of publishers, very likely was so ; but Byron was not to be concealed.   He watched the effect from his Venetian palace, withdrawn out of reach of all the clamorous voices which hailed it with almost universal reprobation, with something of mingled bravado and alarm, like that of a man who has thrown a bomb and waits to see its effect; and though he professes the utmost indifference to that effect, there would seem little doubt that it did move him. The after cantos contain nothing like the story of Haidee for beauty and tenderness; but neither are they so bold in offence. The poet runs away in the voluble easy rattle of his commentary upon the surface of society. Long ere we have got to the end of the stream it has run into a delta of mud and sand, in which the rills of story are lost; and the end is confusion, without either force or meaning of its own, or any connection with what has gone before. The shipwreck and the siege stand out from the midst of the dalliance with all the force of contrast. Few verses have been more constantly quoted than the description of the former, which presents us, when in the midst of a great deal of somewhat grim laughter it touches tragedy, with a very forcible and splendid piece of rhetorical narrative. It is scarcely necessary to allude to the savage onslaught upon the poets of the other school, and especially upon Southey, into which he breaks from time to time, or to the supposed fiercely satirical description of his wife under the character of Donna Inez, with which the poem opens. This is in every respect indefensible, both morally and as a work of art. No poem in the English language that we are aware of, so long and so important, is so unworthy; but its vigour and vitality are as unequalled as are its perversity and cynicism, its fierce abuse and unbridled impurity. There is scarcely a pause or stop in the impetuous and brilliant torrent which pours forth adown plain and hollow, as if from burning springs. It has fallen now into the still current of general literature, and rouses at

least no personal passions; but such was not the case at
the moment of its appearance. Byron's best friends in
London sat in grave committee upon the manuscript, and
shook their heads and would have suppressed it altogether,
as they afterwards suppressed his autobiographical remains.
But the impetuous poet would not listen to them. He
was greatly wounded and offended, it is evident, by the
comments of "my cursed puritanical committee," as he
calls them. "If you had told me the poetry was bad,"
he says "I would have acquiesced; but they say the
contrary, and then talk to me about morality." He
threatens therefore that he will write his best book in
Italian, though "it will take me nine years more
thoroughly to master the language," and declares that he
cares nothing for the English public. "I have not written
for their pleasure," he cries; "I have never flattered their
opinions nor their pride; nor will I. Neither will I
make 'ladies' books' *al dilettar le femine e la plebe.* I
have written from the fulness of my mind, from passion,
from impulse, from many motives, but not for their sweet
voices." This passionate disclaimer is so clearly that of a
man in the wrong as to require no commentary. It is
not the man indifferent to popular applause who protests
with such heat that he does not seek it. No one was
ever more susceptible to it. At a later period he tells
the long-suffering Murray that "the things I have read
and heard," after the publication of the first two cantos,
"discourage all further publication, at least for the
present," and offers pettishly to return the price of the
copyright. Disapprobation took the heart out of him.
"They have not the spirit of the first," he says of the
later cantos. "The outcry has not frightened, but it has
hurt me; and I have not written *con amore* this time.
It is very decent, however, and as dull as the last new
comedy."

The composition of *Don Juan* was stopped half way, at the prayer of Madame Guiccioli, but afterwards resumed. Probably it was intended to be much longer, or at least the poet did not intend that his Pegasus should run away with him into those wide digressions of sharp wit and superficial philosophy, abuse, and scandal, which form the greater part of the poem, and had meant to make his hero illustrate the life of various countries in a much longer succession of adventures. But though his genius had not failed, his life had begun to flag; and to all appearance he let himself be carried away on the current of facile and brilliant verse without taking count where he was going. Probably he was aware that he had lost himself and his purpose, and therefore stopped abruptly with the sudden sensation of impatience and self-disgust which overtook easily a mind so little assured of itself, though so rash and obstinate by times. The graver composition of the plays went on at the same time, and so did the heavy and solemn *Prophecy of Dante*, and his translation of an unreadable Italian poem the *Morgante Maggiore* of Pulci, to which, with his usual strange misapprehension of his own powers, he attached the greatest importance. Pulci was, in his own opinion, the fountainhead from which he got that new spring of poetry which he had essayed in *Beppo*, and made famous in *Don Juan*. It was the rhyme of Hookham Frere's poem of *Whistlecraft*, already referred to; but Byron would not consent to follow the inspiration of Frere. "Pulci," he says, "is the parent not only of *Whistlecraft*, but of all jocose Italian poetry." He did not succeed in interesting Englishmen in this great original, but he made the "light horse gallop" of the measure to be supereminently successful for the discursive treatment he loved, and this was a better demonstration of its merits than any obsolete Italian could have given.

According to all the rules of growth and development, it should have been *Juan* who came first out of the burning fermenting brain of the young poet, and *Childe Harold,* which followed later, out of his maturing mind and calmer intelligence. Had it been so, Byron might perhaps have lived and expanded into greater work and better fame ; but this, unhappily, was not the course of his genius. We have already spoken of the early cantos of *Childe Harold* which brought him at a bound to the very pinnacles of fame. If these first bursts of a poetry still vague and half awakened had so great an effect upon the public mind, what must have been the sensation produced when, flying from real ruin and overthrow, the catastrophe which ended all better hope for him, and made him doubly defiant of a world which he believed had used him so hardly—the passionate pilgrim dashed forth once more over the sea into the unknown, full of anguish and resistance, but with every power heightened, and life itself running doubly strong in his veins ? In the third canto, the new beginning of this great poem, Byron attains his climax. He has never been so near our sympathies, never so near the deeper secrets of life. For the first time he comes within the range of influences more penetrating and sacred than the passions and semi-fictitious despair of his youth. The air is tremulous about him with a possible conversion. It seems to hang on the poise of a breath, whether the perverse, headstrong, capricious, undisciplined soul may not seek refuge, with its wounds and smarting sense of wrong and misery, amid the soft ministrations of nature, in the grateful stillness of hills and waters, of simplicity and peace. Now and then this possibility seems so near that it is all but realised. The contrast of the " clear placid Leman " with the wild world he has abandoned—

"Warns me with its stillness to forsake
   Earth's troubled waters for a purer spring."

He feels the infinity stir around him as he stands in that
solitude where he is least alone ; " the quiet sail is as a
noiseless wing " carrying him away from all impure distractions. " Are not the mountains, waves, and skies a
part of me and of my soul ?" he asks in that musing mood,
which never was so profound and tender :

"And thus I am absorb'd, and this is life ;
   I look upon the peopled desert past,
   As on a place of agony and strife,
   Where, for some sin, to sorrow I was cast,
   To act and suffer, but remount at last
   With a fresh pinion ; which I feel to spring,
   Though young, yet waxing vigorous as the blast
   Which it would cope with, on delighted wing,
Spurning the clay-cold bonds which round our being cling."

The poet never realised these wavering possibilities.
Other influences were too many for him. He went
back to the wretched elements of life, and sank down
from those dawnings of a higher soul to vulgar passion
and vulgarer trite cynicism and philosophy. But we
have the best of Byron in the last half of the *Pilgrimage.*
Everything is stimulated in him : his perceptions, his
natural feelings, his capability of thought, and the more
liquid and larger music of his verse.

CHAPTER III.

SHELLEY——BYRON.

SHELLEY and his companions left Lake Leman in the end of the summer of 1816, leaving Lord Byron there to pursue his course southwards a little later. In November of that same year the tragic incidents to which we have before alluded threw gloom and additional reproach upon the life of the younger poet. Harriet, his young wife, whom he had abandoned nearly two years before, and who in the interval had not lived too wisely or purely, according to the vague accounts given of her by the biographers of Shelley, committed suicide. That this miserable event gave him intense pain almost all agree ; as indeed it is impossible to imagine that a being so sensitive could have been indifferent to such a catastrophe. But it certainly cleared his path of an incumbrance, and in six weeks after, his connection with Mary Godwin was legitimatised by marriage. Thus the theory of Godwin's philosophical sect against marriage as an institution was finally disposed of. Godwin himself had married more than once, notwithstanding his opinions. Shelley, in honourable superiority to them, had married Harriet when she put herself in his power ; but the daughter of Mary Wollstonecraft, already his unwedded companion, might have helped him to maintain his theoretical standard of superiority to all bonds of law, if ever woman could. The

pair, however, visionary as they were, followed the beaten
way of law and order, against which they had rebelled,
as soon as it was open to them ; and in this act the last
spark of energy and meaning which remained in the lawless little band of sectarians died out.   Sacred or not, the
institution was too necessary, too expedient, to be rejected
when the penalties of rebellion were fully realised.

Even in his grief for the catastrophe which swept
poor Harriet out of his path, Shelley, it is said, maintained
his innocence of all blame in respect to the poor girl who
had thus taken her fate in her own hands.   They were
all pitifully young, which is almost their only excuse—
that and their philosophy together.   For youth is cruel,
without meaning it, notwithstanding that it is easy of
access to all emotions.   Its own affairs bulk so largely,
its own feelings preoccupy it so entirely, that it is hard
to give due consideration, from any other point of view,
to the obstacles in its way.   A little later occurred an
incident to which more importance has been attached by
all Shelley's biographers and apologists than the death of
poor Harriet.   "Meanwhile," says Mr. Rossetti, the last
of these defenders of the poet's memory, with fine irony,
"a Chancery suit had been commenced to determine
whether Mr. Percy Bysshe Shelley or Mr. Westbrook
(Harriet's father) was the more proper person to elicit such
intellectual or moral faculties, as the ruling power of the
universe might have gifted the poet's two children with.
In the eyes of a bandaged Justice the retired hotelkeeper
proved to be clearly better fitted for this function than
the author *in esse* of *Alastor* and *in posse* of the *Triumph
of Life*."   From this inflated statement of the case the
reader will derive little real information.   Harriet had
left two children : one a little girl a year old at the time
her husband forsook her, the other a boy born after their
separation, and whom Shelley had never seen.   The chil-

dren had lived with their grandfather all their little lives, and been supported by him ; and in the eyes of the ordinary spectator and of common equity, their father, who did not know them, who had never shown any interest in them, who had been the ultimate cause of their mother's wretched life and suicide and who had just married that mother's supplanter, was evidently anything but a likely guardian of two innocent little mortals, between whom and himself there could be nothing but the mere formal bond of blood. Almost everybody who has mentioned the circumstance has represented it as a rending of the poet's heart, a cruel separation from his offspring ; and no event in domestic history has been more bitterly denounced, or with more passion. Yet these are the circumstances, plainly stated. In the case perhaps of no other pair living would a man's mistress, newly married to him on the death of his wife (which is the plain and brutal way of stating the circumstances), be considered a proper mother and guardian for that wife's daughter ; and it is ludicrous to speak of any real paternal feeling on the part of Shelley towards children whom he never seems to have even inquired about till this moment of conflict. It seems unlikely that any Judge would come to a different decision now than that which Lord Eldon has been devoted to all the infernal gods for pronouncing in 1817. Shelley had to make an allowance of £200, or some say £120 yearly, for the maintenance of the children, and never saw them after. Heaven and earth have rung with proclamations of the injustice of this decision : but it is hard to see in the circumstances wherein its cruelty lay. It half moved Byron to withhold *Don Juan* from the press, lest that publication might throw obstacles between himself and his child, should he ever be in a position to claim her ; but the motive was not powerful enough, though it was an effective thing to say.

VOL. III.

At this time the Shelleys lived at Marlow, where the poet spent much of his time upon the river. It is a pleasure to the imagination to contemplate him out of all the vulgar strife and passionate hot complaints of injustice—to find him here quiet and in obvious ease, though he gave away his money wildly and lived an unthrifty life—floating about the kind and genial Thames, under the shadow of the Bisham woods, among the knotted tangles of the water weeds and floating lilies, his boat floating too in rhythmic leisure and gentle movement, noiseless with the flowing of the water, a soft accompaniment both to life and song. It was on some cliff of Bisham overlooking the river that the *Revolt of Islam* was chiefly written, and there is a wonderful appropriateness in the scene. Something like the flowing of a river is in its linked sweetness long drawn out, an endless gurgling of melodious verse. Time and space, and character and fact, and all limitations, float away as the poet sings his song. It is beautiful; it is heavenly sweet; it is vain as the blowing of the summer air which ruffles the foliage without motive, without meaning, yet is sweet as any sound in heaven or earth. Laon and Cythna are the ideal devoted pair who are to free their race from oppression; but what that race is, or how it is to be freed, no one can tell. The young hero is taken in his first effort and imprisoned high upon a mystic rock, where he has horrible visions. The maiden, escaping from a wonderful cavern under the sea, in which she too has been confined, takes his place and works a momentary victory through the women of the land; but, too magnanimous, they spare the tyrant, who lives to plot and plan and overthrow their work — and at the end perish together upon a great funeral pile, to which envy and fierce prejudice and bigotry drag them, on pretence that the sacrifice of the pair will propitiate Heaven and stop the pestilence. Here,

indeed, they perish; but next moment open their eyes
upon a lovely landscape, and find themselves seated upon
" the waved and golden sand of a clear pool," and are finally
carried off in a pearly boat steered by a child angel, who
turns out to be the child of which Cythna had become
the mother in her cavern—to the island of the blessed.
Nothing can be more vague and visionary than the story,
or more musical than the manner of telling it.   The
reader who attempts to fathom what it means must wade
through shallow oceans of sweetness till he is dazed with
melody; but even then will bring but little away.   The
landscape is like nothing human; it is made up of every
image of beauty that can be heard of or discovered; and
the revolutions that take place in bewildering succession
are equally beyond the reach of the common understanding, which loses itself in the maze.   As the two fair
spirits disappear in the mystic boat, the river over which
the poet's rapt eyes were gazing as he wove his song perhaps touches his mind for a moment, and, though with
decorations unknown to Thames, steals into the concluding strain :—

> " A scene of joy and wonder to behold,
>   That river's shapes and shadows changing ever !
> When the broad sunrise filled with deepening gold
>   Its whirlpools where all hues did spread and quiver,
>   And where melodious falls did burst and shiver
> Among rocks clad with flowers, the foam and spray
>   Sparkled like stars upon the sunny river,
>   Or when the moonlight poured a holier day,
> One vast and glittering lake around green islands lay.

> " Sometimes between the wide and flowering meadows,
>   Mile after mile, we sailed, and 'twas delight
> To see far off the sunbeams chase the shadows
>   Over the grass ; sometimes beneath the night
>   Of wide and vaulted caves, whose roofs were bright
> With starry gems we fled, whilst from their deep
>   And dark green chasms, shades beautiful and white,

> Amid sweet sounds, across our path would sweep,
> Like swift and lovely dreams that walk the waves of sleep.

> " And ever as we sailed, our minds were full
>   Of love and wisdom, which would overflow
>   In converse wild, and sweet, and wonderful ;
>   And in quick smiles whose light would come and go
>   Like music o'er wide waves, and in the flow
>   Of sudden tears, and in the mute caress—
>   For a deep shade was cleft, and we did know
>   That virtue, though obscured on Earth, not less
> Survives all mortal change in lasting loveliness."

This stream of poetry is one which need never end ; it flows on, finding new images at every turn of the lingering unmeasured way. There is no need that anything should come of it ; that there should be incident, or moral, or even meaning. Shelley was always fond, even when his song reached a fuller music, of the " did know," " did spread," " did burst," which jar a little in the melody, but yet do not furnish discord enough to harm the cadence. The *Revolt of Islam* is the longest of all his poems, and the last which any but a student is likely to turn to now.

In 1818, Shelley and his family went to Italy, and among other wanderings the poet visited Venice and Lord Byron, renewing the friendship which had been begun on Lake Leman. Of this visit the poem called *Julian and Maddalo* was one of the results. It was not the first essay he had made in narrative poetry, which seems to have attracted him at this period of life, but it was a much higher flight than *Rosalind and Helen*, which preceded it. These two tales, if tales they can be called, stand alone in his poetry. Perhaps they were a conscious attempt in a new channel, perhaps the fruit of some suggestion ; but, whatever was the cause of their production, it is evident that this medium did not please him, and he returned to it no more. *Julian and Maddalo* is inter-

esting from the glimpse it gives us of the two poets in
their second meeting.   There is no record in verse of
Byron's estimate of the companion and fellow-traveller of
whom, at a moment of his life so important in his history,
he had seen so much ; but there was a link of connection
between them in the little person of the poor baby Allegra,
Miss Clairmont's child, who in her infancy had been sent
to her father in Venice, and who, happily for her, closed
her existence in a very few years, and thus got rid of a
maze of unhappy circumstances which must have over-
shadowed her bitterly enough had she lived.   It was upon
some business connected with this infant that Shelley went
to Venice, and she, too, comes into the story.   "Whilst
I waited, with his child I played," the poet says—

> " A lovelier toy sweet Nature never made,
>   A serious, subtle, wild, yet gentle being,
>   Graceful without design and unforeseeing,
>   With eyes—oh speak not of her eyes !—which seem
>   Twin mirrors of Italian heaven, yet gleam
>   With such deep meaning, as we never see
>   But in the human countenance : with me
>   She was a special favourite, I had nursed
>   Her fine and feeble limbs when she came first
>   To this bleak world ; and she yet seemed to know
>   On second sight her antient playfellow,
>   Less changed than she was by six months or so."

It is, however, the description of Byron and the picture
of one of his best known habits which is specially interesting, bringing before us the scene with all its enchantments, and the two poets in the central light, young and
with so many of the richest gifts of nature, yet so little
satisfied or happy :—

> " I rode one evening with Count Maddalo
>   Upon the bank of land which breaks the flow
>   Of Adria towards Venice : a bare strand
>   Of hillocks, heaped from ever-shifting sand,

Matted with thistles and amphibious weeds,
Such as from earth's embrace the salt ooze breeds,

     •   •   •   •   •

This ride was my delight.   I love all waste
And solitary places ; where we taste
The pleasure of believing what we see
Is boundless, as we wish our souls to be :
And such was this wide ocean, and this shore
More barren than its billows ; and yet more
Than all, with a remembered friend I love
To ride as then I rode ;—for the winds drove
The living spray along the sunny air
Into our faces ; the blue heavens were bare,
Stripped to the depths by the awakening north ;
And, from the waves, sound like delight broke forth
Harmonizing with solitude, and sent
Into our hearts aërial merriment.
So, as we rode, we talked ; and the swift thought,
Winging itself with laughter, lingered not,
But flew from brain to brain—such glee was ours,
Charged with light memories of remembered hours,
None slow enough for sadness : till we came
Homeward, which always makes the spirit tame.

     •   •   •   •   •

Our talk grew somewhat serious, as may be
Talk interrupted with such raillery
As mocks itself, because it cannot scorn
The thoughts it would extinguish :—'twas forlorn,
Yet pleasing, such as once, so poets tell,
The devils held within the dales of Hell
Concerning God, freewill and destiny :
Of all that earth has been or yet may be,
All that vain men imagine or believe,
Or hope can paint or suffering may achieve,
We descanted, and I (for ever still
Is it not wise to make the best of ill ?)
Argued against despondency, but pride
Made my companion take the darker side.
The sense that he was greater than his kind
Had struck, methinks, his eagle spirit blind
By gazing on its own exceeding light."

The rest of the tale is supposed to illustrate the vanity

of Shelley's sanguine view of life, and the justice of the
gloomier aspect under which it appeared to Byron.   No
doubt it is a real reminiscence of many a discussion of
the kind, when Shelley, an eager optimist, ardent in easy
plans of liberating nature, and still keeping a longing hold
upon the gospel according to Godwin, met with the cynicism of the elder poet, the man worn with dissipation and
many a downfall, and glad to attribute to fate and necessity
the evils which he could not escape from.   The description of Venice which follows is singularly beautiful, most
finely touched in liquid clearness and light, in all its glow
of sunset colour and quick-falling magical light.

This year and the two or three following were the
climax of Shelley's genius, as indeed they were all that
remained to live of his disturbed and unsettled life.   He
wrote in rapid succession his greatest poems one after the
other—the *Prometheus*, in some respects the most perfect
work of the age; the *Cenci*; the *Epipsychidion*, and many
others.   We are not aware of anything in the English
language that can be fitly placed by the side of the great
ideal drama, beautiful as a vision, glowing with imagery
and song, yet great and imposing as the marbles of the
gods, which came suddenly forth from amidst the Alastors
and Laons, and their swamps and marshes of verse, and
set itself at once in the high places above criticism.
Something, no doubt, of the old perversity of the boyish
Atheist, who was never content save when hurling defiance
at the heavens, was in the poet's choice of the rebellious
Titan, the god-defier and vanquisher, as his hero.   Though
it is but an official god that is to be dethroned, yet the
idea is dear to him; and even in the aspect of imperial
Jove, the cloud-compeller, the king of gods and men, there
is nothing to conciliate the intellectual iconoclast, to whom
the very idea of law and rule is obnoxious.   But though
this lurks in every line of the suffering Titan's challenge

and stern disdain of all his enemy can do, yet there is no commonplace blasphemy in the poem. Prometheus, upon his rock immovable, capable of nothing but suffering and constancy, cowing his victor even while he endures all the agonies that Jupiter sends, is a magnificent conception. He is comforted by the melancholy and dignified voice of the Earth, the great mother for whom he suffers, and by the softer pitying presence of Ione and Panthea, who sit by him through his vigil veiling their lovely faces in their wings, when the furies dart upon the silent sufferer and torture him; but yet Prometheus is alone, all-enduring, resolute as the rock on which he is bound. His figure rises with all the effect of a noble picture against the lurid sky, full of fiery and cruel light. " Ah me, alas ! pain ever, for ever !" This opening overawes and absorbs even the reader least disposed to understand an ideal representation so far beyond and above the forces of humanity. The Thalabas and Kehamas, even the Man- freds and Cains, vanish before a conception so great, clothed in verse so melodious and noble. It is like nothing that had ever been seen before in the poetry of the north. There is a veil over our perfect understanding in many cases. The spirits and their voices, though beautiful, are confusing; they are too like each other, or our faculties lack clearness to keep the threads of being separate. In classic times, when the earth ran over with visionary life, and wild and lovely intellectual creatures lurked in every brook and every tree, character and indi- viduality had not begun to be needful. This is the greatest drawback to the modern mind in comprehending the visions of classical antiquity, or rather those modern adaptations of them, in which a consciousness of this difficulty always lurks. But the group of Prometheus commends itself to the eye as well as to the ear. It is cut out for us as in living marble, and the high and noble

verse in which the heroic Titan utters his soul seldom falls
below the tragic dignity of the situation.   On the other
hand, the sweetness and devotion of the great woman-
spirit remind us more of the theories of those religious
enthusiasts who believe in divine duality and a mother-
God than of the mere softnesses of the classic nymphs.
Asia has the greatness and power which become a divinity:
and even her sister-spirits are above the dimensions of the
human.   These grand outlines are somewhat vague ; they
are too little concise, too unlimited in speech, for even the
ideal drama.   Indeed, there is scarcely a single dramatic
element in the great Mystery, as it rises slowly amid
ethereal music, with one great voice pealing by times in
stately sweetness above all artifices of oratory, between us
and the skies.   This is the part of the poem which, to our
thinking, is the greatest ; but its lyrics still stand unrivalled in the language.   Sometimes there is a touch in
them of the quaint and delightful no-meaning of some of
Shakspeare's snatches of spirit-song, but in most cases the
lovely melody still retains a thread of intellectual power,
and the soft cadences as they fall carry an echo of
thought.   To compare them with the hymn-book choruses
of *Manfred* would be to throw into almost ludicrous light
the *banalité* and laborious matter-of-fact of those productions.   The song of Asia, so often quoted, conveys so true
a picture of the character of Shelley's poetry altogether,
and its effect upon the sympathetic reader, that we extract
it, not so much as an example of beautiful verse as for the
description it contains :—

> " My soul is an enchanted boat,
>   Which, like a sleeping swan, doth float
> Upon the silver waves of thy sweet singing ;
>   And thine doth like an angel sit
>   Beside the helm conducting it,
> Whilst all the winds with melody are ringing.
>   It seems to float, ever, for ever,

> Upon that many-winding river,
> Between mountains, woods, abysses,
> A paradise of wildernesses,
> Till, like one in slumber bound,
> Borne to the ocean, I float down, around,
> Into a sea profound, of ever-spreading sound.
> Meanwhile thy spirit lifts its pinions
> In music's most serene dominions,
> Catching the winds that fan that happy heaven;
> And we sail on, away, afar,
> Without a course, without a star,
> But by the instinct of sweet music driven,
> Till through Elysian garden islets,
> By thee most beautiful of pilots,
> Where never mortal pinnace glided,
> The boat of my desire is guided."

" This poem," Shelley says, in prose almost as ornate
as his poetry, " was chiefly written upon the mountainous
ruins of the Baths of Caracalla, among the flowery glades
and thickets of odoriferous blossoming trees, which are
extended in many widening labyrinths upon its immense
platforms and dizzy arches suspended in the air.   The
bright blue sky of Rome, and the effect of the vigorous
awakening spring in that divinest climate, and the new
life with which it drenches the spirit to intoxication,
were the inspiration of the drama."   Unless it had been
written in the groves of Ida, on the slopes of Olympus,
it could not have had a more fitting scene.

This great work was followed at a short interval by
the terrible and impassioned drama of the *Cenci*.   That
Shelley should have chosen so horrible a story shows how
curiously his musical genius and tender soul were disposed towards the most fantastic and incredible glooms of
imagination.   He could not bear to see or think of pain,
but his mind had an unnatural pleasure in horrors which
are beyond the common range of criminality altogether,
and cruelties too black for merely human conception.
There is something in the primitive simplicity and abso-

lutism of such a nature, rejecting all modifications, and dealing only with first principles, which makes it compatible with the most sensitive gentleness to impute the fiercest capabilities of crime to those who disagree with it. No Puritan had ever a keener vein of bigotry in him. He would not have burned or beheaded, but he did worse: he thought the enemies of freedom and of free thought were capable of pursuing himself relentlessly, and attempting his assassination in real life: and in poetry it was his pleasure to imagine, as easy and delightful to the minds he hated, such unnatural crimes as make the hair stand upright on our heads.   Probably he believed, in all sincerity, that a worshipper of the God whom he regarded as cruel and merciless, the God of punishment and wrath, He who commanded the destruction of the Canaanites and the slaying of Agag, was capable of any monstrous outrage upon human nature.   In pursuance of this wild theory he makes the hideous reprobate Cenci, not a mocker or false believer, but pious after a fashion, imploring God's curse upon his knees, and believing it will come.   Besides this polemical impulse, which never deserted him, his mind had a natural inclination towards extremes.   The contrasts which he preferred were darknesses as of hell in alternation with the sunny noonday—not mere passing clouds and vapours.   No doubt it was those natural tendencies which made the most revolting of historical incidents attract him.   The pain and freezing horror of it will keep the drama of the *Cenci* from ever being popular: but few readers will have any difficulty in granting the claim made by Shelley's disciples, that it is the finest tragedy of the age.   To tell the truth, this is not saying much, for the age was poor in dramatic art, as England has continued to be.

But there is nothing poor or feeble in this wonderful production.   It is totally unlike anything that Shelley

produced either before or after.   The self-restraint which
banished from its nervous dialogues so much of his natural
exuberance of detail and imagery, shows a power with
which we should not have credited him but for this
example, and nothing in his previous work could have
prepared the reader for the distinctness of conception,
such as it is, with which these terrible figures are framed.
It would be hard to say they are natural; there is
little humanity in them; but the extraordinary image of
the father burns against the background with a diabolical
force and determination which is indescribable.   We
know of no such bad man in all poetry.   Shakspeare's
Richard holds a very different position in the world of
imagination; he is curiously fashioned, shadowed out and
rounded against the troubled scene with all his subtle
gifts, his specious arguments, and fine pretences.   But
Cenci is unprovided with any of these gradations.   He has
not even the excuse of a great ambition.   His ghastly
triumph in the news that his sons are dead has no
sufficient purpose; nor has the worse outrage upon his
daughter.   It is evil for evil's sake that he gloats in, and
derives a fell enjoyment from, and the highest gratification he anticipates is working such utter debasement of
soul in his victims, that the crime he forces them into
will become an inspiration to them also.   Cenci himself
has never known what innocence was.   His early friend
has no recollection of him save one of wickedness :—

> " I stood beside your dark and fiery youth,
>   Watching its bad and bold career, as men
>   Watch meteors ; but it vanished not.   I marked
>   Your desperate and remorseless manhood : now
>   Do I behold you, in dishonoured age,
>   Charged with a thousand unrepented crimes."

Such a creation can scarcely be called human : it is
the symbol of guilt which pleases the primitive mind,

without relentings, without complication, all bad and black and absolute; but it has a hideous ideality and life. Beatrice, on the other hand, resembles little the sad, half-childish half-heroic martyr of Guido's picture, which in its wonderful anguish of spent tears and exhausted hope, is one of the most touching images Art has handed down to us, and one of the best known. The outraged heroine of Shelley is a far more passionate and powerful spirit. There are no softenings in her, no shrinking from the vengeance, which her unimaginable wrong demands. And indeed the mistake in her is, that she is too strong to make it possible for us to believe in the outrage at all. Such a woman would have resisted to the death, and would not have been overcome. This is the flaw in the conception, the failure which the reader feels in spite of himself. Her proud and fiery spirit, however, is no type of excellence, but bears the oil in it of being Cenci's daughter. The scene in which she overawes the actual murderer, and forces him, by the power of her constraining eyes and indignant eloquent address, to withdraw the confession extorted by the rack, and (falsely) to declare her innocent, is fine and exciting, but degrades Beatrice from any ideal eminence. The only expedient for a heroic woman in such circumstances would have been to stand strongly upon the justice of her cause and vindicate her act. She might have been moved by the impulse of self-defence at first, and faltered; but in cold blood could never have sent her tool to death with a lie on his lips. Putting aside these defects, however, all that she says is poured forth with noble fire and energy. Beside her all the other personages of the drama grow pale—the shrinking attendants, the gentle Lucretia, the vacillating Giacomo, the deceitful Orsino, are weak and ghost-like: but her mien is ever grand, and her utterances powerful. The *Cenci* stands by itself in the intensity of its gloom and passion; a work to be read once with excitement and awe, but which the general reader would be little apt, for his own pleasure, to turn to again. It is far more like the Greek drama in the unity of its single purpose and movement than the rich and irregular variety of Shakspeare. Shelley was of the former, not the latter world. His sympathies with men were all theoretical; he had no brotherly insight into their ways, or appreciation of their wants, though he would have bought justice for them and freedom, according to his conception, with his blood—or anybody else's. But his world was the absolute, not the real. Sometimes this raised his poetry into a confused but lovely empyrean far above the comprehension of the general; but sometimes, too, led him to failure, and to substitute a lower creation for a higher, as in the case of Beatrice, who, such as she is, a pale and terrible figure, stands distinct against the poetical firmament with an altitude and bearing entirely her own.

Among the poems which followed there are several of which it is very difficult to speak. Such strange yet beautiful rhapsodies as *Epipsychidion* and the *Witch of Atlas* defy all the comments of the critic. The former is a strain of impassioned love addressed to "a beautiful soul," the noble Italian lady who would seem to have inspired Shelley with a spiritual passion. Whether it were only spiritual, it is needless to inquire. The language of passion is always subject to mistaken interpretation; but the reader can scarcely help reflecting that the bond of marriage, which neither husband nor wife thought necessary, was a very useful safeguard to Shelley and Mary. So far as a meaning can be traced through the sweet wilderness of verse, the poet would seem to identify in his Emilia the ideal which he has been pursuing all his life—the one perfect woman of his dreams. Their opportunities of meeting were few; but their letters were of the most impassioned description,

and this poem is one long hymn of adoration to the
" Spouse ! sister ! angel !" " too late beloved, too soon
adored," whom he describes as the " Pilot of the fate
whose course has been so starless." The passion in the
poem, however, is too abstract to offend the most sensi-
tively moral, and it is beautiful as running water, or the
sound of his own *West Wind,* or any other inarticulate
melody. Amid its indistinct loveliness, however, here is
one curious little passage, which shows the confusion of
Shelley's own mind as to ordinary human ties :—

> " I never thought before my death to see
> Youth's vision thus made perfect.   Emily,
> I love thee ; though the world by no thin name
> Will hide that love, from its unvalued shame.
> Would we two had been twins of the same mother !
> Or, that the name my heart lent to another
> Could be a sister's bond for her and thee,
> Blending two beams of one eternity !
> Yet were one lawful and the other true,
> These names, though dear, could paint not, as is due,
> How beyond refuge I am thine.   Ah me !
> I am not thine : I am a part of thee."

There must have been no inconsiderable heartache
among the little group at Pisa, however it was distributed,
when these lines were written ; although, perhaps, in the
fragmentary lyrics of the poet's last days there was matter
still more dangerous ; but we need not inquire into the
sentiments which save in these beautiful verses have
left no other record. Love, even when expressed in the
loveliest poetry, is less lovely when it breathes forth
devotion to a number of adored objects. The *Witch of
Atlas* is more mysterious still than the anthem of passion
which is inscribed to Emilia Viviani. There are readers
who will understand—or at least who will be so carried
along the stream of poetry, like Asia in her enchanted
boat, that they will seem to understand these beautiful

utterances of mystery ; but no critic could define them, and it is unnecessary to add anything to the many expressions of admiring bewilderment which already exist. Other poems of varying beauty and splendour we must be satisfied to name in the same way—the *Triumph of Life*, a fine unfinished allegorical dream, the confused dramatic sketch called *Hellas*, and many more. In *Adonais*, which is an elegy to the memory of young Keats, just dead in Rome—the *avant-courier* preceding into the unseen this young and brilliant group of short-lived poets—we have the thread of meaning which many of the other productions of this period want so much. Shelley was not, according to his letters, so great an admirer of Keats as he seems in his verse ; but his indignant spirit had been roused by the common idea of the time, that the poor young poet was the victim of a review—

> " And that the soul, that very fiery particle,
>   Had let itself be snuffed out by an article,"

as Byron says, with somewhat cruel levity. This idea fired the revolutionary, to whom critics were but another kind of tyrants oppressing the free-born, and in the flame and fire of his sudden partisanship and wild grief over the slaughtered, this poem was written. It is worthy of a more perfect inspiration. If it has not the succinct splendour of *Lycidas*, it counts next after that wonderful lament, and is a fitting and noble monument to the young poet. Though it was somewhat hard to assail a harmless reviewer as " a deaf and viperous murderer," and though the foundation of all this scathing denunciation was a mistake, yet the verses which enshrine the memory of that gifted boy are as beautiful as if they had sprung from pure love and sorrow :—

> " Peace, peace ! he is not dead, he doth not sleep—
>   He hath awakened from the dream of life—

'Tis we, who lost in stormy visions, keep
With phantoms an unprofitable strife,
And in mad trance, strike with our spirit's knife
Invulnerable nothings.—*We* decay
Like corpses in a charnel ; fear and grief
Convulse us and consume us day by day,
And cold hopes swarm like worms within our living clay.

" He has outsoared the shadow of our night ;
Envy and calumny and hate and pain,
And that unrest which men miscall delight,
Can touch him not and torture not again ;
From the contagion of the world's slow stain
He is secure, and now can never mourn
A heart grown cold, a head grown grey in vain ;
Nor, when the spirit's self has ceased to burn,
With sparkless ashes load an unlamented urn.

" He lives, he wakes—'tis Death is dead, not he ;
Mourn not for Adonais.—Thou young Dawn
Turn all thy dew to splendour, for from thee
The spirit thou lamentest is not gone ;
Ye caverns and ye forests, cease to moan !
Cease ye faint flowers and fountains, and thou Air
Which like a mourning veil thy scarf hadst thrown
O'er the abandoned Earth, now leave it bare
Even to the joyous stars which smile on its despair !

" He is made one with Nature : there is heard
His voice in all her music, from the moan
Of thunder, to the song of night's sweet bird ;
He is a presence to be felt and known
In darkness and in light, from herb and stone,
Spreading itself where'er that Power may move
Which has withdrawn his being to its own ;
Which wields the world with never wearied love,
Sustains it from beneath, and kindles it above."

These lines do not sound much like the production of
one who had signed himself " Atheist" in the levity of a
traveller's book, and on every more serious occasion when
an opportunity was offered him ; but it does not seem
that Shelley doubted immortality, though he doubted
God : and poetical ethics are always vague. " That

Power which wields the world with never-wearied love"
is the hardest of all things to keep out of true poetry,
which, in its very nature and essence, turns towards the
divine, whatever its possessor may think or say.

There remains to notice only that portion of Shelley's
poetry which is his most indisputable title to fame—those
lovely little lyrics which are dear to all. If Shelley's
productions were all swept out of the world except those
which are preserved in Mr. Palgrave's admirable little
book, the *Golden Treasury*, we doubt much whether the
loss would seriously or generally affect his claims to
immortality. The *Ode to the West Wind*, the *Skylark*, the
Spirit of Delight, the *Lines written at Naples*—"in dejec-
tion," as the title goes—those which were composed
among the Euganean Hills, and many a nameless snatch
of song, breathing infinite suggestions of melody and
thought, are, of all he has left us, the most dear to the
common heart. Fanatics may prize Shelley's mystic
utterances, and students do their best to fathom them for
ages, without making the least impression upon the wider
human audience; but the heart and the ear which are
closed to the charm of these shorter lyrics are dull indeed,
and unworthy the effort of a poet; the memory is unfur-
nished in which they do not lurk to sweeten solitude and
give expression to many a wistful thought and dreamy
fancy. Some of them embody the very soul of pensive
thoughtfulness:—

> " We look before and after,
>   And pine for what is not ;
>   Our sincerest laughter
>   With some pain is fraught—
> Our sweetest songs are those that tell of saddest thought."

It is hopeless to attempt to indicate one after another
these beautiful songs of the imagination and heart; the
reader wants no guide nor introduction here.

The life Shelley spent in Italy in these fertile and abundant years was full of friends, and though also full of agitations, would seem to have had its share of happiness. The curious correspondence which is to be found in the volume, published since these pages were written, of Southey's letters to Caroline Bowles, comes in strangely in interruption of the softer record. It seems almost cruel to remind so irresponsible a being as Shelley, once he had escaped the atmosphere of real life which, more or less, is always to be found in England, of the tragedy of poor Harriet and the misadventures of his early life, as Southey does with a stern virtue which, in any other circumstances, we should approve. The elder poet did not know how soon the inexorable shadows were to close round that young and visionary life, which at all times had played with its existence, nor ever fathomed the real meaning of the phantasmagoria with which it surrounded itself. But as a matter of fact, we do not love Shelley the less for his old friend's somewhat pitiless indictment. We cannot think of him indeed, with our knowledge of all that was going to happen, without so pitiful a sense of approaching fate, that our forgiveness of all his vagaries is secured beforehand. And yet it is difficult to blame Southey, who was right also from his point of view ; and sadly disappointed besides in the youth whom he had loved and considered in the shortsightedness of man as another self, whom he could understand and help over his difficulties. This little episode of severe condemnation comes like the visit of a gloomy seer, alarming in momentary solemnity, yet soon got over, into the records of the little Italian coterie, where all was wild and astray, yet full of enjoyment and of the pleasurable yet sometimes almost tragic inquietude of youthful life.

In 1821 Shelley went to Ravenna to visit Byron, and induced him to join the little company of friends at Pisa.

One consequence of this renewed intercourse was an invitation sent to Leigh Hunt, a poor man with a family of children and a sick wife, who had been one of Shelley's warmest friends in his early days in London, and to whom he had already done innumerable kindnesses, to come to Italy, for the purpose of joining Byron and himself in a literary enterprise, the idea of which they had struck out between them. It is difficult to disentangle the rights of this story from the three or four versions of it which are given by the different actors in the transaction. By one we are told it was Byron's idea; by another that the suggestion was first made by Shelley, with a view to benefit Leigh Hunt; by Leigh Hunt himself, that it was to be a joint undertaking, Lord Byron being the originator of the scheme: and by Byron, that he was himself drawn (we think he does not hesitate to say inveigled) into it by the brothers Hunt for their own profit. This is one of the literary misunderstandings which are most unpleasant to read of and least edifying to investigate. The plan was to start a quarterly review or magazine, to be called the *Liberal*, and published in London, though written in Italy, and which was to afford a medium for the poems and speculations and ideas of the poetical brotherhood and their retainers. Shelley seems to have had but little to do with the scheme, but it was he who invited with eager kindness the friend whom he had already served so often, and with whom and his family both Mary and he were on the most intimate and cordial terms. The Shelleys and their friends, Captain Williams and his wife, with whom they formed almost one household, had gone to the village of Larici, on the eastern Riviera, for their summer quarters, when the Cockney poet and journalist arrived, after a long and miserable voyage, at Leghorn. Shelley and Williams had a short time before been made happy by the acquisition of a pleasure boat, "a small

schooner," which they called the *Don Juan,* and in which
they had sailed about those happy coasts like two school-
boys, full of delight in their new toy, through May and
June, in the lovely Italian summer, rash and joyous, with
one sailor boy for their crew, and all the temerity of
ignorance.   The two set out " in high spirits" in their
little cockleshell, coasting along the most beautiful shore
in the world, to busy Leghorn, to meet the stranger—
whom Shelley installed in his own house at Pisa, and
welcomed with enthusiastic kindness.   After a few days'
delay to see his friends established, and renew the talks
and confidences of old, Shelley and his companion set out
together in their boat, to return to their temporary home.
The description given by Captain Trelawney, one of the
members of this intimate society, of the evening on which
they set sail, reads almost like a bit out of one of the
many narratives of imaginary voyages which Shelley
delighted in.   Just so would he have painted the fatal
evening on which Alastor or Laon, the heroes of his youth,
set out to meet an evident fate.

" It was almost dark, though only half-past six," Trelawney says;
" the sea was of the colour, and looked as solid and smooth as a
sheet of lead, and covered with an oily scum.   Gusts of wind swept
over without ruffling it, and big drops of rain fell on its surface,
rebounding as if they could not penetrate it.   There was a commotion in the air, made up of many threatening sounds coming upon
us from the sea.   Fishing craft and coasting vessels, under bare
poles, rushed by us in shoals, running foul of the ships in the har-
bour.   As yet the din and hubbub were that made by man : but
their shrill pipings were suddenly silenced by the crashing voice of
a thunder-squall that burst right over our heads.   For some time
no other sounds were to be heard than the thunder, wind, and rain.
When the fury of the storm, which did not last for more than twenty
minutes, was in some degree cleared, I looked to seaward anxiously,
in the hope of descrying Shelley's boat——"

But the reader knows that in that blast Shelley's wayward, beautiful, and wealthy genius, not yet fully de-

veloped, had taken flight, and was lost to all mortal mediums of communication for evermore.

Strange stories are told of supernatural warnings and intimations which had been made to him during that early summer, of impending fate.   He saw, or thought he saw, the appearance of the little Allegra, who had died a few weeks before in her Venetian convent, rise out of the sea, and smiling, clap her hands at the sight of him.   He had been called from his bed by a cloaked figure, which, leading him into another room, threw back its hood and disclosed his own features.   On another occasion some of his friends saw Shelley, to all appearance, walking near them, when he was certainly in another place; as Sir Robert Peel is said to have seen Byron in London streets, when he was in Venice.   Those curious indications of instinctive faith in the supernatural seem strange in a man who had so gloried in his unbelief—but to be sure it was God, and especially the Christian God, whom he disbelieved, and not the unseen.   What is perhaps more extraordinary is the constant disappearance in a boat of all the creatures of his fancy.   Generally it is a dream river up which they thread their course as they disappear from mortal sight; but whether it be death or translation, this is always the medium.   In his own case it was the quickly excited, soon allayed *tourment* of that soft Italian sea, by which he made an instantaneous transition from warm youth, and life, and poetry, and friendship, into the unknown.

It is unnecessary to linger upon the oft-told tale of the burning of the recovered bodies, when weeks after the sea gave up its dead.   It was said at first that those funeral rites were exacted by the authorities, but this does not seem to have been the case, and the high-flown ultra-poetical spectacle was evidently the suggestion of some one among the excited band of young men, distracted by the shock and horror of the sudden catastrophe, yet not without a certain theatrical sense that their heathen rites were the finest tribute that could be paid to the poet.   Leigh Hunt gives a painful picture of a scene which was too much for the highly strained nerves of spectators so sensitive and excitable. He relates how Byron and himself fell into wild mirth as they drove away, with that flame still scorching their eyes, and their souls harrowed by the unprecedented sight; they laughed and shouted to the reproachful night in the wild half madness of pain, trying to forget the horror of it.   Thus, by sea and by fire, what had been Shelley was scattered to the elements, of which his eager tremulous nature, his soul alit with wandering lights, his wild rebellious spirit, his tender heart, and the poetry which embodied every tone of natural music and every strange turn and twist of spiritual caprice, might have been framed.

The connection between Lord Byron and Leigh Hunt was short-lived, and in every way unhappy.   In all the letters of the former he makes it appear that his connection with Hunt and his periodical was not of his seeking, an impression which seems to be quite contrary to the facts of the case ; but it was a painful position for both —the friend who united them being thus snatched from between them a few days after the arrival of the poor and harassed man of letters, whose faithful friend Shelley had been for so long.   The *Liberal* failed completely, notwithstanding the publication in it of Byron's *Vision of Judgment*, and other poems by his hand : and of all that Leigh Hunt himself could do—and though an unthrifty man, he was never unpopular as a writer.   But Byron, too, was now at the end of his poetical career.   He had poured forth his soul in various ways, and in many an unaccustomed channel ; he had ranged over the whole gamut of poetical utterance, from the dialogues of the loftiest angels to the rattle of *mondain* commentary, modern politics, and scandal, and he had not in any found the satisfaction for which his soul craved. He believed that his popularity in England was forsaking him, and the universal voice of criticism which had been raised against the immorality of *Don Juan* had, even while it flattered, shaken deeply a mind which, though rashly self-willed and venturesome, never had any real confidence in itself. That the public had sustained a shock in its fidelity to a poet who, notwithstanding moral disapproval and all the social persecution which he supposed he had been subjected to, had secured above any other its steadfast allegiance, seems to be proved by the fact that his *Vision of Judgment*, the fierce satire with which he annihilated Southey, found no publisher, and had to see the light in the *Liberal*, along with the tedious translations from Pulci in which he took a perverse pleasure. All this quickened the discontent, the restless desire for some new excitement—or nobler determination to make a new beginning and do something in the world of more actual effect than poetry—which was fermenting in his mind. " If I live ten years longer, you will see that it is not over with me—I don't mean in literature, for that is nothing—but you will see that I shall do something, the times and fortune permitting, that, like the cosmogony of the world, will puzzle the philosophers of all nations," he writes. And it was now that those proposals were made to him by the committee of Greek sympathisers in London which decided his fate.

Here seemed, indeed, the new opportunity he wanted. Byron had little sympathy with those who were his immediate social inferiors at any time. From the day when a schoolboy at Harrow he protested against the flogging of a comrade because he was a lord, till his latest breath, a love of peerages and titles which goes the length of vulgarity, and which makes the great poet in certain phases cruelly resemble the British snob, that revelation of modern genius, had been strong in him. But this did not interfere with a practical liking for "the people" as represented by servants and dependants, and a theoretical interest in the emancipation of oppressed countries, and the restoration of freedom to such classic races as the Italians and Greeks, both of which were then under the yoke of other powers. He had joined the Carbonari some time before, and had gone through an interval of anxious expectation, looking for a rising, and fully disposed to lend his aid in every way to the hoped-for revolution. That project had come to nothing; but the time seemed to be ripe for the deliverance of the Greeks, and every generous impulse was in favour of that race, from which all our traditions of art and poetry and wisdom have come. Weary of all things, and disgusted with most, seeing, as he thought, his very fame slip from him, with some real enthusiasm for the cause and an eager desire for a new opportunity of distinguishing himself, Byron threw himself into this romantic expedition. He went out like a new crusader to conquer and set free the sacred lands of poetry and freedom. All that was in him, both good and bad, was roused for this undertaking. It was a great, noble, romantic enterprise, worthy of his rank, and transferring to another and, he thought, more splendid sphere the superiority which his genius had achieved : and there was at the same time a touch of melodrama in it which pleased the other part of him, the weaker part of the author of the *Corsair*. It is needless to enter into the sad tale. He went away in a kind of masquerade of greatness on which approaching fate and genius throw to us nowadays a dignifying solemnity, notwithstanding the mock heroics that were in it. But his constitution was broken and his days numbered, and after a most distressing illness, mismanaged and miserable in every way, he died at Missolonghi in April 1824, about two years after the scarcely more sad catastrophe which ended the life of Shelley. His last words, inarticulate and not understood, indirectly concerned the tragedy of his life; the names of his child, his wife, and sister, were made out by his distracted attendant, without anything more of the final explanations or last messages which his spirit, confused among the mists of death, intended to send to them. And thus, in loneliness and trouble and sorrow, this being so wonderfully endowed, and who might have had so glorious a career, passed away into the darkness. A more sad conclusion could not have been imagined. On his thirty-sixth birthday, which occurred less than three months before, he had written some verses, not on his highest level, but with something of the same sentimental-romantic cast to which he had given vent at the greatest crisis of his life, anticipating for himself "a soldier's grave." But even this was not granted to his ambition, and all that he could do for Greece was to soothe in some degree intestine clamours and sacrifice a great deal of money. No outburst of new power, no blaze of new fame, was permitted to the tried spirit to make up for the failure of its life.

Thus ended the second group of the poets who were the glory of the generation preceding our own, and who formed with their elder brethren such an epoch of literary greatness as has seldom crossed the severer path of history. The young Keats, of whom we have yet to give an account, and whose connection with this greater pair is accidental more than real, had glided out of the world before them, like a pale herald or page to announce the coming of the princes. The elder men who had preceded them in the world of letters, and lent them, if not inspiration, at least the genial suggestion which woke their individual voices, outlived them long, seeing them rise

and fall like meteors. We will not attempt to make any
further comparison between the two bands of poets; they
were essentially different in genius, and bore up each a
separate side of that poetic crown which, next to the
Shakspearian, distinguishes this age as the greatest in the
history of our language. It is a favourite pursuit with
many students of history to trace the high tides of intellectual energy to the immense stimulation of such a
political event, for instance, as the French Revolution, and
much has been said of the effect of that extraordinary
crisis in human affairs upon the development of so great
a school of poetry in England. But we are unable ourselves to see the connection, so far as the earlier group
is concerned. Wordsworth, Coleridge, Southey, and the
lesser minds who were connected with them, felt, indeed,
the momentary influence which a great contemporary
event must inevitably exercise upon sensitive spirits; but
their minds were cast in an entirely different mould, and
save that Wordsworth probably got from his Revolution
experiences, the fine theory which runs through much of
his poetry, as to the uses of misery and suffering, and their
beneficial, if painful, agency on the world, it is impossible
to point to any effect which the convulsions of political
life had upon them. But Byron and Shelley were the
children of the Revolution. The spirit of wild discontent
on one side and wilder visionary longing for a new system
and form of life on the other had got into their veins.
Obedience, discipline, and order, and all the established
sanctities of home and family, of law and government,
were to them tyrannical prejudices of the past. Their
minds were restless all their life long with that fever
which they had sucked in at their birth, which so many
secondary circumstances account for, yet which may well
be believed to have taken its origin from the wild ferment
in the air, the hot and fiery commotion, the blood and

flames that reddened earth when those angels of divination, confused yet receptive, first lighted upon it and took their earliest survey of its affairs through wondering childish eyes. They did not know what they would be at, any more than the populace did which found a vent for its blind misery in spreading the like around it, and exacted a wild vicarious atonement indiscriminately from the innocent, for the wrongs done by the guilty. To both these uneasy souls the conditions of Revolution lasted all their lives long: they never got out of that fatal atmosphere. Wildly rejecting all guidance, without leader or following to steady them upon their way, they had but their own uncertain instincts, their own wild impulses, to guide them; and to glorify these impulses, and make of them the only divine guides, was the object, so far as they had an object, of much of their poetry and of the greater part of their lives. Even what they loved became repulsive to them when it was associated with the idea of duty. The fantastic freedom of a classic Faun, to roam where it would, to enjoy as it would, to dart away at every impulse, was in Shelley's ethereal nature, only half human and altogether irresponsible: though his intellect tangled him in theories of political justice, in fantastic schemes for the amelioration of the race, and his child's heart of pity and tenderness made him incapable of denying kindness or help to any supplicant—save those who had a lawful claim upon his service. Byron was of the earth earthy—a totally different kind of being. He did not stand upon the right of doing wrong, like his companion spirit; he followed the law of his appetites and senses, without any doubt on the point that it was bad to do so, but a braggart's pleasure in the badness, as a proof of his courage and power of rebellion against heaven itself, which he was never unwilling to appease privately by acknowledgment of his insubordination. His was in every

way the lower side of the great rebellion. He had all the
restless uneasiness, all the sense of a world out of joint, of
wrongs to be avenged, and bitter opposition to all authorities and exactions of duty; but he was a cynic where
Shelley was an enthusiast, and hoped nothing from the
race, to which, notwithstanding he too showed a contemptuous prodigal pity when any individual pang came
under his eyes.

Peace to their troubled spirits! The heart bleeds to
contemplate them, so young, so full of noble gifts, dropped
so early out of all operation of those experiences of life
which might have brought a higher development and perhaps a nobler element of tranquillity and satisfaction into
their lives. We are far from believing in such waste of
genius as that their noble faculties are lost. By this
time, perhaps—who can tell?—these changed and perfected voices, in fullest harmony and measure, are prepar-
ing for us the songs to be sung in heaven.

PERCY BYSSHE SHELLEY, born 1792 ; died 1822.

Published Zastrozzi and St. Irvyne before 1810 (?).
Printed for private circulation, Queen Mab, 1813.
Published Alastor, 1816.
          The Revolt of Islam, 1817.
          Rosalind and Helen, 1819.
          Prometheus Unbound, 1820.
          Cenci, 1820.
          Epipsychidion, 1821.
          Hellas, 1821.
          Julian and Maddalo (published after his death), 1824.
          The Witch of Atlas, posthumous.
          Adonais.
          Smaller poems.
          Many fragments in prose, unpublished.
          Other fragments to be found in the Essays, Letters,
              etc., edited by Mrs. Shelley ; and in the Shelley
              Memorials, edited by Lady Shelley.

GEORGE GORDON BYRON, born 1788 ; died 1824.

Published Songs of Idleness, 1807.

English Bards and Scotch Reviewers, 1809.
Childe Harold, Cantos I. and II., 1812.
The Giaour, 1813.
The Bride of Abydos, 1813.
Corsair, 1814.
Lara (published with Rogers's Jacqueline), 1814.
Hebrew Melodies, 1815 (?).
Siege of Corinth, 1816.
Parisina, 1816.
Childe Harold, Canto III., and Prisoner of Chillon, 1816.
Manfred, 1817.
Don Juan, Cantos I. and II., 1819.
Marino Faliero, 1820 (?).
Don Juan, Cantos III. IV V., 1821.
Cain, 1822.
Don Juan, Cantos VI. VII. VIII., 1822.
   ,, ,, ,, IX. X. XI., 1823.
   ,, ,, ,, XII. XIII. XIV., 1823.
   ,, ,, ,, XV. XVI., 1824.
Two Foscari.
Sardanapalus.
Hebrew Melodies.
The Dream.
Short Poems.
Heaven and Earth.

CHAPTER IV.

JOHN KEATS.

THE youngest of this young group, connected with Shelley by natural links of congenial spirit and temperament, as well as by some actual acquaintance and kindness, but fiercely thrust aside and disowned by Byron, cannot be dissociated from their larger and, young though they were, maturer figures.   The distance between twenty-four and thirty is not very much in years, but it makes a marvellous difference in development, and even to Shelley Keats was not much more than a boy full of ambition and promise. John Keats was born in 1795, and was consequently three years younger than Shelley, and seven years younger than Byron.   He was not like them, born, as people say, "a gentleman," but belonged to that middle class which, in those days, kept itself much more closely within its own boundaries, and did not invade the high places as now. His family had much respectability and a little money, but the parents both died early, leaving their children to the care of strangers, and bequeathing a delicate constitution to two at least of their sons.   One of his brothers died at a still younger age than the poet, and he himself seems to have been always a delicate youth, accustomed to much care and anxiety about his health.   " The publication of three small volumes of verse, some earnest friendships, one profound passion, and a premature death,'

are, as his kind and sympathetic biographer, Lord Houghton, touchingly says, " the only incidents in his career."
His poems, though they have held their ground from that
time to this, are more preludes and overtures in poetry
than anything else, and he had little time to show what
manhood was in him, and had not that command of money
and leisure which enabled his contemporaries to emancipate
themselves from the ordinary bonds of life. Byron was
a ruined peer, and Shelley a rich man's prodigal son : but
even the poverty of wealth is better than the well-to-do-
ness of the humble, and confers a certain fine superiority
to fate. Keats was in no way superior to fate. His
friendship with Leigh Hunt brought him within the little
literary coterie of which that gentle journalist was the
head : and he had met Shelley in its little assemblies,
where poetry was the great subject, and the neophytes
babbled perpetually of green fields. The epithet of the
Cockney school bestowed upon this band by the sharp-
tongued critics, was not without reason, for Leigh Hunt's
enthusiasm for everything that was green and growing
has a tone of exaggeration in it which sounds like that
of a man whose garden was a flower-box in a window,
and his extravagances of furnishing and decoration—
though far enough, no doubt, from what a minor poet
would think necessary now — afforded contemptuous
amusement to the stalwart writers of the Blackwood
school. No doubt this pale youth, with his angelic blue
eyes and long hair, flitted out and in of that lower circle
of society in London which we have attempted to indicate.
He attended Hazlitt's lectures on the poets, and wrote
long letters about them to his friends, several of whom
were poets like himself, as they all thought in those days,
—but not like Keats as it turned out :—and he had the
freedom of Haydon's studio, who was then a rising painter,
with, as everybody thought, all the world before him, to

whom even Wordsworth, as well as the younger fry, addressed sonnets.   The occupation of young Keats in those days was that of a medical student, and he seems to have gone manfully through the preliminary work of the profession to which he was destined, though it revolted him, as may be easily imagined.   To thrust a worshipper of beauty such as he was, while still so young and always so sensitive, into the dark revelations of disease and the horrors of anatomy, must have been to subject him to an ordeal almost unendurable : and all the advantage his studies eventually gave him was the painful enlightenment by which he could decide on his own case, and foresee the inevitable end of his first attack of illness.   But poetry and perpetual poetical communion with so many who were like-minded sweetened his uncongenial toil. Once, it is said, he met Coleridge while walking with Leigh Hunt, no doubt in one of the suburban lanes between Hampstead and Highgate.   After a little cursory talk, during which, probably, the modest stripling stood silent, they parted : but a minute after, Keats, his enthusiasm bursting through his shyness, rushed back to beg that he might shake hands with Coleridge.   No doubt it was a thin and hot and humid hand which was thrust into that of the elder poet ; for he said, " There is death in that hand," as the young enthusiast rushed away.

Keats, however, was not Cockney in his inspiration. Though he was no scholar, his mind was Greek rather than English.   It is not wonderful that a highly educated youth, fed upon Greek poetry from his earliest dawn of perception, should turn back upon the classic ages as the true and only fountains of poetical loveliness and truth.   But Keats knew these glories only at secondhand, and the fulness of understanding with which he jumped at them looks almost like divination.   His mind answered to the far-off touch of the ancient divinities before he

knew what they were. He has left in his sonnet on
Chapman's Homer an admirable description of the effect
produced upon him by his first introduction to the Greeks
and their divine fables—

> " Oft of a wide expanse, had I been told,
>   That deep-brow'd Homer ruled as his demesne :
>   Yet did I never breathe its pure serene,
> Till I heard Chapman speak out loud and bold :
> Then felt I like some watcher of the skies,
>   When a new planet swims into his ken ;
> Or, like stout Cortez, when with eagle eyes,
>   He stared at the Pacific—and all his men
> Look'd at each other with a wild surmise—
>   Silent, upon a peak in Darien."

This great new sea of inexhaustible story and vision
which the young reader "shouted" with delight to discover was the very element of his soul. He flung himself into it with a comprehension and feeling which few
of its profoundest investigators ever attain. Had he
found his inspiration in his own century, in the atmosphere which he and his contemporaries were breathing,
we, for our part, would have thought the choice wiser.
But such was not the bent of his genius. He turned
from the confusions of his own age, which he had neither
strength nor inclination to fathom, to the calm and distant land of shadows, where gods and goddesses came
down to men, where Endymion wooed Diana, and the
Sun-god was superseded on his throne—with the relief
at once of physical weakness and natural disposition.
He was not robust enough for political strife, or to struggle
as his contemporaries were doing with noisy questions
about the Regent's morals or manners, or the corruptions
of the State. It was so much easier and more delightful
to escape into the silvery brightness, the magical dreams
and dews of Olympus, even as reflected in dim mirrors of
English, and amid the commonplace surroundings of our

latter days. From the first glimpse we have of him in his letters, amid the weak boyish jokes and banter which are not worth preserving or reading, there occur continual references which show how early poetry had become his chief object in life. Those whom life endows more abundantly with other interests may play with their inspiration, feeling towards that divine gift as, according to Byron, men do towards a scarcely stronger passion—

> " Man's love is of man's life a thing apart,
> 'Tis woman's whole existence."

This was the case of Keats in respect to the heavenly gift, which was all that redeemed his dim existence to him. In poetry his was the woman's part—it occupied all his thoughts. " I find I cannot exist without eternal poetry," he says at a very early period; " I began with a little, but habit has made me a leviathan. I had become all in a tremble from not having written anything of late; the sonnet overleaf did me good—I slept the better last night for it." There is something hectic in this eagerness, as if the fervid boy already divined how little time he had in the world to exercise his gift.

He had made considerable progress in his medical studies when, either the need of poetical expression became so urgent or the encouragements of his friends led him to believe that he had in his genius a means, not only of delight but of feasible occupation. Early in 1817, when he was twenty-two, he went to the Isle of Wight, in order to " be alone and improve himself," as he says, and evidently with the intention of testing his powers in some greater effort than he had yet attempted : and here *Endymion* was begun. His mind was full of the importance, almost solemnity of this outset. " I have asked myself so often why I should be a poet more than other men, seeing how great a thing it is, how great things are

to be gained by it, what a thing to be in the mouth of
fame, that at last the idea has grown so monstrously beyond my seeming power of attainment that the other day
I nearly consented with myself to drop into a Phaeton,"
he writes to Leigh Hunt in the midst of a trifling letter
full of the usual semi-poetical chatter of the coterie.   But
he seems at the same time to have held himself aloof
from the perpetual discussions, criticisms, and laudations
with which such a society receives the productions of its
members, and retained his independence.   " If poetry comes
not naturally as the leaves to a tree, it had better not come
at all," he says, and with the true spirit of an artist adds
a little later, " I am anxious to get *Endymion* printed, that
I may forget it and proceed."   This is like anything rather
than the puling boy which he was once represented to be.

   The story of *Endymion* does not require any description
here.   The poet leads us through endless glades, through
enchanted ravines, by fountains and streams of fairy
beauty, with his love-lorn youth, who is devoured by an
overpowering passion for an immortal, far greater and
more beautiful than any earthly maiden.   The charm of
the mystery, and the intoxication of a love almost too
great for mortal faculties, absorbs and abstracts altogether
the shepherd prince, who is not yet worthy to join his
lady in the skies, and who does not even know which of
the divinities it is who has raised him to this dizzy
elevation of visionary passion.   The development of
romantic life which the poet has given to the pair of
lovers and their secret meetings is just such a filling out
of the old fable with the new existence of modern genius,
as gives the legend a delicate human charm.   It never
attains to the melody of Shelley's verse ; but remote as
the subject is from human experience, it is a little nearer
the solid ground than the adventures of Laon and Cythna:
for Keats never loses hold of his little silvery thread of

narrative, and keeps all his descriptions and musings within a certain relation to it. *Endymion* is not a great poem. It is not perfect in its melody even, but full of numberless little jars and breaks of poetical discord. The oft-quoted line with which it begins, and which has become a sort of copy-book commonplace by dint of usage, is Leigh-Huntish, and a perfect emblem of the sentimental half-sham half-slang used by the little poetical tribe who decorated their parlours with green boughs and statuettes, and considered themselves priests of beauty and nature. "A thing of beauty is a joy for ever:" it is the very sentiment of those little meetings where all was melody and nonsense and poetical definition and ornament, and where art was not, nor nature. But the poet goes far beyond his keynote, and in the leisure of youth lingers over lovely images, half complete, and glimpses of the divine—not indeed of the spiritual kind, nor embodying a noble moral, or any elevation of the human towards a sublimer sphere—but the divine of classical dreams and visions in which personal bliss and the soft intoxication of pleasure were all that was dreamed of as perfection. The sweet and aimless song has no theories in it such as Shelley was bound to interweave in his wildest wandering visions. Keats, though he was so little apart from his great contemporary in age, was no child of Revolution. He wanted nothing but to roam about the unimaginable tangles of the dewy woods and meet his goddess, humouring his humanity by long despondencies and privations of her presence, till it flashed upon him in a moment, with that sudden note of joy and sudden bursting of the darkness into light which makes every darkness suggestive, and every corner a hiding-place beyond which rapture lurks, to the instinct of youth. It is this which makes Keats the favourite of young readers. His song is the song of youth and natural delight.

This artless utterance had but a harsh welcome from the world. The hot animosity which politics excited, and the prejudice with which the little community of the suburbs, in all its mingled criminality of sentiment and sweetness, of Radicalism and impecuniosity, was regarded, found vent upon the boyish production of a young man who cared little about politics and had but a transitory connection with the coterie. Why Wilson, in all his genial bigness, should have foamed at the mouth over Leigh Hunt it is wonderful to imagine, save that there is a kind of soft pretension which irritates more than greater sins : but the poor young poet, supposed to be a disciple of his school, was still more savagely used by the censors of literature on all sides. *Blackwood*, in a cruel mood, advised him to go back to his gallipots, and sneered at the starved apothecary after a brutal fashion of the time which has happily disappeared from our usages now-a-days. And no one treated him more contemptuously than Byron, who could not find epithets nasty enough to vent his disdain in, and who, when Jeffrey generously stepped into the field to maintain the cause of the unfortunate youth, declared with bitter spitefulness that he himself no longer cared for the applause which he shared with such a being. So far did all these assaults go, that it was the common belief of the time that Mr. Gifford, in the *Quarterly* (the poet of Anna), had killed Keats—a supposed guilt which called forth the fierce and eloquent denunciation of Shelley in the *Adonais*. But this was not true, though no doubt the critic deserved what he got for some other iniquity, if not for that. The young poet bore these attacks with manly and modest firmness. He was " far more annoyed " by the cool indifference of Wordsworth—who remarked only, " It is a pretty piece of Paganism," when the *Hymn to Pan* was read to him—than by the more public abuse with which he was assailed.

" I begin to get a little acquainted with my own strength
and weakness," he says with dignity to some anxious
sympathisers : " my own domestic criticism has given me
pain without comparison beyond what *Blackwood* or the
Quarterly could inflict." And here is a vindication of his
youthful work which it would be difficult to surpass in
candour or manliness. The reference is to a letter which
had been published in the *Morning Chronicle* in defence
of the young poet.

" J. S. is perfectly right in regard to the 'slip-shod Endymion.'
That it is so is no fault of mine. No ! though it may sound a little
paradoxical, it is as good as I had power to make it by myself.
Had I been nervous about it being a perfect piece, and with that
view asked advice, and trembled over every page, it would not have
been written ; for it is not in my nature to fumble. I will write
independently. I have written independently *without judgment :* I
may write independently and with judgment hereafter. The Genius
of poetry must work out its own salvation in a man. It cannot be
matured by law and precept, but by sensation and watchfulness in
itself. That which is creative must create itself. In *Endymion* I
leaped headlong into the sea, and thereby have become better
acquainted with the soundings, the quicksands, and the rocks, than if
I had stayed upon the green shore and piped a silly pipe, and taken
tea and comfortable advice."

Keats neither responded to his critics by savage retalia-
tion like Byron, nor broke a bloodvessel as he was reported
to have done, but continued on his way with a composure
and lofty meaning very remarkable in so young a man.
" I will assay to reach to as high a summit in poetry as
the nerve bestowed upon me will suffer," he says. " The
faint conceptions I have of poems to come bring the blood
frequently into my forehead. . . . I feel assured I should
write from the mere yearning and fondness I have for the
beautiful, even if my night's labours should be burnt every
morning, and no eye ever shine upon them." "This is a
mere matter of the moment," he writes a little later to his
brother in America; " I think I shall be among the

English Poets after my death." Few men have stood with firmer self-possession yet humility, to receive the often maddening sharpness of those critical spears which hurtled through the air with virulence so uncalled for.

Keats had a harder blow to sustain some time after in the death of his brother, "poor Tom," the consumptive youth over whom he had watched for long. The seeds of the same disease were evidently in himself before, but it was in the spring, after Tom's death, that he returned one evening to Hampstead, where he was living with a friend, very ill and much agitated. He had driven there on the outside of the stage-coach, and had caught cold. "Getting into bed, he slightly coughed and said, 'That is blood; bring me the candle,' and after gazing on the pillow, turning round with an expression of sudden and solemn calm, said, 'I know the colour of that blood, it is arterial blood; I cannot be deceived in the colour. That drop is my death-warrant. I shall die.'" A more touching scene could scarcely be imagined. He was twenty-three, and the first fascinations of a most passionate love had caught hold upon him. "If you would have me recover," he said pathetically to the friend, Mr. Charles Brown, with whom he was living, "flatter me with a hope of happiness when I shall be well." The object of his love lived in the next house, and in a collection of letters to her, recently published,—a very pitiful but perhaps unnecessary publication,—there is a series of touching little notes, imploring her from his sick-bed, sometimes to come to him, sometimes not to come, as the fluctuations of sickness demanded. "I will wait patiently till to-morrow," he says. "Send me the words 'Good-night,' to put under my pillow." "I read your note in my bed last night, and that might be the reason of my sleeping so much better. Send me every evening a written Good-night." "If I am to recover, the day of my recovery shall see me by

your side, from which nothing shall separate me. If
well, you are the only medicine that can keep me well."
The fluctuations of this bitter drama are heartrending.
After a while the poor sick lad began to feel himself a
clog upon the girl he loved, and was stunned by the news
that she was about to leave home, and that they were to
be separated; and though unable · to conceive how he
shall support such a blow, " I must be patient," he says
pathetically, " and in the meantime you must think of it
as little as possible." When this danger is abated, he
follows her in his imagination as she moves about. " You
will have a pleasant walk to-day. I shall see you pass.
I shall follow you with my eyes over the heath. Will you
come towards evening instead of before dinner ? When
you are gone 'tis past. If you do not come till the evening I have something to look forward to all day." Poetry
could not express more powerfully than these simple words
the longing of the sick heart for the object of its love.

Before this melancholy time, which was indeed the
beginning of sorrows, Keats had written the *Pot of Basil*,
The Eve of St. Agnes, *Lamia*, and several of the smaller
poems, which are to our thinking the noblest of all : and
the fragment of *Hyperion*, which is generally acknowledged
as his greatest effort. The latter production has been the
subject of extravagant praise. Byron, the poor poet being
dead, describes this poem vaguely but grandiloquently as
seeming to be " actually inspired by the Titans, and as
sublime as Æschylus," and Shelley describes it as " surely
in the very highest style of poetry." It is very different
from the easy grace and irregular sweetness of *Endymion*.
The subject of *Hyperion* is the dethroning of the ancient
gods, a grand and sombre theme, in which we might have
supposed a certain relation to the *Prometheus* of Shelley,
had not the production of the younger poet preceded that
of the elder. There is something of the same marble

stateliness and grandeur in the first presentation of the
subjects of the poem.   How great was the progress which
the poetic youth had made from the time of his pretty
sentimentalising about "the thing of beauty" will be seen
at once in the noble opening of this great fragment.

> " Deep in the shady stillness of a vale
>   Far sunken from the healthy breath of morn,
>   Far from the fiery noon, and eve's one star,
>   Sat grey-haired Saturn, quiet as a stone,
>   Still as the silence round about his lair ;
>   Forest on forest hung about his head
>   Like cloud on cloud.   No stir of air was there,
>   Not so much life as on a summer's day
>   Robs not one light seed from the feather'd grass,
>   But where the dead leaf fell there did it rest.
>   A stream went voiceless by, still deaden'd more
>   By reason of his fallen divinity
>   Spreading a shade : the Naiad 'mid her reeds,
>   Press'd her cold finger closer to her lips.
>
>   Along the margin-sand large foot-marks went,
>   No further than to where his feet had stray'd,
>   And slept there since.   Upon the sodden ground
>   His old right hand lay nerveless, listless, dead,
>   Unsceptred ; and his realmless eyes were closed ;
>   While his bow'd head seem'd listening to the Earth,
>   His ancient mother, for some counsel yet.
>
>   It seem'd no force could wake him from his place ;
>   But there came one, who with a kindred hand
>   Touch'd his wide shoulders, after bending low
>   With reverence though to one who knew it not.
>   She was a Goddess of the infant world ;
>   By her in stature the tall Amazon
>   Had stood a pigmy's height : she would have ta'en
>   Achilles by the hair and bent his neck ;
>   Or with a finger stay'd Ixion's wheel.
>   Her face was large as that of Memphian Sphynx,
>   Pedestall'd haply in a palace-court,
>   Where sages look'd to Egypt for their lore,
>   But, oh ! how unlike marble was that face,

How beautiful, if sorrow had not made
Sorrow more beautiful than beauty's self.
There was a listening fear in her regard,
As if calamity had but begun,
As if the vanward clouds of evil days
Had spent their malice, and the sullen rear
Was with its stored thunder labouring up.
One hand she press'd upon that aching spot
Where beats the human heart, as if just there,
Though an immortal, she felt cruel pain :
The other upon Saturn's bended neck
She laid, and to the level of his ear
Leaning with parted lips, some words she spake
In solemn tenour and deep organ tone :
Some mourning words, which in our feeble tongue
Would come in these like accents ; O ! how frail,
To that large utterance of the early gods !"

This is in a very different strain from the languorous
melody of *Endymion*. To Keats himself it appeared too
like Milton. "I have given up *Hyperion*," he says ;
"there were too many Miltonic inversions in it." But we
do not think the reader now will think the similarity very
great. Fine as this is, however, the young warmth and
fanciful luxuriance of the earlier poem has perhaps a
stronger hold upon the general mind, which understands
a love-tale, even when the beloved maiden is a goddess,
better than the sentiment of Godhead dethroned.

It is not, however, even upon *Hyperion* that Keats's
best title to fame is founded, at least with the general
reader. The beauty of his lyrics is, above everything else,
the charm that endears him to the popular mind ; and we
might say once more, that if all his works, except those
preserved in Mr. Palgrave's delightful little volume, were
to die out of recollection, his *Ode to a Nightingale*, that to
Autumn, the loveliest embodiment of the " season of mists
and mellow fruitfulness," that *On a Greek Vase*, which
contains so wonderful a description of the immortal life
of the past, arrested in a moment of fullest activity and pre-

served for ever by art: would still secure his immortality. These verses are above criticism, and cannot be read but with a gentle rapture, that supreme satisfaction of ear and mind which makes us linger and repeat and part unwillingly with the liquid lines. "The admirable *Ode to a Nightingale*," says Lord Houghton, "was suggested by the continual song of the bird that, in the spring of 1819, had built her nest close to the house, and which often threw Keats into a sort of trance of tranquil pleasure. One morning he took his chair from the breakfast-table, placed it on the grass-plot under a plum-tree, and sat there for two or three hours with some scraps of paper in his hands. Shortly afterwards Mr. Brown saw him thrusting them away as wastepaper behind some books, and had considerable difficulty in putting together and arranging the stanzas of the ode." So true was it, that as he himself says, his love of the beautiful would have made him write even without the stimulus of publication. This was at the moment when his heart was most full, and everything within him at the highest tide of feeling. His young brother was dead; the sole passion of his life had begun: love and grief had touched the depths within him; and he himself, alas! though he did not know it, had begun to falter upon the edge of his premature grave.

It was in the end of 1818 that his brother died. In the summer following his letters to the lady whom he loved so passionately began; but it was not till early in 1820, after the fatal chill which has been described, that these letters began to reflect the miserable certainty which was creeping upon him, that his love was one of those which could never have an earthly close. The *Letters to Fanny Brawn*, which have been published very recently, have all the makings of a tragic poem in them. "Health is my expected heaven, and you are the Houri," he says, when recovery seemed still possible. "My mind," he writes in another letter, " has been the most discontented and restless one that ever was put into a body too small for it. I never felt my mind repose upon anything with complete and undistracted enjoyment—upon no person but you. When you are in the room my thoughts never fly out of the window; you always concentrate my entire senses." When he improves a little, he tells her of his impatience, which increases as he feels himself on the borders of health, and that she has made him think more seriously of his illness than it deserved: for " how horrid was the chance of slipping into the ground instead of into your arms —the difference is amazing, love ! " In one little note he cries out with enthusiasm that he could build an altar to her for staying at Hampstead to be near him ; yet in the next more soberly assures her that she is wrong in supposing that he is displeased because she has gone to town and not stayed at Hampstead after all. " God bless my sweet love ! " he adds—" illness is a long lane; but I see you at the end of it, and shall mend my pace as well as possible." As summer advanced his health improved. His last volume, containing *Isabella*, *Lamia*, and several of the shorter poems, was published, and he began to think of settled occupation. But ere long all his prospects were darkened again ; the spitting of blood, which had been his brother's chief symptom, returned, and the doctors ordered him to a warmer climate for the winter. " They talk of my going to Italy," he cries in despair to his Fanny. " 'Tis certain I shall never recover if I am to be so long separate from you ;" though in the same breath he breaks out into wild reproaches that she does not know what it is to love : " I have heard you say that it was not unpleasant to wait a few years," he cries with passionate wonder over such a sentiment. The letters that follow grow more and more miserable in their passionate dissatisfaction :—

" Every hour I am more and more concentrated in you," he says ; " everything else tastes like chaff in my mouth ;" but he adds in the same letter—" For all this I am averse to seeing you ; I cannot bear flashes of light and return into my gloom again. . . . If my health would bear it, I could write a poem, which I have in my head, which would be a consolation for people in such a situation as mine. I would show some one in love, as I am, with a person living in such liberty as you do. Shakspeare always sums up matters in a sovereign manner. Hamlet's heart was full of such misery as mine is when he said to Ophelia, 'Go to a nunnery—go, go !' Indeed, I should like to give up the matter at once ; I should like to die. I am sickened at the brute world which you are smiling with. . . . The world is too brutal for me ; I am glad there is such a thing as the grave. I am sure I shall never have any rest till I get there."

By this time the poor young poet had got jealous of his dearest friends ; suspicions that Fanny's thoughts were divided between himself and Brown, and wild imaginations of the freedom with which she would move about and enjoy herself, while he was suffering and far away, made his soul sick. At last he seems to have started quite suddenly, accompanied by the young painter Severn, who risked his whole career by his determination to accompany the ailing and miserable young man to Rome. " Keats did not even give notice to Brown, " though at this moment I should be without pence were it not for his assistance." His jealous, wounded, hopeless heart took a kind of consolation in bursting all bonds that linked him to his former life. He plunged into the unknown, like Byron's strong swimmer, who plunged into the sea to forestal fate. They set out quite suddenly with some show of cheerfulness on the part of the sufferer, though the ink was scarcely dry of the letter in which he had poured forth the burden of his misery. " Keats," Severn wrote, " looks very happy ; for myself (in the delight of his heroic friendship) I would not change with any one." They sailed from London to Naples, one of those terrible lingering voyages which are now no longer a necessary aggravation of the always dismal journey in search of health. On shipboard the unhappy young poet wrote to the friend whom he suspected—let us hope without cause —of being his rival, yet whom he still believed in, and could not forsake without a sense of wrong :—

"I wish to write on subjects that will not agitate me much. There is one I must mention, and have done with it. Even if my body would recover of itself, this would prevent it ; the very thing which I want to live most for will be a great occasion of my death. I cannot help it ; who can help it ? Were I in health it would make me ill ; and how can I bear it in this state ? . . . I wish for death every day and night, to deliver me from these pains, and then I wish death away, for death would destroy even those pains, which are better than nothing. Land and sea, weakness and decline, are great separators, but death is the great divorcer for ever. . . . I seldom think of my brother and sister in America ; the thought of leaving Miss —— is, beyond everything, horrible—the sense of darkness coming over me. I eternally see her figure eternally vanishing. Some of the phrases she was in the habit of using in Wentworth Place during my last nursing ring in my ears. Is there another life ? Shall I awake and find all this a dream ? There must be ; we cannot be created for this sort of suffering."

Thus the poor young fellow wrote, tormenting himself by endless thought, seeing miserable visions, unable either to reconcile himself with life and love, or to make up his mind to their abandonment. Then in an interval of the sickening storm within and without, when the winds and the waves lulled a little, on some night when the sky was blue, and his soul at wistful rest, no longer swept by angry clouds—he for the last time lifted up his trembling voice between heaven and earth—

"Bright star ! would I were steadfast as thou art,
　　Not in lone splendour hung aloft the night,
And watching, with eternal lids apart,
Like Nature's patient sleepless Eremite,
The moving waters at their priest-like task
　　Of pure ablution, round earth's human shores ;

> Or gazing on the soft new-fallen mask
>   Of snow upon the mountains and the moors ;
> No !—yet still steadfast, still unchangeable,
>   Pillow'd upon my fair love's ripen ng breast,
> To feel for ever its soft fall and swell,
>   Awake for ever in a sweet unrest ;
> Still, still to hear her tender-taken breath,
> And so live ever—or else swoon to death."

Thus the troubled and anguished human creature, driven by the winds and tossed, like the never-resting water, he who had made so many songs in his little day of all lovely things, has fixed for us for ever the calm impartial shining of this star, last light of earth that penetrated the growing darkness. One more terrible letter came from Naples, as soon as the forlorn travellers landed, always about *her*, and the misery of being parted from her. "There is nothing in the world of sufficient interest to divert me from her for a moment," he says ; "Oh, that I could be buried near where she lives. I am afraid to write to her, to receive a letter from her—to see her handwriting would break my heart, even to hear of her anyhow ; to see her name written would be more than I can bear. . . . My dear Brown, for my sake, be her advocate for ever. I cannot say a word about Naples. I do not feel at all concerned in the thousand novelties around me. I am afraid to write to her. I should like her to know that I do not forget her. Oh, Brown, I have coals of fire in my breast. It surprises me that the human heart is capable of containing and bearing so much misery." He ends by imploring his friend, when he writes, "If she is well and happy put a mark thus X." A few weeks later another letter came from Rome, with an attempt at cheerfulness and a kind of pathetic ghostly banter. "If I recover, I will do all in my power to correct the mistakes made during sickness, and if I should not, all my faults will be forgiven." . . . Then he adds

with the fleeting tearful smile of weakness, " I can scarcely
bid you good-bye, even in a letter. I always made an
awkward bow. God bless you.——JOHN KEATS."

Apparently these were the last words he ever wrote.
This was in November 1820, and he lingered painfully
till February 1821. At the very end of his days there
came a letter from the too much beloved, a mere glance
at which tore him to pieces ; it was put unread into his
coffin. And thus ended life and love together, so far as
mortal eyes can see.

This wonderful passion, so hectic and feverish, so
devouring and unsatisfied, was the only human influence
that helped to kill the young poet. Love, and not Mr.
Gifford in the *Quarterly*. It was not even she that did
it, but the horror of being forced from her, and the want
of faith in her faithfulness. But love is a more seemly
and a more dignified slayer than a critic, —— if it were
possible to look thus lightly at a conclusion so full of
anguish. He directed that the words " Here lies one
whose name was writ in water," should be put on his
grave. But he was more right in the earlier youthful
confidence with which he pronounced that he should be
among the poets of England after he died, than in this
mournful sentence on himself. No poet who has done so
little bears a higher fame.

JOHN KEATS, born 1795 ; died 1821.

Published Poems, 1817.

Endymion, 1818.

Hyperion, Isabella, etc., 1820.

CHAPTER V.

MOORE——MONK LEWIS——THE SMITHS, ETC.——PEACOCK——
THEODORE HOOK——JOHN GALT.

WE have done perhaps some injustice, if not to the
permanent position, at least to the contemporary fame of
Moore by giving him so small a place in this record.
Whether Byron and Shelley were perfectly sincere in
their expressions of admiration it would be difficult to
divine, for there is perhaps a certain exaggeration permis-
sible and natural in one poet's expressed opinion of another
poet who is his friend and admirer, especially when the
younger man and newer songster is referring to a previously established reputation. "Lord Byron has read me
one or two letters of Moore to him, in which Moore
speaks with great kindness of me, and, of course, I cannot
but feel flattered by the approbation of a man my inferiority to whom I am proud to acknowledge," says Shelley;
and Byron throughout writes to his friend, the only one
of all his literary contemporaries for whom he owns any
warmth of affection, with perpetual expressions almost of
enthusiasm for his poetical powers. These appear very
strange to us now when Moore's reputation has dropped
from the highest to a very subordinate place in literature,
and when all his confectionery compositions, his Eastern
tales,——and even the contemporary satires which were
effective in their day, have alike fallen into the limbo

whence there is no redemption.   His songs still retain, and will always retain, a certain place in the popular memory, but we dare not venture to say that this would have been the case had they not been linked to the beautiful national melodies with which he was so well inspired as to connect them.   He belongs to the number of those writers who, like Dives in the parable, had their good things while they were living : and, no doubt, with his gay temper and gentle epicureanism, Moore himself would have much preferred this to the meagre living and posthumous praise of greater poets.   Many of his melodies are touching and tender, many of them full of sparkling gaiety and life.   There is scarcely any one who does not know the first line, probably the first verse, of scores of those facile and graceful compositions.   It is scarcely needful to recall them to the reader ; and though in this age of classical music, the simplicity of the ballad has fallen out of fashion, yet the taste for it is too widespread and too natural to be more than temporarily in abeyance. Even now, in the height of a musical renaissance, there are thousands of people who will be moved by one of Moore's songs, sung with feeling and expression, against the hundred connoisseurs who will think it beneath their notice.

" She is far from the land where her young hero sleeps,
    And lovers around her are sighing,
But wildly she turns from their gaze and weeps,
    For her heart in his grave is lying.

" She sings the wild song of her dear native plains,
    Every note which he loved awaking,
Ah ! little they think who delight in her strains,
    That the heart of the minstrel is breaking.

" He had lived for his love, for his country he died,
    They were all that to life had entwined him ;
Nor soon shall the tears of his country be dried,
    Nor long shall his love stay behind him.

" Oh ! make her a grave where the sunbeams rest,
    When they promise a glorious morrow,
They'll shine o'er her sleep, like a smile from the West,
    From her own lov'd island of sorrow."

This is the perfection of verse for the poet's purpose
—to be sung, not read. Its meaning needs no second
thought, it is full of picturesque and tender suggestion,
yet never overbalances the air by too much poetry. A
pathetic story and a passionate national sentiment are
concentrated in it with exquisite grace and smoothness.
The Irish singer may be excused if he feels that he has
done something for his country when he sings such a
refined epitome of its woe. But beyond this there is little
to say, and Moore had no revelation of his race to give,
to bring it near to the general heart. He had enough
nationality for this pathetic sentiment, and for a poetical
appreciation of the hopeless wrongheaded heroism of those
poor young Irish rebels who flung themselves against the
strength of England like children against a locked and
bolted door. But he had nothing to tell of his country,
no insight into it or means of interpretation. Many have
been the wrongs of Ireland, and her disabilities in the
march of human progress ; but none greater than this, for
which Providence alone is responsible, that in the allot-
ment of genius she got, instead of Burns and Scott, only
Tom Moore and Miss Edgeworth, excellent artists both,
but with the thinnest burden of prophecy, the most limited
revelation. If Scotland had been endowed no better, it
might not, perhaps, have affected her manufactories (but
even for this we should not like to undertake to answer),
but it certainly would have modified her position most
strangely, and restricted her development. Burns made
the face of his country luminous, and carried the songs of
its peasantry, the loves of its cottages, into the sympathy
and friendship of the world. But Moore's communications

were of a strictly drawing-room character, and Ireland might have been lost in the mists of the South Seas for anything he has to tell us of her inner heart and being. St. James's and polite society were heaven to the sociable little Dublin beau, who would not for the world have had the ladies suppose that he knew anything of Paddy save his jokes and lightheartedness, the conventional drapery that has hid him for ages. The great poet who is born a peasant is little likely to do much for himself in the present, or perhaps in any conditions of the world. But how much he is able to do for his country! Ireland, however, as yet, has never had the smallest promise of a Burns.

It is evident, however, that Moore's faculty was thought very highly of by his contemporaries. The terrible Jeffrey, chief slaughterer of the innocents, against whom every great writer of the age had a grievance, descends from his throne of darkness almost to plead for the aid of Moore in the great review—a most remarkable testimony to his powers. The sugary bubbles of *Lalla Rookh* brought him in no less a sum than £3000, and his *Irish Melodies* seem to have procured him, for many years, an income of £500 a year. These are substantial proofs of popularity. His *Life of Byron* will always remain the most trustworthy and genuine of the poet's records. Even in its partiality it is never false, and we doubt if any one could have held the balance more steadily, or discriminated with sounder sense, the wonderful gifts of genius, and the dangerous tendencies of character which made his friend and hero so great and so miserable. His connection with Byron altogether is one of his chief claims upon the recollection of posterity. In the beginning of that connection Moore certainly gave as much or more than he received of social distinction and semi-patronage, and all that Byron did for him in later years was to involve him

in a painful debt and still more painful discussion. When
Moore visited Venice in 1819, Byron presented him with
an extraordinary mark of regard in the shape of his own
autobiography, a precious packet of manuscript, full of the
most intimate experiences of that stormy life about which
the world was so curious. Moore, no doubt, like so many
other people, was in want of money, which perhaps, Byron
was expected to help him to — for there is repeated
reference to the fact that this precious packet, which
would have excited public curiosity to the utmost, was
excellent security, upon which Murray would not refuse
to make an important advance. With the condition that
it was not to be published till after his death, Byron
seems to have contemplated with satisfaction the publication of these memoirs and the commotion they would
produce, and afterwards added, on several occasions, to the
MS. in Moore's hands, or rather in the hands of Murray,
whither they had been transferred as security for £2000
advanced to Moore. When the poet died so prematurely
and with so little warning, this MS. naturally became the
object of many eager and anxious thoughts. Some conflict about the property and Moore's right of redeeming it
from the hands of the publisher we need not enter into.
As a matter of fact, Moore paid back the £2000, and
reluctantly, as may well be supposed, but honourably,
submitted the manuscript to the examination of a sort of
small committee, representing Byron's wife and sister, by
whom it was destroyed. Many regrets and some vituperations have been spent upon this act. Lord John
Russell assures us that he read the MS., and that the
sacrifice of it was but a trifling loss to the world. In the
face of many admirers of Byron's letters and personal
revelations, it may seem a bold thing to say that we
should be little surprised if this were strictly true. To
ourselves it has always seemed that the letters and

journals, so far as they have been published, were far too hurried and superficial, too full of levity and the swing and haste of the moment, to be at all worthy of so great a poet : nor can we imagine that his reputation would be increased by any further accumulation of such material, putting aside altogether the likelihood that what he had to reveal might have been little conducive to either public or private advantage. Anyhow, it was Moore and not the wealthier friends—the rich wife and relations—who bore the expense of this holocaust, which is a wonderful testimony to his high spirit and honourable feeling. On the other hand, we may allow that his *Life of Lord Byron* made up in some degree for his sacrifice. It brought a substantial recompense in money, and added to his reputation—and those results would, no doubt, have been in a great measure prevented by the stronger interest of any personal chronicle issued with the authority of Byron's name.

Moore wrote a life of Sheridan in the earlier part of his career, and also a memoir of Lord Edward Fitzgerald, and executed a considerable amount of miscellaneous literary work. He lived to be an old man, dying so late as 1852 ; and for the expiation of any literary sins he may have perpetrated, left his own hapless memory to the care of Lord John Russell, who, too busy in the affairs of State to spend much time in the execution of such a commission, shovelled up all the unfortunate poet's scraps and notes into a sort of wastepaper-basket of eight volumes, where they lie for the investigation of any reader, who may think it worth his while to produce for himself, out of these incoherent materials, some idea of the lively intelligence and good-humoured genial character of the author of *Irish Melodies*. These everyday jottings and familiar communications are always kind, affectionate, and cheerful, and give us the utmost satisfaction as to

Moore's moral and domestic character: but they are
trivial, as the sweepings of any man's study would probably be. Had he dealt unkindly by Sheridan or Byron,
this treatment would have been poetic justice. But he
did not do so. His own work is always conscientious
and careful. The friendly and sensible little man did his
very best for his heroes, so that the cruelty with which
he has himself been treated is all the greater. It is a
lesson to poets to resist the allurements of social ambition, and rather to trust a brother hack in literature than
a statesman and a noble peer.

It is almost vain to attempt a reproduction of all the
lighter figures which embellished Society at this period,
and made literature fashionable. The larger shades of
Mackintosh, Brougham, and Hallam, who gave dignity to
the assemblies at Holland House, have been already
mentioned, and demand treatment more serious. But in
the general London world there is no appearance more
characteristic and amusing than that of the quaint little
magician, with his trifling countenance and his mask of
horror, Matthew Gregory Lewis, known to everybody in
his own time and ours as Monk Lewis, though in these
days not one reader in a thousand has any acquaintance
with the romance which earned him that name. He was
the son of a rich man who held a lucrative post under
Government, and had abundant private means, and of
a pretty fantastic fine lady, fond of fine company, of
music and musicians, and all the curiously mixed and
heterogeneous society which fashion and the arts make
up between them. The boy was brought up in his
mother's drawing-room, giving his childish opinions with
quaint precocity upon every subject, from a classical sonata
to a lady's headdress, and keeping his mother's friends
in amusement. When he was still a schoolboy, quarrels
arose in his home, which resulted in a separation between

his parents, and the pretty, proud, frivolous mother, left her husband's house. Henceforward, the precocious boy became her affectionate friend, protector, and champion, dividing his schoolboy means with her, when her thought-less expenditure had exhausted her own, writing her long tender letters about all that was going on, sympathising, guiding, deferring to her opinion, confiding all his plans, literary and otherwise, to her. A more touching picture could not be than that of this curious pair, in themselves so imperfect, the faded, extravagant, foolish, but loving mother, and her fat little undergraduate, so sensible, so tender, so constant, so anxious to anticipate all her wants, scarcely betraying the consciousness that these wants are sometimes unreasonable, and while he pours out all his heart to her, still remaining loyally just and faithful to the father, whose liberality he will not hear impugned. At sixteen the youth had already written a farce which he hoped Mrs. Jordan would think worthy of her acting, and two volumes of a novel, though neither of them seem to have seen the light : and from that time his pen seems never to have been laid down. His play of the *East Indian* was actually accepted and acted when he was very little older, the profits of it being intended as a present for his mother, who managed this part of his business for him, having apparently kept up her con-nection with actors and the artist world generally. " Should I not obtain a farthing from the *East Indian*," he says, however, " I trust I have a much surer prospect of making you a little present than depends upon the humour of a gallery. The volume of poems of which I spoke to you in my last letter are now completed, and by July I trust I shall get them copied out fair and in a fit manner to put them into the hands of a publisher. I have no doubt of selling it. . . . Whatever this work produces, you may reckon upon every farthing of it as

your own.   If the *East Indian* succeeds, I shall set about
arranging *Adelaide* for representation.   The opera of *Felix*
could easily be brought out upon the strength of my first
play.   In short, I have a number of irons in the fire, and
I think some of them must answer my purpose."   The
young man was nineteen when he set this catalogue of
productions upon paper, and cheerfully confident in his
powers.   *The Monk* was written when he was twenty.
It had been begun some time before and laid aside, but
when the young author read the *Mysteries of Udolpho*,
which he considered " one of the most interesting books
that has ever been published," he resumed his interrupted
work, and in two weeks produced the " romance of between three and four hundred pages " upon which his
future fame was built.   *The Monk* was published in 1795.
Mrs. Radcliffe's books had given the public a taste for
wonder and mystery, and this had special piquancies of
its own to refresh the jaded appetite.   It leaped into
immediate fame.   " This singular composition," says a
contemporary critic, "which has neither originality, morals,
nor probability to recommend it, has excited and will
continue to excite the curiosity of the public, such is the
irresistible energy of genius !"   Such, we may add once
more, are the inconceivable delusions of contemporaries ;
but Monk Lewis's genius was at least as much the laugh-
ing-stock of his generation, as an object of admiration to
them.   By some good people the production, however,
was taken so seriously, that the Attorney-General of the
day was " instructed by one of the societies for the suppression of vice, to move for an injunction to suppress
its sale."   We should be disposed to say now that it is
hardly up to the mark of a " penny dreadful," even in
point of literary merit.   The horrors are of the crudest
description, and there is neither character nor force of
writing to redeem them.   Mrs. Radcliffe is incomparably

superior. There must have been something in the contrast between the fat little boyish person, blubber lips and
beady eyes, of the author, and the atrocities he lisped
forth so innocently, which tickled Society. It is scarcely
possible to conceive any more serious reason for his
fame.

A year after *The Monk* came the *Castle Spectre*, a
drama of the same description, which once more was
received with great favour by the public, and was followed
by many other plays, one of them an extraordinary composition, which the author calls a monodrama, *The Captive*,
in which the stage is held by one sole performer, representing a lady unjustly confined in a madhouse, whose
frantic appeal to her gaoler, and afterwards her long
soliloquy to herself and hearers, to prove that " I am not
mad, I am not mad," interrupted only by dumb show, the
attempt of a frantic madman to get into her cell, and
finally the arrival of her deliverers, when she has almost
raved herself into real madness—produced the most extraordinary effect upon the audience. " Never did Covent
Garden present such a picture of agitation and dismay.
Ladies bathed in tears, others fainting, and some shriek-
ing with terror—while such of the audience as were able
to avoid demonstrations like these, sat aghast with pale
horror painted on their countenances." The temerity of
the young author of twenty-one who could venture on
such an innovation is as extraordinary as the effect produced, which no doubt was owing to the powers of the
actress, and the melodramatic force of the situation.

The family history of the Lewises was shortly after
disturbed by an incident which plunged them into unimaginable terror. The mother, separated from them, yet
not shut out from their kindness, and to whom Matthew
clung with so much devotion, took a step which threatened
to sever all the ties still left between them. She wrote

a novel! When this terrible fact was known, her son, with a panic almost beyond words, rushed to pen and ink, to implore her to suppress it. By every motive which can move a woman, he abjures her to make this sacrifice. To be sure there were reasons why it might be doubly painful to such a household to be brought under the criticism of the time, to which personal gossip was delightful; but the horror with which her son contemplates the mother's authorship is doubly amusing at the present moment, when to write novels has become so common an accomplishment.

"I do most earnestly and urgently supplicate you, whatever may be its merits, not to publish your novel," he says. "I cannot express to you in language sufficiently strong, how disagreeable and painful my sensations would be were you to publish any work of any kind, and thus hold yourself out as an object of newspaper animadversion and impertinence. I am sure every such paragraph would be like the stab of a dagger to my father's heart. It would do a material injury to Sophia; and although Maria has found an asylum from the world's malevolence, her mother's turning novel writer would, I am convinced, not only severely hurt her feelings, but raise the greatest prejudice against her in her husband's family. As for myself, I really think I should go to the Continent immediately upon your taking such a step. . . . Be assured the trade of authoress is not an enviable one. In the last letter I had from poor Mrs. K——, she said that if she could but procure for her children the common necessaries of life by hard labour, she would prefer it to the odious task of writing."

This is a sermon which would greatly surprise an intending novelist of the present moment. Mrs. Lewis gave in to the terrible penalties thus set before her, and sacrificed her work, which no doubt—as would probably be the case with a great many competitors for fame—was the best thing she could do. "I always consider a female author as a sort of half-man," her severe counsellor goes on to say. Poor lady, though he is so kind to her, he does not spare any little literary vanity of which she may

have been possessed.   " I never before heard of you being
accused of having written *The Monk*.   This goes more to
put me out of humour with the book than all the fury"
with which the critics had assailed it; and he adds with
disdainful irony, " I am quite of your opinion when you
say that it would be better for you, as a woman, to write
dull sermons than *The Monk*, not merely on the score of
delicacy, but because *a dull work will prevent its author
being much talked of*, a point, in my opinion, of all others
the most desirable for a woman to attain."   To see this
little cock-sparrow of two-and-twenty thus laying down
the law is very comic.   These were the days when Mr.
Collins in Miss Austen's novel declared that he was aware
no " elegant female" ever accepted a proposal at the first
asking, and when it was still popularly accepted as a rule
that it was no disgrace to a woman to be clever or
instructed, so long as she did not show it—" a tragedy *not*
intended for publication," even the severe "Monk" had no
objection to.

But though he objected to her authorship, Lewis was
very tender to his mother, and the story of their constant
intercourse, and the reversal of positions which is natural
when a precociously sensible, cool-headed, and affectionate
boy becomes the protector and guardian of a flighty parent,
is pretty, and amusing, and touching in a breath.   He
was a foolish little fellow upon the outside, frothy and
fictitious in his work, which was always more laughable
than impressive; but in his domestic relations, and, later,
in the larger duties which cost him his life, he was a
little hero.

In 1801, out of the midst of all the finest society in
London, and travelling with the Duke of Argyle in his
landau, as he describes to his mother, he came to Scotland,
and encountered in Edinburgh young Walter Scott, a
Scotch advocate, on his promotion, newly married and

happy, but as yet undistinguished, fond of old ballads, and
trying his skill in translations from the German. Scott
told Allan Cunningham, years after, that he had never
been so elated as when "the Monk" asked him to dinner
at his hotel. The odd little Englishman, with his round
projecting eyes and boyish person, "the least man I ever
saw," was that wonderful thing, a successful and famous
author, and his notice was something to be proud of.
Lewis was eager to get contributions for the *Tales of
Wonder* which he was then collecting, and of which he
informed his new acquaintance "a ghost or a witch was
a *sine qua non;*" and they seem to have formed at once
a cordial acquaintance, with something in it—save the
mark !—of patronage and genial condescension on the part
of the visitor. Lewis would seem to have carried his
kindness so far as to set on foot negotiations for the
publication of Scott's translation of *Goetz von Berlichingen.*
What was more remarkable was the correspondence which
passed between "the Great Unknown," as he may well
be called in such a conjunction, and his literary patron,
whom he describes as "a martinet in rhymes and num-
bers." The idea of Monk Lewis schooling Scott in style
and versification is highly comic; and the lectures were
"severe enough, but useful eventually," the amiable giant
says. Scott's "first serious attempts in verse" were thus
brought to light. *The Eve of St. John, Glenfinlas,* and
several other of his early poems, were published in Lewis's
collection. But by this time the temporary fame of *The
Monk* had begun to fail, and, nobody knowing the mightier
figure which was thus conjoined with this, the *Tales of
Wonder* created no particular impression upon the mind of
the public. This collection contained the famous ballad
of *Alonzo the Brave,* which, as the majority of readers
nowadays have, we fear, entirely forgotten, was written
as a serious and awe-inspiring poem, and not as a burlesque.

Lewis had been living in great comfort during three years of literary activity, with a pretty cottage at Barnes full of all sorts of dainty nicknacks, in which he received the fashionable world, and even entertained, if not angels, princesses—and chambers in the Albany, luxuries such as few men of letters had any chance of. But in 1812 his father died, and he became at once a rich man. Many delightful stories are told of his kindness and beneficence. The little man with his round eyes went about like Haroun Al Raschid, seeing miseries which nobody else saw, and enjoying, no doubt, the excitement of sending an anonymous bank-note with all the suddenness and un-fettered liberality of a gift from heaven. There is one instance of the kind showing his readiness both in wit and charity, which we may permit ourselves to tell. He was passing through a country town in which was a company of strolling players, whom he went to see. A young actress of the company, hearing who he was, took the somewhat audacious step of calling upon him at his inn and begging something from him, "any trifle" unpublished, to give *éclat* to her approaching benefit. Lewis promised her a little piece called the *Hindoo Bride*, for which she was to come next day; but, on looking through his papers, found that he had not got it. Not knowing what to do, he went out for a stroll to think over the dilemma in which he found himself, and was forced to take shelter from a shower in a little shop, through the door of which he heard a conversation going on in an adjoining room. He recognised the voice of his petitioner, and listened. The actress was telling her mother what she had done, and it appeared from the conversation that she was the support of the old lady, who on her part, though gratified by the result, feared that the girl might have exposed herself to remark by her boldness. Lewis went back to his inn, and put up a fifty pound note in a letter, in which he informed his visitor that the *Hindoo Bride* was not to be found. " I have had," he said, " an opportunity of witnessing your very admirable performance of a far superior character in a style true to nature, and which reflects upon you the highest credit. I allude to a most interesting scene in which you lately sustained the character of ' The Daughter ! ' Brides of all denominations but too often find their empire delusive, but the character you have chosen will improve upon every representation." He left the town the same night, avoiding all thanks and explanations.

No one could be better qualified to understand and appreciate the filial virtues. One of his pleasures on coming into his fortune was to establish his mother in a pretty house, decorated to the last inch of its space, not perhaps in what we should consider as good taste now-adays; but different opinions prevail in different periods as to that indefinable quality. In the little entrance-hall of this " white cottage," opposite the door, there was a cupboard, made by " some matter-of-fact person," one of those admirable conveniences which it is now the fashion to admire. But the new inhabitant had a soul above cupboards. She turned it into a bower of painted roses and honeysuckles, encircling " a magnificent mirror," beneath which " was represented a low white gate, half open, disclosing a winding path and shady perspective of wood and water." This was what was thought the finest of decoration in the beginning of the century. Lewis and his mother would have painted the panels of the cupboard door with bristling perpendicular daisies or lilies had they done their decorations now.

Part of the property left to Lewis by his father consisted of estates in Jamaica, and the kind and conscientious little man had always determined to make himself acquainted with this portion of his possessions, which at

that time meant so much more than it does now.   He
went to Jamaica accordingly in 1816, and his account of
his arrival and residence there, and of the tumultuous
simple joy of the negroes whom he could not bear to hear
calling themselves his *slaves*, is a far more interesting and
worthy recollection than his bleeding nuns and mysterious
monks.   On his return he visited Italy and Switzerland,
and it was on this occasion that we find him with the
poets on the Lake of Geneva.   Of that meeting, as the
reader will recollect, one remarkable literary token remains in Mrs. Shelley's *Frankenstein*, called into existence
by his suggestion, in the wet summer days they spent
together.   There is another relic of the occasion, which
has an interest of its own of a different kind.   It is a
codicil to Lewis's will, framed in the interest of the
slaves who had gained his heart.   Convinced that they
could not be fitly protected unless under the eye of
" their proprietor," he resolves to secure their safety " to
the very utmost of that power which the law allows me,"
leaving upon his heirs the obligation of spending three
months in Jamaica every third year, of preserving intact
all the privileges and regulations which he had given and
made for the advantage of the negroes : and forbidding
the sale of slaves.   All this is laid down in the most
stringent and solemn words, with directions that the succession shall pass over every one who refuses to fulfil
these conditions, and " solemnly branding with the names
of robbers and usurpers of property not belonging to
them" any who may endeavour to set aside the will, or to
avoid the performance of its obligations.   This document
is signed, as witnesses, by Byron and Shelley both; and
it is a memorial of their meeting which is of the very
highest interest.   Lewis went back to Jamaica a very
short time after, and left the island to return home in
May 1818 ; but he died on the passage, a sacrifice to his

own humanity and sense of duty. Thus nobly ended the
life of the butterfly of society—a bad poet and indifferent
romancer, but kind and honest and true, a good son and
master, resolute to do his duty by all dependent on him.
He might have written better verses without being worthy
of so much praise.

Another pair of writers to whom society owed a great
deal of amusement were brought to the knowledge of the
world by a contemporary incident, which would not at
first sight have seemed a likely one to produce so much
fun and frolic. Drury Lane Theatre, which had been,
like most theatres, burnt down, was completed and about
to be reopened in October 1812. The directors thought
that an ode from some of the many poets of the time
would be an appropriate feature in the ceremonial of the
opening, and they were so far before their age as to
bethink themselves of the fine expedient of putting up
the privilege of writing this address to public competition.
It is not likely that any of the poets whose names have
survived to this time would avail themselves of such an
invitation, and consequently, among the huge number of
addresses received, not one was found good enough for
the purpose. The situation struck the lively wits of two
mirth-loving young men, great in fugitive verses both, but
with little idea of serious authorship—James and Horace
Smith, the sons of a wealthy solicitor, himself of literary
tastes and some reputation. Some one suggested the
publication of a supposed selection from the condemned
poems, and the brothers caught at the idea with glee.
There was but six weeks to prepare the volume; but this
did not discourage them, and they hastily divided between
them the authors whose peculiarities they thought most
fit for the purpose. The result was a little book which,
written at first as a mere *jeu d'esprit*, has held its ground
for the last half century, and is perhaps more generally

known now than many of the great poets, whom, with a
keenness and lightness of touch which was never dulled
by ill nature, it held up to the genial laughter of the
lookers-on. The writers give an amusing account, in
their preface to an edition published in 1835 — more
than twenty years after — of the difficulty they found in
getting their joke into print after having hurried through
its composition. The caution of the publishers had
nearly spoilt their fun and ours. " 'What have you
already written ?' was his first question, an interrogatory
to which we had been subjected in almost every instance ;"
they tell us in their description of this difficulty. The
young authors had no answer to give, and in consequence
of this the *Rejected Addresses* were themselves over and
over again rejected. But at last one more discriminating
than the rest was found—as that wise man generally is
found—to take the risk ; and the success was so rapid
and decided that the authors themselves were unfeignedly
astonished. The idea tickled the public ; and the imitations were very good, better sometimes than the models
they copied. Scott was even more delighted than was
the general reader with the parody of his own style. " I
certainly must have written this myself," said that fine-
tempered man. Lord Byron wrote to Mr. Murray with
unusual benignity—" Tell him I forgive him, were he
twenty times our satirist." And Mr. W. Spencer, a name
well-nigh unknown to our days, but not considered then
so much below the level of Scott and Byron, declared
that the audacious versifier was the man of all others
he wished to see. There was consequently no drawback
upon the pleasure of the amusing little performance,
which in all its airy malice pleased everybody. It it
impossible to refuse a laugh to the imitations of Wordsworth, Coleridge, and Southey, or not to admire the
admirable dexterity with which the peculiarities of Scots

and Crabbe were caught. As was inevitable, the collection includes several parodies of poets whose style has long ceased to be known to any one: but that is not the satirist's fault.

Those light-hearted wits did little afterwards to justify the sudden and wide reputation they had thus acquired. The younger, Horace, strayed into prose writing, and was the author of at least one novel, *Brambletye House*, which acquired a good deal of reputation; but James, though he wrote a great many verses in the same jocular vein, never progressed again beyond mediocrity. It was not indeed, his intention to seek the public ear again. " James," says his brother, " implicitly adhered to his favourite position, that when once a man has made a good hit he should rest upon it, and leave off a winner. . . . Having won the prize which seemed to him the only worthy object of contention—a welcome reception wherever he went, and a distinguished position in society —he wanted all motive for further and more serious exertion." He wrote at a later period several dramatic sketches for Charles Mathews, for which he was paid £1000. " A thousand pounds for tomfoolery," he says himself with admiring wonder, adding what Mathews had said, " You are the only man in London who can write what I want—good nonsense." Sometimes, however, the nonsense James Smith wrote was not over good, for writing nonsense is a very fatiguing operation. But he was always genial and kind: " his good sayings were heightened by his cordial good-nature, by the beaming smile and the twinkling eye." And he was always fond of society, and above all of the society of persons of distinction. He loved a lord, like most Englishmen, and still more he loved a lady. When Keats met the two witty brothers at dinner, they did not harmonise with his youthful gravity. " They only served to convince me

how superior humour is to wit," he says tartly. "These
men say things which make one start without making one
feel: they are all alike, their manners are alike, they all
know fashionables, they have all a mannerism in their
very eating and drinking, in their mere handling a
decanter. They talked of Kean and his low company.
'Would I were with that company instead of yours,' I
said to myself." But Keats was jaundiced, and probably
did not from his cold heights of poverty and deprivation
understand the well-off and peaceful people down on the
sunny level of wealth and comfort. And youth is slow
to understand wit. James Smith was one of those genial
and amiable old bachelors who are always so popular in
society. We know most of him, because Horace outlived
him and affixed a brief biographical sketch to his
Memoirs. Otherwise the merits of their great work seem
to have been pretty equally divided between them.
James contributed a large share of the best of the compositions; but Horace was the author of the *Tale of
Drury Lane, by W. S.,* which is perhaps the first of all.

The brothers were fond of the brilliant little coterie
established by Lady Blessington at Kensington, not very far
from the supreme arbiters of taste and fashion at Holland
House. Lady Blessington herself was a fashionable novelist
of some pretensions, and so was Lady Caroline Lamb,
another of the beauties of the period, whose novel *Glen-
arvon,* an extinct performance, attracted a little attention
then, the hero of the piece being supposed to be Byron,
who had disastrously crossed the poor lady's life in the
period of his brief glory in London. Lady Blessington
also contributed something to the Byron literature, mani-
fold as it was. But these light and passing butterflies of
literature, ephemera of a moment, can scarcely be reckoned
as belonging at all to its history. Their names cling to
those of the greater persons to whom some chance associ-

ation attached them, but that is all that can be said.
Lady Morgan is a name of somewhat greater importance,
and her *Wild Irish Girl* has some right to the honours of
a national story.   But she too and most of her works
have vanished from the permanent acquaintance of the
country, as so many others have done who were notable
enough in their time.   Spencer, Luttrel, Sotheby, Lord
Thurlow, and many another, where shall we find any
record of them now ?

Of a very different order was the writer who, though
appearing little in fashionable society, is connected so
closely with one of the last group of poets that his place
must fall somewhere near Shelley's in the records of
literature.   Thomas Love Peacock, one of the friends to
whom Shelley did the kindest service at a moment when
he was in no superfluity of wealth himself, became acquainted with the poet in 1812, when he was living in
Wales with his young wife Harriet, shortly after their
marriage.   Peacock was some seven years older than
Shelley, a young man whose education had been irregular,
and (as usual) without the University brand, but who was
an accomplished scholar, of a keen intellect, and much
eccentric satirical power.   How a man with so clear an
eye for the follies of his neighbours should have formed
so warm a friendship with the enthusiast boy, so wayward
and visionary, it is difficult to make out ; but he did so,
and continued so much the trusted friend of the poet that
he was named the executor of his will, though they had
not seen each other for some years before Shelley's death.
He has left us a record of that much-vexed and discussed
period of Shelley's life, the time of his separation from
Harriet and elopement with Mary, and all the events that
flowed from these acts, into which it is not necessary
now to enter, save to say that it is perhaps the most un-
impassioned and impartial account, doing justice to the

unfortunate Harriet, though without any breach of his friendship with Shelley. Peacock's reputation, however, rests upon the curious series of novels, if novels they can be called, *Headlong Hall, Nightmare Abbey, Crotchet Castle,* etc., which he has left behind him, books which are scarcely stories, though there is an artificial and whimsical thread of narrative to link their often brilliant conversations and discussions together. These, we were about to say, are unique in literature ; but they have served as a model in our own day to other productions of a similar character, not so incisive and terse, and far from being so amusing. But Peacock was for many years alone in the curious vein of satire which he discovered. His method is somewhat artificial ; and we can imagine the dismay of the ordinary novel-reader who should suddenly find himself confronted by the caustic fun and amusing dialogue of *Headlong Hall* or *Nightmare Abbey* when in search of an innocent romance. Perhaps it requires the zest of a consciousness, that were we not somewhat superior ourselves, we should not enjoy them, which has disposed such as have come under his spell to regard Peacock with something like enthusiasm. His first book, *Headlong Hall,* published in 1816, introduces us to a curious company, in which each individual is the representative of a theory, and shapes his talk accordingly—one being a " perfectibilian," another a " deteriorationist," and another a " statu-quo-ite,"—very rude symbols indeed of what can scarcely be called types of character so much as abstract figures representing each an opinion which each feels to be triumphantly proved right by every new change of circumstances. Among these oddities, Dr. Gaster plays the moderating part indicated by his name, and carries a savoury odour of good cheer through all the sharp repartees and bold assertions of the antagonists ; while Squire Headlong—who, when it is suggested to him that it is his duty to marry and continue his noble race, cries out with cheerful readiness, " Egad! that is very true; I'll marry directly"—furnishes a most amusing figure. This kind of satire is very easy and impersonal, and leaves the withers entirely unwrung of society in its usual forms; and it is absolutely artificial, and like nothing that ever was seen among mortals. But the fun is very skilful, sometimes dazzling, and always eccentric and amusing. *Nightmare Abbey* is still more wildly unlike anything that ever was in heaven or earth; but here we have what is intended for a sketch of Shelley in the hero of the piece, Scythrop Glowry by name, the only son of the master of Nightmare Abbey, and of a race given up to gloom. Gloom, however, is not the characteristic of the heir, but rather a confused energy and restlessness of mind and imagination, often very amusingly described, though we cannot but think it must have been a considerable test of Shelley's friendship for the writer to accept it as a joke. Here is an introductory sketch:—

" Scythrop proceeded to meditate upon the practicability of reviving a confederation of regenerators. To get a clear view of his own ideas, and to feel the pulse of the wisdom and genius of the age, he wrote and published a treatise, in which his meanings were carefully wrapped up in the monk's hood of transcendental technology, but filled up with hints of matter deep and dangerous, which he thought would set the whole nation in a ferment; and he awaited the result in awful expectation, as a miner who has fired a train awaits the explosion of a rock. However, he listened and heard nothing, for the explosion, if any ensued, was not sufficiently loud to shake a single leaf of the ivy on the towers of Nightmare Abbey; and some months afterwards he received a letter from his bookseller, informing him that only seven copies had been sold, and concluding with a polite request for the balance. Scythrop did not despair. ' Seven copies,' he thought, ' have been sold. Seven is a mystical number, and the omen is good; let me find the seven purchasers of my seven copies and they shall be the seven golden candlesticks with which I will illuminate the world.'"

The vagaries of this visionary youth, and how he

compels his father's consent to his engagement with an
ineligible young lady, by appearing before him with a
skull in his hand, supposedly filled with some fatal liquid,
which he vows he will drink if his petition is refused;
but when the consent is given, and the father, rushing in,
disturbs an agitated interview by a sudden " Bless you, my
children!", and suggests the naming of the wedding-day,
responds with an embarrassed " Really, sir, you are so
precipitate"——is most whimsically and cleverly told; and
so is his final embarrassment between the conflicting
claims of two ladies, with both of whom he is in love :——

" He could not dissemble to himself that he was in love at the
same time with two damsels of minds and habits as remote as the
antipodes. The scale of predilection always inclined to the fair
one who happened to be present; but the absent was never
effectually outweighed, though the degrees of exaltation and depres-
sion varied according to accidental variation in the outward and
visible signs of the inward and spiritual graces of his respective
charmers. Passing and repassing several times a day from the
company of the one to that of the other, he was like a shuttlecock
between two battledores, changing its direction as rapidly as the
oscillations of a pendulum, receiving many a hard knock on the
cork of a sensitive heart, and flying from point to point on the
feathers of a super-sublimated head. This was an awful state of
things. He had now as much mystery about him as any romantic
transcendentalist or transcendental romancer could desire. He had
his esoterical and his exoterical love. He could not endure the
thought of losing either of them, but he trembled when he imagined
the possibility that some fatal discovery might deprive him of both.
The old proverb about two strings to a bow gave him some gleams
of comfort; but that concerning two stools occurred to him more
frequently, and covered his forehead with a cold perspiration."

This is a bold picture to make of a friend, and one
who, at the moment, was standing in a much more
tragic position of the same kind between his Harriet and
his Mary. But it throws a curious light upon the
character of Shelley, in which there certainly was——
notwithstanding his great genius——something elvish and

faun-like, with starts of sudden boldness and timidity like a wild creature.

Character, however, is not Peacock's forte—his personages are all abstract, and harp upon their one string with wonderful cleverness often, but with the monotony which is inseparable from the literary puppet. In his two later works there is a difference in this respect. Dr. Folliot, in *Crotchet Castle*, carried out and continued in Dr. Opimian in *Gryll Grange*, is a well-defined personage: the old-fashioned acute man of the world, in the shape of a squire-parson, a scholar, and a gentleman, with a caustic wit, and a great taste for and comprehension of the good things of this life—disliking all innovations and novelties, and very ready to meet any antagonist in the warfare of words, a conflict in which, however antiquated his opinions may be, his wit and readiness of resource are as like as not to have the best of it. The author himself would seem to have resembled in many things this favourite character. His mixture of fine understanding and prejudice, of brilliant dialectic skill and pugnacious wrongheadedness is as remarkable as his power. These were days in which men were not ashamed to give their prejudices full scope, and to characterise their enemies with unscrupulous vigour. And Peacock had all the hostilities of his literary sect—with a furious contempt for the critics, especially Jeffrey and his brotherhood, and a hatred still deeper for the excellent Southey, who—one scarcely can tell how—seems to have been singled out as the recipient of all the vials of their wrath.

Of the many verses with which these eccentric stories are studded, we must quote a portion of one, which is to be found in the *Misfortunes of Elphin*, a Welsh romance of vague chronology, of the times of Arthur, which is told with admirable humour and mock gravity. The

first lines of this *War Song of the Dinas Vawr* will be
found, if they chance to strike the reader's ear and fancy,
to be one of those utterances of genius which prove
applicable to all the circumstances of life.

> " The mountain sheep are sweeter,
>   But the valley sheep are fatter ;
> We therefore deemed it meeter
>   To carry off the latter.
> We made an expedition,
>   We met a host and quelled it,
> We found a strong position,
>   And killed the men who held it.
>
> " On Dyfed's richest valley,
>   Where herds of kine were browsing,
> We made a mighty sally,
>   To furnish our carousing.
> Fierce warriors rushed to meet us,
>   We met them and o'erthrew them ;
> They struggled hard to beat us,
>   But we conquered them and slew them.
>
> " As we drove our prize at leisure,
>   The king marched forth to catch us ;
> His rage surpassed all measure,
>   But his people could not match us.
> He fled to his hall pillars,
>   And ere our force we led off,
> Some sacked his house and cellars,
>   While others cut his head off.
>
> .   .   .   .
>
> " We brought away from battle,
>   And much their land bemoaned them,
> Two thousand head of cattle,
>   And the head of him that owned them.
> Ednyfed, King of Dyfed,
>   His head was borne before us ;
> His wine and beasts supplied our feasts,
>   And his overthrow our chorus."

In this ironic banter and *reductio ad absurdum* Peacock
has no superior. His books themselves will probably

seem tedious to the hasty reader, but even he will find
in them innumerable suggestions which subsequent
writers have made capital of. His wine and beasts
have helped us to many feasts since his day.

Peacock held for many years an important post in
the India House, in which he succeeded James Mill.
And when he retired, he was succeeded by that stern
philosopher's son, John Stuart Mill, whose fame is still
fresh among us. These were all much greater men than
Charles Lamb, the beloved Elia, who scribbled so many
years away at a humbler desk under the same roof.

Another name which stood high among contemporaries, and occupied, in the opinion of many men, a
position entirely different from that which would be
allowed to him now, was Theodore Hook, a novelist of
much temporary reputation, a successful journalist, and
what was perhaps of more importance to his reputation
than either, a wit and epigrammatist of the highest
acceptance in his day.

"That the author of *Sayings and Doings* stands in jeopardy of
passing away rapidly from the memory of man, cannot indeed for
a moment be believed," writes his biographer. "So long as taste
for the higher works of fiction endures, *Maxwell*, *Gilbert Gurney*,
etc., must ever take high place and precedence on our shelves;
and we have no more doubt that a century hence the spectre of
Martha the Gipsy will haunt the imaginations of our great-grand-
children, while endeavouring to trace out, in the area of some
gigantic Grand Junction Railway Station, the site of what once
was Bloomsbury Square, than that the narrator of the tale himself
would have readily given his last half-crown to any red-cloaked
old lady who might have happened to solicit alms after nightfall
in that neighbourhood. His literary fame is safe."

Alas! Bloomsbury Square still remains in unblemished
respectability, but who knows anything of *Martha the
Gipsy*? It was no earlier than 1848 that these words
were written, not much more than thirty years ago; but

the literary fame which the writer flattered himself was
so "safe" has disappeared like last year's snow.   Hook
made his appearance in the world, at a very early age, as
the author of some farces of the lightest description.

> "Gods ! o'er those boards shall Folly rear her head
>   Where Garrick trod, and Siddons lives to tread ?
> On those shall Farce display Buffoon'ry's mask,
>   And Hook conceal his heroes in a cask ?"

says Byron, sparing nobody in his *English Bards*.   Hook
had been at Harrow with the noble poet.   He lived, as
his biographer delights to think, to pay back this satiric
line tenfold in the criticisms of the *John Bull*.   But in
the meantime his youth was in itself a farce in innumerable scenes, full of frolic and mischief, and every wild
device by which a young madcap could keep himself and
his friends in laughter.   His jokes sometimes had issues
which were more disagreeable than ridiculous, but he
never cared very much for that, and they were innocent
enough so long as he was merely a dare-devil boy,
balancing on the edge of society, and playing innumerable
pranks, in which there was perhaps some serious intention
of getting himself into notice as well as the pleasure of
the folly itself.   In 1812, when he was twenty-four, he
got an appointment to a responsible post at the Mauritius,
which, but that there was a good income involved, must
have evidently been as unsuitable for him as any appointment ever was.   But the days of patronage were not then
over, and the young scapegrace gaily undertook the office,
in which, as a matter of course, from sheer carelessness
and incapacity to understand business or anything else
that was serious, he fell into great trouble before long.
It was natural enough that he who could not manage his
own small financial concerns, should soon be proved unable to manage those of a colony, and the failure was so
great that he was sent home in half-a-dozen years as a

prisoner, under military escort. This alarming action on
the part of the authorities came to little when he got back
to London, except a burden of indebtedness which weighed
him down for years; but which he managed to shake off
somehow or other, though it reappeared like a spectre in
his life from time to time. He came back in 1819, and
a year after had so far recovered his spirits and freedom
that we find him in the full excitement of a new newspaper, the *John Bull,* of which he was partly the originator,
and which he conducted at first in mysterious hiding, but
afterwards openly for many years. *John Bull* did not
originate in a very lofty inspiration. These were the days
when Caroline of Brunswick, the shabbiest and least
reputable of injured queens, was fighting her poor cause
against her still less reputable husband, with a great expenditure of feeling and sympathy on the part of the
people, founded rather on horror of him, than any real
love for her. The *John Bull* was begun for the purpose
of maintaining the cause of the King, by very unsavoury
methods, against this unfortunate Princess, who stood in
royal George's way; and Hook was in no way superior to
this degrading office. When any lady ventured to show
herself at the shabby little court where Caroline held such
state as was possible, she instantly became a mark for the
arrows of this band of shabby assassins. Where all is so
pitiful, King and Queen, defenders and assailants, it is
hard to know how to characterise this odious mission.
All that scurrility and scandal could do was aimed at
every individual who entered the doors of Brandenburgh
House, so that when at length the unhappy Queen died,
and got free of her troubles, the *John Bull,* a full-grown
London newspaper, tottered in its career and felt its
occupation gone. It is not a very noble beginning, neither
was the nature noble of the man who thus rushed into the
lists in such a cause. But it is difficult for us now to

enter into the fierce and coarse polemics of this conflict, which does not enlist our sympathies on either side—for the Queen was as unattractive a victim as the King was an unelevated oppressor. Hook's novels are not of much higher class than his journalism. They abound in caricature, not even the caricature of invention, but that of actual portraiture, all his broadest sketches being easily identified by those who knew him, and by society in general. They were clever enough to be largely read at the time, but nothing can be more entirely dead than these galvanically vivacious productions are now, nor is there enough even of contemporary life in them to make it worth while to recall them to the reader.

Theodore Hook was distinguished among his contemporaries, still more than by his novels or his journalism, by the curious gift of improvisation which he possessed, and by a taste for the broad farce of mystification, practical jokes played upon all sorts of people, which it needed a dauntless impudence as well as a great deal of ready wit and unbounded cleverness to carry out. Thus he would go and force his way into a dinner party in a house where he was absolutely unacquainted, by the cleverest subterfuges, making himself, as soon as he had got a footing, so amusing and delightful to his host and the party, that the impertinence was more than condoned. All this was very amusing in the doing, and somewhat amusing in the telling, though it soon palls upon the reader; but it is not a very elevated or satisfactory mode of amusement, and few lives could be less dignified or worthy than that of this poor man of letters, this Yorick of infinite fancy and frolic, whose existence was good to nobody, not even to himself. Never was there more festivity and apparent enjoyment, more fun and noise and frivolity, but seldom an existence so barren, with so little to show for the gifts which nature had lavished, and which were but so many more means of

failure to the unfortunate upon whom they fell.   He died
in 1841 at the age of fifty-three, pitifully pursued by
debts and embarrassments to the very edge of the grave.

It has been somewhat difficult to find a place for one
of the most characteristic of Scotch novelists—John Galt.
With the literary circles in Edinburgh he had not the
remotest connection, nor, if we except the moment in
which this odd and vulgar Scot, pushing his devious way
about the world, crossed the path of Byron, had he any
literary associates at all.   The early part of his life was
spent in what is vaguely called "business," and in
processes of self-culture such as go on among young
clerks and working-men of a superior order, and which,
though admirable in themselves, rarely qualify the groping
student who has thus to stumble along the paths of
knowledge without guidance, to instruct the world.   Galt
was not successful in his early attempts in his office in
Greenock, nor does he seem to have been more so in
London, whither he removed early in the century, when
a young man of five or six and twenty.   His account of
himself in his *Autobiography* is by no means clear, but
gives us a confused picture of commercial embarrassments,
meetings of creditors, and other unpleasant accompani-
ments of failure, amid which his own attitude of cleverness
and self-confidence is always pleasing to the narrator.   A
self-opinionated Scotsman of the vulgar type, shrewd yet
reckless, self-admiring, knowing nothing better than his
own little world of the Mechanics' Institute, or local
library committee (for perhaps it was too early as yet for
Mechanics' Institutes)—how such a man could have been
admitted to the ranks of literature at all would puzzle
extremely the reader who, without knowing anything
more of Galt, should stumble upon this dull record of
himself.   When trade failed, however, he took to book-

making, and, travelling for the purpose it would seem—
as he might have travelled for the purpose of getting
orders in drysaltery, a more likely occupation—met Byron
in the East on several occasions by the chances of the
road, and formed an acquaintance upon which, at a later
period, he presumed to write a life of the poet. This was
some time about 1810, when the first cantos of *Clide
Harold* were being written. Afterwards Galt went to
Canada as agent of a company, and there worked for a
number of years, colonising and founding townships, and
encouraging emigration, but always thwarted and disap-
proved of by the authorities at home. It was on his
return from this undertaking, unsuccessful as before, when
he was about forty and considerably worn by knocking
about the world, that he fell, by chance as it would seem,
upon the vein of rich metal in his disorderly intellectual
possessions.

Up to this time, with a mind little cultivated but full
of self-consequence, and an obtuse Scottish incapacity to
perceive the things which he could not do, he had written
besides his travels, only dramatic productions, which
Scott, notwithstanding his constant kindness, characterises
as " the worst tragedies that ever were seen." But at
last it seems to have occurred to the always active-minded
adventurer to turn his eyes back to the life with which
his youth had been familiar—the homely coteries of his
native country, the village groups among which he had
been born. By what extraordinary magic it was that the
man who, writing his own life in precisely the same
localities and among the same classes, produces nothing
that is not vulgar, wearisome, and commonplace, should
the moment he got into the realm of fiction find means
to put before us the quaintest group of characters, all
real, lifelike, and original, racy of the soil and true to
nature, but not vulgar at all—is the most extraordinary

literary miracle : but so it was.   The *Ayrshire Legatees*,
the *Annals of the Parish, The Entail*, and even *Sir Andrew
Wylie*, though the humour of the last is broader and the
atmosphere less pure, are in their way wonderful repre-
sentations of the national life in out-of-the-way corners
of Scotland, impossible to be omitted in the literary
annals of the country.   Galt was not, like Scott, a master
of his art ; he had none of the genial breadth of observation, the noble comprehension of humanity, which belong
to great minds.   But what he did know he knew minutely
and by heart.   His was the simple realism with which
imagination has scarcely anything to do ; not a record of
life read by lights of higher perception and insight, but
of facts scarcely modified at all save by the machinery of
story-telling.   His Mrs. Pringle could, no doubt, have
been identified to the very ribbons on her cap : and all
the little individualities, so minutely set forth, of every
simple but guileful actor on the little scene, belong to the
very certainty of primitive life, in no way elevated or
idealised, true, yet with a lower kind of truth than that
with which the imagination has to do.   This sort of
portrait-painting, in which there is little harm, perhaps,
when the subjects are found in Scotch villages, is in most
cases a dangerous craft, and a very poor expedient to
replace art.   Fortunately it neutralises its own mischievous
tendencies by being very rarely successful.   But in Galt's
best work the imitation of nature is so close, and the life
so thoroughly penetrated and known, that the picture
almost reaches the higher level of real art.

As was to be expected, the author himself conceived
his best efforts to be of a kind more ambitious.   His is
no fiery spirit intolerant of criticism, and he is willing to
accept as much praise as any one will bestow on the
simplicities of his Ayrshire stories ; but he is still a little
wounded that *Ringan Gilhaize*, the story of a martyr-

covenanter, of which he says with an injured tone, " My memory does not furnish me with the knowledge of a novel of the same kind," should not have gained the appreciation which he feels sure it deserved, and that the *Majolo,* a book in which he had endeavoured to make his hero " feel precisely what Buonaparte is reported to have felt," should have been " absolutely neglected" by the public. On the other hand, his " amiable friend the Earl of Blessington" paid him " perhaps the most pleasing compliment" he ever received, by remarking upon the character of Lord Sandford in *Sir Andrew Wylie,* that " it must be very natural, for in the same circumstances he would have acted in a similar manner," without seeming to have " the least idea that he was himself the model of the character." This was the principle of his work throughout. But the simple wonderment of his group of country folk with their sudden accession of fortune, amid the sights of London—the current of their thoughts, all moulded in the narrowness of the parish, the gleams of mother wit, sometimes ludicrous, sometimes wise, the background of honest goodness never too good, and the unfailing store of " pawky " humour and sense — are in their way as good as anything can be. The miracle is, as we have said, that the very same people are intolerable bores and vulgar nuisances in the real story of his life, whom here in fiction he makes the most amusing companions. Nothing more flat and vulgar than the autobiography, nothing more genuine, humorous, and original than the stories. In this way Galt is a greater wonder than Scott himself.

We will not even attempt to put upon record the number of trashy publications to which Galt's name is attached. Travels, biographies, tragedies, books without number rattled from a pen so commonplace save in one direction, that it is inconceivable why they were published at all;

but among all this dross the one clear streamlet, like
a burn in his own homely, tuneful country side, the
district which brought Burns into the world as well as
this strangely-gifted humourist, goes on with a cheerful
tinkle ever worthy the attention of the passer-by, and
ever pleasant, fertilising, adorning. A man who has done
so much as this has the best of claims upon his country
to have all the rest forgotten.

We have omitted to notice among the writers of Scotland a name which, however, like Galt's, is but little connected locally with Scotland, though no more genuine
Scot could be, either in his works or sentiments, than
Allan Cunningham, "honest Allan," one of those men,
peasant-born and but barely educated, who, by dint of
something which we must call genius, though not great
enough to reach an exalted rank, have made their way
out of the fields and workshops into the world of literature. Nothing but that spark of a divinity uncontrollable
and subject to no laws, which, like the winds, goes
"where it listeth," could account for the appearance here
and there of such a simple and stalwart figure, in regions
so different from those which brought him forth. Allan
Cunningham was all the more remarkable that he not
only brought out of a gardener's cottage enough of the
faculty of Song to find him a place in the poetic records
of his country, but also out of the stonemason's yard some
perception of art which made him capable of becoming
the trusty assistant and head workman of a great sculptor.
His connection with Chantrey is still more remarkable
than his connection with literature, for art exacts a harder
apprenticeship than has ever been required for authorship. Perhaps it was the faithfulness of the man, and
steady devotion, that made him capable for this post,
rather than any insight into art. He was the author of
several songs which are not unworthy of a place in the

language of Burns, and a great deal of hard - working composition, *Lives of Painters,* and other respectable productions, a *History of Literature Biographical and Critical,* with some novels which will not bear much criticism. " Honest Allan," says Sir Walter Scott of him, " a leal and true Scotchman of the old cast. A man of genius besides, who only requires the tact of knowing when and where to stop, to attain the universal praise which ought to follow it." The sight of such a man in the haunts of authors and artists in London, with his shepherd's plaid over his shoulder, his rustic breeding, and flavour of the soil, is one of the most remarkable in all the circle of strange sights. He had much intercourse with Sir Walter, and with many others of the best men of the day, and was adopted fully into that world so foreign to his race. His songs are the chief things that remain of him. This most simple, but by no means most easy branch of poetical composition has always been a special gift of Scotland, where, at the same time, many voices kindred to " honest Allan's—those of Lady Nairne, whose fame, like that of Lady Anne Lindsay, depends on one song, of Motherwell, and Tannahill, and several other congenial spirits—were then flourishing. It is with an apology for previous omission that we mention them here. And on the same argument, we may add the name of another Scot of other pretensions, William Tennant, a man of education and literary skill who was not so fortunate as Allan, but lived and died a poor schoolmaster, without ever issuing out of his little native sphere. A long poem in the measure of *Whistlecraft* and *Don Juan,* but preceding both, the subject of which is *Anster Fair* and the heroine Maggie Lauder, could scarcely be carried into fame or the general knowledge except by the greatest gifts of genius. And these Tennant certainly did not possess. But his verse has much of the freedom and flow of the greater productions

in which the same medium was adopted, and has power
enough to make the chance reader regret that it had not
a little more—enough at least to raise such a skilled
manufacture to something more than merely local fame.
Where Tennant got the measure we are not informed.
That he should have drawn it direct from Pulci and the
Italians seems unlikely; but it is at least remarkable
that a form of poetry which was afterwards to become so
famous should have first stolen into English in this humble
and unnoticed way.

THOMAS MOORE, born 1779; died 1852.

Published Translation of Anacreon in 1800.
        Little's Poems, 1801.
        Odes and Epistles, 1806.
        Lalla Rookh, 1817.
        The Fudge Family in Paris, 1818.
        Rhymes for the Road, 1819.
        Loves of the Angels, 1823.
        Fables for the Holy Alliance, 1823.
        The Epicurean, 1839.

MATTHEW GREGORY LEWIS, born 1775; died 1818.

Published The Monk, 1796.
        The Castle Spectre, etc., many Dramatic Works and
          Operas at different times betwixt 1797 and 1812.
        Tales of Wonder, 1801.
        Bravo of Venice, 1804.
        Feudal Tyrants.
        Tales of Terror.
        Romantic Tales.

JAMES SMITH, born 1775; died 1839.

Published Rejected Addresses, 1812.
       ,,   ,,   22d edition, 1851.
        Comic Miscellanies contributed to various periodicals,
        reprinted after his death.

HORACE SMITH, born 1779 ; died 1849.

Published Brambletye House, 1826.
      Tor Hill.
      Zillah.
      Adam Brown, etc.

THOMAS LOVE PEACOCK, born 1785; died 1866.

Published Headlong Hall, 1816.
      Melincourt, 1817.
      Nightmare Abbey, 1818.
      Rhododaphne.
      Maid Marian, 1822.
      Misfortunes of Elphin, 1829.
      Crotchet Castle, 1831.
      Gryll Grange, 1860.

THEODORE EDWARD HOOK, born 1788 ; died 1841.

Published A number of Farces and Operettas between
      1805 and 1821.
      Sayings and Doings (first series), 1824.
         ,,   ,,   (second series), 1825.
         ,,   ,,   (third series), 1828.
      Reminiscences of Michael Kelly, 1826.
      Maxwell, 1830.
      Life of Sir David Baird, 1832.
      The Parson's Daughter, 1833.
      Jack Brag, 1837.
      Births, Deaths, and Marriages, 1839.
      Love and Pride, 1833.
      Gilbert Gurney, 1835.
      Gurney Married, 1839.
      He continued to publish Novels and Magazine
      Articles to the end of his life.

JOHN GALT, born 1779 ; died 1839.

Published The Ayrshire Legatees, 1820.
      Annals of the Parish, 1821.
      Sir Andrew Wylie, 1822.
      The Provost, 1822.

Published The Entail, 1823.
          The Steamboat.
          Ringan Gilhaize.
          The Spaewife.
          Lawrie Todd.
          The Owner, 1824.
          Bogle Corbet, 1831.
          And many others.

ALLAN CUNNINGHAM, born 1784 ; died 1843.

Published Several Songs in Cromek's Remains of Nithsdale and
          Galloway Song, 1810.
          Sir Marmaduke Maxwell, 1822.
          Paul Jones.
          Lives of Painters.
          History of Literature.

WILLIAM TENNANT, born 1785 died 1848.
          Published Anster Fair, 1812.

CHAPTER VI.

MARIA EDGEWORTH——JANE AUSTEN——SUSAN FERRIER.

THERE is a curious symbolism in the names which stand at the head of this page——three women representing with great fitness the three countries that form Great Britain, all writing the same language, and embodying to a great extent the same ideal, yet revealing each the characteristics of her race in a manner as amusing as it is instructive. Miss Ferrier, the youngest of the group, was somewhat cast into shade by the apparition, close beside her, of the greatest of novelists, yet, nevertheless, kept her place and reputation notwithstanding Sir Walter. The others held undisturbed possession of the field, and were each supreme on her own ground. Novel-writing——though we are apt to say that it never attained such general extension as now——has always been a popular art, and perhaps at no period since literature began to have a history, did it ever happen that the story-teller was absent from the beadroll. But there had been a lull after Richardson and Fielding, and their successor Smollett. The two latter, we presume, making every allowance for the change of manners, never could have been considered suitable for domestic reading: and the gradual development of an ever-increasing audience brought necessities with it which probably had some occult power in quickening the feminine imagination, and calling into being that pure-minded and delicate art which

was found to the amazement of all beholders to be capable
of delighting and amusing the public without infringing
the finest standard of morals.   Richardson had meant well
—he had supposed and everybody had said that *Pamela*
was the support of virtue, an example for womankind.
But neither Fielding nor Smollett was solicitous about
virtue.   They were "robust" masters of the art of fiction,
with no sort of affectation about them ; their books were not
meant for the women—and probably at that period women
were not very much considered in the audience to which
writers in general addressed themselves.   But a change
had evidently come about in this respect at the end of
last century.   Whether it was Rousseau and the French
Revolution who did it, or whether it was the waking up
in divers places of such genius among women as creates
its own audience and works its own revolution, it is difficult to tell.   Mary Wollstonecraft, who was the most
likely to be influenced by these foreign powers, wrote bad
stories in the old style, and probably Maria Edgeworth
and Jane Austen knew very little of Rousseau.   It is as
hard to decide how they were produced as it is to trace
any other awakening of a new thing in poetry or art.
They were as much a new source of life and meaning as
were the poets their contemporaries, and arose—because
it was in them—mysteriously out of the gentle darkness,
each a particular star.

It is curious to note the difference between their contemporary Mrs. Inchbald and these ladies of the new light.
The *Strange Story*, with its graceful talent and individuality, belongs to the eighteenth century altogether.   It
deals with no definable development of human nature, and
has in it no real study of life.   It is a surprise to us to
realise that *Pride and Prejudice* was actually written
earlier than that curious romance, though it did not till
some time after see the light.   Mrs. Inchbald is of the

past, and her production is almost archaic; but Jane
Austen belongs to humanity in all periods, and Miss Edgeworth is even more clearly natural and practical. The
life of average human nature swept by no violence of
passions, disturbed by no volcanic events, came suddenly
uppermost in the works of these women as it had never
done before. Miss Austen in particular, the greatest and
most enduring of the three, found enough in the quiet
tenor of life which fell under her own eyes to interest the
world. Without ever stepping out from the shelter of
home, or calling to her help a single incident that might
not have happened next door, she held the reader, if not
breathless, yet in that pleased and happy suspension of
personal cares and absorption of amused interest, which is
the very triumph of fiction. She had not even a new country
to reveal like Miss Edgeworth, or a quaint and obscure
region of odd manners and customs like Miss Ferrier.
She had nothing to say that England did not know, and
no exhibition of highly-wrought feeling, or extraordinary
story to tell. The effect she produced was entirely novel,
without any warrant or reason, except the ineffable and
never-to-be-defined reason of genius which made it possible
to turn all those commonplace events into things more
interesting than passion. It would be difficult to find
anything nearer witchcraft and magic. Why we should
be so much amused and delighted by matters of such
ordinary purport, and why a tiresome old woman or
crotchety old man, whom, in real life, we would avoid,
should become in print an exquisite diversion, is one of
the most unaccountable of literary phenomena. But so
it is. And as we mark the growth and rise of the new
flood of noble poetry at the meeting-point of the two
centuries, we should be negligent of one of the first duties
of a historian if we did not note likewise the sudden
development of purely feminine genius at the same great

era. Female writers have never been wanting. In the dimmest ages there has always been one here and there adding a mild, often a feeble, soprano to the deeper tenor of the concert. How it is that these have never risen to the higher notes and led the strain, as the feminine voice does in music, we need not inquire. Women are very heavily weighted for any race, but it can scarcely be that circumstances account for an inferiority so continual. But the opening of an entirely feminine strain of the highest character and importance—a branch of art worthy and noble, and in no way inferior, yet quite characteristically feminine, must, we think, be dated here in the works of these three ladies. Women's books before had either been echoes of those of men, or weakly womanish, addressed to "the fair" like so many productions of the eighteenth century. The three sister novelists who came to light in the beginning of the nineteenth, were, in their own way, as remarkable and individual as Scott or Fielding, and opened up for women after them a new and characteristic path in literature.

Miss Edgeworth was the first to appear in the field, and she had the advantage of an altogether new and untrodden ground. She was born in 1767, the eldest child of the gay young philosopher referred to by Miss Anna Seward, the husband of the beautiful Honora Sneyd, and of various other charming women, but whose chief distinction is that he was the father of his daughter. Maria was the child of his first marriage—a marriage contracted before he was twenty, and soon ended. Three wives and three families followed, and the house at Edgeworthstown was a very full one; but Mr. Edgeworth and his eldest daughter seem to have been each other's most tender and faithful friends through all the many incidents of his life. He was a man full of whims and crotchets and boundless self-confidence, fond of writing, and occupying himself

busily in systems of education and benevolent conspiracies
of all kinds for the public good. Byron, when he met the
great novelist and her father in London, gave vent to a
witty saying which characterises them very cleverly. *She*
looked, he thought, the simplest of ordinary little women,
as if she could scarcely write her own name, while *he,* on
the contrary, looked as if nothing else was worth writing
—an admirable description. One or two somewhat laborious treatises, on *Practical Education,* on *Irish Bulls*—are
said to be the joint production of father and daughter, and
Miss Edgeworth herself has left it on record that she had
recourse to her father's ready wit and invention in all her
difficulties. " I am sure," she says, " that I should never
have written or finished anything without his support."
Many of her books are introduced by a little address from
him full of genial self-complacency, as of a man who felt
himself the author not only of the books but of the mind
that produced them, and consequently deserving of double
credit. " My daughter," he says with an evident roll of
satisfaction in his voice, " asks me for a preface to the
following volumes : from a pardonable weakness she calls
upon me for parental protection : but in fact the public
judges of every work not from the sex, but from the merit
of the author." The crow of the cock, stepping gallantly
out in front of his womankind, has been not unfrequently
reproduced by proud yet semi-apologetic relatives introducing the works of female authors to the world.

Maria Edgeworth was a half-grown girl, at the moment
when observation is most vivid, when she was taken from
England, where she had been born, and up to her
thirteenth year educated, to her home in Ireland ; and no
doubt the contrast struck her with wonderful keenness
and force. It is a scene she is fond of repeating. Lord
Glenthorn in *Ennui* and the young Lord Colambre in the
Absentee, are both led through the amusing experiences

of an arrival, from all the prejudices and decorums of
England into the very heart of the reckless, thriftless,
contented, witty, scheming, and faithful population of the
unknown country; from which they both have derived
their means without any knowledge of either the land or
the people. No doubt her own recollections gave force
and animation to the picture. It was not, however,
through the means of a youthful hero and captivating
Irish heroine—personages whose charms literature has
always been ready to acknowledge—that Miss Edgeworth
first opened up this unexplored and novel region to the
public. Her first work had no enlivening of youthful
love, no cheerful hopes of amelioration to recommend and
soften the picture. *Castle Rackrent*, which was her first
publication (in 1801), and which is one of the most
powerful and impressive of her books, is devoted to the
miserable story of improvidence, recklessness, and folly,
by which so many families have been ruined, and which
is linked with so much that is attractive in the way of
generosity and hospitality and open-handedness, that the
hardest critic is mollified unawares, and the sympathetic
populace, which is no adept in moral criticism, admires
with enthusiasm while he lasts, and pities, when he has
fallen, the culprit who is emphatically nobody's enemy
but his own.

The story is told by an Irish retainer, faithful to his
master to the very death, and though heartbroken when
ruin comes, as proud of the lavish prodigality and beneficence of the house, and even of its wild waste and profusion, as if these had been the chief claims of "the
family" to honour. It was a bold proceeding upon the
part of a young author to stake her fortune upon a book
in which there was neither love nor marriage, nor any of
the well-worn romantic expedients for holding the reader's
attention. It is the story of the ruin of a family, gradu-

ally worked out as it descends from generation to generation with a power which is at once amusing and tragical.
There are incidents in the story which it is to be hoped
were not common even in the worst state of Ireland, such
as that of the imprisonment in her own house of Sir Kit's
wife, but this powerful picture has been generally accepted
as a true rendering of the miserable existence and downfall
of many a house. The "family" is one of high descent
and pretensions, with a very good estate in possession, and
the *éclat* of a much finer one which had been theirs, and
which still gives them a right to think themselves the
first people in the district. It is free of the usual incon-
venience of a large number of sons and daughters, for the
prevailing recklessness of the race, and its constant need
of money, leads one representative after another into a
loveless or repugnant marriage, and not an heir is born so
long as we follow its history in the ungenial house. From
first to last an endless and aimless prodigality is the rule,
with the one exception of the second baronet to whom we
are introduced, Sir Murtagh, who represents the reverse
sin of avarice, and who with his wife is continually grind-
ing and crushing the people, exacting every kind of gift
and profit from them. This pair are remorselessly drawn.
"This for certain," says Old Thady, the hanger-on who
tells the tale, "the new man did not take at all after the
old gentleman : the cellars were never filled after his
death, and no open house, or anything as it used to be ;
the tenants even were sent away without their whisky.
I was ashamed myself, and did not know what to say
for the honour of the family, but I made the best of a bad
case, and laid it all at my lady's door, for I did not like
her anyhow, nor anybody else. . . . I always suspected
she had Scotch blood in her veins." Sir Murtagh and his
lady manage their estate in a manner which affords an
excellent contrast to the dissipation of the others, and

throws also a curious light upon the habits of the period.
The description reads something like the exactions of a
grand seigneur in France before the Republic.   The table
at the castle was kept provided with " duty fowls, duty
turkies, and duty geese . . . for what with fear of driving
for the rent, or Sir Murtagh's lawsuits, they (the tenants)
were kept in such order, they never thought of coming
near the hall without a present of something or other."

" As for their young pigs, we had them, and the best bacon and
ham they could make up, with all young chickens in spring ; but
they were a set of poor wretches, and we had nothing but misfortunes with them, always breaking and running away.   This, Sir
Murtagh and my Lady said, was all their former landlord, Sir
Patrick's fault, who let 'em all get the half-year's rent into arrear.
There was something in that, to be sure.   But Sir Murtagh was as
much the contrary way ; for let alone making English tenants of
them, every soul, he was always driving and driving, and pounding
and pounding, and canting and canting, and replevying and replevying, and he made a good living of trespassing cattle ; there was
always some tenant's pig, or horse, or cow, or calf, or goose trespassing, which was so great a gain to Sir Murtagh that he did not like
to hear me talk of repairing fences.   Then his heriots and duty
work brought him in something, his turf was cut, his potatoes set
and dug, his hay brought home, and, in short, all the work about
his house done for nothing ; for in all our leases there were strict
clauses heavy with penalties, which Sir Murtagh knew well how to
enforce ; so many days' duty work of man and horse from every
tenant he was to have and had every year ; and when a man vexed
him, why, the finest day he could pitch on, when the cratur was
getting in his own harvest, or thatching his cabin, Sir Murtagh
made it a principle to call upon him and his horse ; so he taught
'em all, as he said, to know the law of landlord and tenant."

This was in the happy days when Ireland had a parliament of her own, and home rule was unbroken : and
under a landlord native to the soil, a descendant of the
old kings, one of the same race and same creed as the
unhappy dependants whose blood he sucked.   But with
all these exactions and robberies the landlord did not

thrive. "He used to boast that he had a lawsuit for every letter in the alphabet," and out of forty-nine suits " he never lost one, but seventeen," which was his way of throwing away his substance. Sir Murtagh died of passion in a quarrel with his wife " about an abatement," and his younger brother reigned in his stead. " A fine life we should have led," says Thady, " had he staid among us — God bless him! He valued a guinea as little as any man; money to him was no more than dirt, and his gentleman and groom, and all belonging to him, the same." Sir Kit, however, found Castle Rackrent dull, and " went off in a whirlwind to town," leaving everything to his agent, and keeping up a continual demand for money. " He had the spirit of a prince, and lived away, to the honour of his country, abroad, which I was proud to hear of." The state of things under the rule of the agent, and the constant drafts for money of the owner, are described as follows :—

"He ferreted the tenants out of their lives ; not a week without a call for money, drafts upon drafts from Sir Kit ; but I laid it all to the fault of the agent ; for, says I, what can Sir Kit do with so much cash, and he a single man ? But still it went. Rents must be paid up to the day, and afore ; no allowance for improving tenants, no consideration for those who had built upon their farms : no sooner was a lease out, but the land was advertised to the highest bidder, all the old tenants turned out, when they spent their substance in the hope and trust of a renewal from the landlord. All was now set at the highest penny to a parcel of poor wretches, who meant to run away, and did so, after taking two crops out of the ground."

Amid all this Miss Edgeworth gives scarcely any indication of disturbance among the peasants, or secret societies, or any attempt at agitation. To be sure, there was an insurrection breeding, the unfortunate attempt of '98, during the period embraced by her story, of which she gives some small incidental account in another work,

representing the country folk, however, as but little and
very superficially agitated, and the tremendous burdens
upon them in respect to their occupation of the land as
wholly inoperative in the matter.   Whether she is a
competent authority or not on this point we cannot tell;
but she was an eye-witness, and knew what she was
talking about.

Sir Kit got out of his difficulties by marrying an ugly
Jewess, whom he shut up in her room for some years,
because she refused to give up her jewels to him; till he
was finally shot in a duel, to the great grief of the whole
country side.   "He was never cured of his gaming
tricks; but that was the only fault he had, God bless
him," says the pious Thady.   He was succeeded by Sir
Conolly (or Condy for short), who was "the most universally beloved man I had ever seen or heard of," and
whose story of wild waste at once of money and affections
and life is so complete, and the gleams of honourable
feeling that flash out of the wretchedness of his bankrupt
condition, so affecting—that the reader is touched by the
pitiful tale, and notwithstanding his whisky punch, the
smell of which revolts his unloved wife, and the madness
of his hopeless career altogether, regards with a pang the
miserable end of the spendthrift, who falls a victim at last
to whisky and misery in a wretched little house, whither
he has retired, after making over his castle to Jason
O'Quirk, the too-quickwitted son of old Thady, who has
grown upon his master's misfortunes, as wicked attorneys
do everywhere.   The reckless poor gentleman, who fore-
stalls his inheritance, by advances, before he has got it,
and begins a great deal worse than nothing: who is
swept into a marriage he has no desire to make, and
which is decided at last by the toss of a halfpenny: and
who will not be troubled about his expenses or about
anything else in the world, but floats on helpless to

destruction, and dies at last of a drunken bet, is contemptible enough from every moral point of view; but
the love and admiration and sorrow of the faithful old
retainer, who tells the tale——the remnants of a higher
nature in the victim——and the utter misery and tragic
sweep of fate with which he is carried away, have a
heart-rending effect.

"There was none but my shister and myself left near him of
all the friends he had. The fever came and went and lasted five
days; and the sixth he was sensible and said to me, knowing me
very well, 'I'm in burning pain all withinside of me, Thady.' I
could not speak, but my shister asked him would he have this
thing or t'other to do him good? 'No,' says he 'nothing will
do me good now;' and he gave a terrible screech with the torture
he was in—then again a minute's ease—'Brought to this by drink,'
says he. 'Where are all the friends?—Where's Judy?—Gone,
hey? Ay, Sir Condy has been a fool all his days,' said he; and
this was the last word he spoke, and died. He had but a poor
funeral after all."

The young author who began her career by a tragedy
so homely yet so profound as this must have been as
courageous as she was able. It was a revelation of the
deepest of national disabilities, a type of character so wayward yet so winning, so hopelessly facile, so obstinate and
immovable, so generous and so selfish, that the moralist
could but stand by in despair and feel the impotence of
all exertion. In her other Irish stories which followed,
Miss Edgeworth took advantage of a more attractive plot,
and of the more ordinary *motif* of romance——the perennial
love-story. In *Ennui* we have a number of pictures more
cheerful but equally characteristic, the humours of the
peasant being more entertaining, and even in his worst
development of thriftless *insouciance* never so hopeless
as the follies of his master; while in the *Absentee* we are
permitted to hope for a remedy of all evils, and rapid
substitution of a heaven upon earth for the wretchedness

of the agent's remorseless sway, by so easy an expedient
as the return of the absentee family.   The novelty of the
circumstances set before us in these studies, and the dis-
similarity of many points in the Irish character to the
experiences of the English reader, never hinder our
recognition of the life and nature which make the whole
world kin.   The shiftless careless cotter, sitting content
with the squalor of his lot, and embarrassed only by the
botheration of all attempts to better it : full of gratitude,
affection, and faithfulness to all natural ties : far happier
in the dash and daring of a hairbreadth escape than in
national security and good order ; touched with instantaneous impulses for good or evil, ready in understanding
and still more ready in wit—who has for all this time
been our favourite type of the Irish peasant, is chiefly
Miss Edgeworth's creation ; and nobody before her had
revealed the fine gentleman, gallant, handsome, and
manly, but as indolent of mind as the cotter, and letting
everything go with still more fatal facility, whose pitiful
consciousness of something better in him is never extin-
guished even by the low vices and degraded company to
which he falls, but never does anything more for him
than gild the ruin of his hopes and prospects.   Nor has
this exponent of national character failed to see the
stealthy treachery which is the reverse side of the instinctive, spaniel-like, uncritical devotion of the race,
or the bitter avarice and grasping acquisitiveness which
varies the profusion and prodigality of the spendthrift.
What Miss Edgeworth failed in was the gift of throwing
a romantic and elevating interest over her country as Sir
Walter did for his.   She interests and excites the reader,
but sets before him no picture which he longs to see, no
society which he would like to join.   There are no historical associations to attract him, and little but the
painful problems of social misery to solve.   Though she

writes with genuine love for her country, she communi-
cates no enthusiasm for it. To be sure, enthusiasm had
little or no existence in her own perfectly well-balanced
and over-educated soul.

The Tales in which Miss Edgeworth took upon her
to expound the world of fashion are less successful than
her national sketches, but many of them are well worth
reading; and if it is difficult to believe in the grossness
of the dandy as shown in some of her sketches of a period
so recent as the beginning of this century, the sprightly
graces of her heroines, and the admirable good sense
which they display in all the entanglements of their respective stories, are always agreeable. Her *Tales for
Children* and *Parent's Assistant* enjoyed an enormous
popularity, which has not lasted, we fear. Probably the
virtues of the model young persons whom she holds up
to the admiration of the youthful world are too matter-of-
fact to please a young imagination. Our sympathy per-
versely goes astray from Ben, who buys a comfortable
greatcoat, to Harry, who chooses a green and white
archery uniform instead; and we are less angry with
Rosamond for admiring the purple jar in the chemist's
window than with her mother for permitting the child to
buy it. Good sense and practical education are admirable things, but they may be carried too far. It was the
lot, however, of Maria Edgeworth to be trained in one of
those somewhat appalling family seminaries of all the
virtues, where nothing escapes the system of education,
and everything is made subservient to the moral discipline of the house. It is scarcely fair, however, to assert
—as is so often done—that her imagination is deficient,
that she has no enthusiasm, nor anything more elevated
in her than the dominion of plain sense, and the honesty
which is the best policy. We have already indicated the
tragedy of *Castle Rackrent*, where she has succeeded,

amid details of petty and even vulgar vice, in giving such touches both of pity and terror as raise the miserable drama to poetic rank. She never again strikes quite so high a note, but the picture of King Corney in *Ormond* is as striking and full of pathos as that of Sir Condy. Perhaps her admirable papa, who cut and carved her manuscripts at his will, declaring that to write was her part, and to amend and criticise his, may have subdued her tragic vein.

But nothing can be more pleasant than the picture she has left us of the close communion and partnership which existed so long between her father and herself. Sometimes it was he who invented the stories, and she who wrote them down—as was the case in respect to her tale of *Patronage*, it must be allowed one of the least successful of her productions, and the most open to the charge of flatness and matter-of-fact treatment. But ordinarily it was she who brought her skeleton tale to her father, to be by him considered and weighed in the critical balance. She lived at home in all the freedom and cheerfulness of the large and full household; seeing wife succeed wife in the government of the mansion, and family after family fill up the many rooms. The younger daughters, children of Mrs. Honora or Mrs. Elizabeth, were married or died in their bloom; but Maria still lived peacefully on, her father's companion and counsellor, growing quietly into maturity, till, no doubt, in her gentle and ripe maidenhood, she became the elder of the two, a sort of indulgent senior to that ever energetic, ever active personage who was capable of so many loves, and renewed his youth periodically in a new marriage. They must have got to be something like brother and sister as she grew old and he young, marrying at fifty-four a lady who was younger than Maria. But nothing seems to have impaired their tender union, or the warm and cheerful placidity of the family life.

Her books were received with great favour, and her reputation at once reached the highest place. " Without being so presumptuous as to hope to emulate the rich humour, pathetic tenderness, and admirable tact which pervade the works of my accomplished friend," said Sir Walter Scott in the preface to the *Waverley Novels*— when, after so long a period of concealment, he at last revealed himself publicly to the world which had guessed his secret so long—" I felt that something might be attempted for my own country of the same kind with that which Miss Edgeworth so fortunately achieved for Ireland —something which might introduce the natives to those of the sister kingdom in a more favourable light than they had been placed hitherto ;" and he describes " the extended and well-merited fame of Miss Edgeworth, whose Irish characters have gone so far to make the English familiar with the character of their gay and kindhearted neighbours, that she may truly be said to have done more towards completing the Union than perhaps all the legislative enactments by which it has been followed up," as one of the inducements which led him to complete and publish *Waverley*. The sincere compliment of imitation could not have been paid in a nobler way ; and one of the prettiest episodes in the too-hospitable life at Abbotsford is the visit of Miss Edgeworth to her great contemporary.

" The next month—August 1823—was one of the happiest in Scott's life," writes Lockhart. " Never did I see a brighter day at Abbotsford than that on which Miss Edgeworth first arrived there. . . . The weather was beautiful, and the edifice, and its appurtenances, were all but complete ; and day after day, so long as she could remain, her host had always some new plan of gaiety. One day there was fishing on the Cauldshields Loch and a dinner on the heathy bank. Another, the whole party feasted by Thomas the Rhymer's waterfall in the Glen—and the stone on which Maria that day sat was ever afterwards called Edgeworth's Stone. A third day we had to go further afield. He must needs show her, not Newark alone, but all the upper scenery of the Yarrow, where ' fair hangs the apple frae the rock ;' and the baskets were unpacked about sunset, beside the ruined chapel overlooking St. Mary's Loch : and he had scrambled to gather bluebells and heath-flowers, with which all the young ladies must twine their hair,—and they sang, and he recited, until it was time to go home beneath the softest of harvest moons. Thus a fortnight was passed—and the vision closed ; for Miss Edgeworth never saw Abbotsford again."

While Maria Edgeworth was growing into maturity in her Irish home, frightened by the rebellion, but never losing her faith in her countrymen, a younger girl in an English rectory in Hampshire, with nothing about her beyond the calmest everyday circumstances, began, quite unprovoked by outward stimulation, to exercise a gift still finer and more subtle than that of her Irish contemporary. Jane Austen, who was born in 1775, was eight years younger than Miss Edgeworth. She was a shy and quiet girl, with the keenest insight and gently cynical penetration, hidden under a pretty humour and softly trenchant banter. The way in which she tenderly laughs at, and turns outside in, the young nephew to whom she addresses some pretty letters, published in the little anecdotical memoir not long since given to the world, betrays her use in private life of the keen and exquisite derision which is one of her favourite weapons in her art. She was only about twenty in her sheltered and happy life at home in the end of the old century, when she wrote what might have been the outcome of the profoundest prolonged observation and study of mankind—what is, we think, the most perfect of all her works—*Pride and Prejudice*. It must have been in her father's parish, in the easy intercourse of village or rural life, that she saw, probably without knowing she saw, so many varieties of human nature. No feasible inducement was before her to bring this strange endowment to life; no hothouse training in moralities and the creed of universal instructiveness; no restless literary papa to set her an example; no unknown society or manners to reveal. An excellent ordinary strain of honest gentlefolks, peaceably tedious and undistinguished, and anxious to make it apparent that their Jane knew nothing of literary people, and was quite out of any possibility of association with such a ragged regiment, was the family that give her birth. She wrote—no one can tell why—out of native instinct, preferring that way of amusing herself to fine needlework,—telling stories, as Burns rhymed, "for fun," with no ulterior views. She was pretty, sprightly, well taken care of—a model English girl, simple, and saucy, and fair. It is almost impossible to imagine that she who traced all the vicissitudes of long and faithful love in the delicate and womanly soul of Anne Elliot can have been entirely without such experiences in her own person; but if so, her life shows no trace of the hidden episode, and all is plain and unexciting and matter-of-fact in the little record. Her success in her lifetime is said to have been small, and her own eagerness about the reception of her books scarcely rises above the little girlish excitement of a successful mystification, as when *Pride and Prejudice* is read aloud to a serene rural auditor, without any hint of the authorship, and Miss Jane exults in the interest aroused. The girlishness of her own estimate throughout is as amusing as any of her characters. "Fanny's praise is very gratifying," she writes. "Her liking Darcy and Elizabeth is enough; she might hate all the others if she would." How Miss Austen would have delighted to draw with delicate malicious touches the pretty young authoress, careful of the effect to be produced by her lovers, and quite unconscious of the superiority of "the others," the wonderful Bennet family, the

ever-to-be-remembered Mr. Collins, and all the infinite
humours of that little world! At the same time there
is this warrant for that innocent bit of sentimental preference, that Miss Austen's lovers, at least in this book,
have a character and individuality much superior to most
of the *jeunes premiers* we meet in fiction. Darcy is not
a mere walking gentleman or Elizabeth a featureless
angel; but it brings us very near to the young woman
who, in her girlish innocence, must have been little more
than the handmaiden and secretary of her own genius,
to find her pretty Elizabeth, the high-spirited bright girl
in whom, no doubt, her own young ideal was expressed,
so near to her heart. "I must confess," she says, "that
I think her as delightful a creature as ever appeared in
print, and how I shall be able to tolerate those who do
not like *her* at least, I do not know."

These lines were written when the book was published, when Miss Austen had reached the maturity of
thirty; but the work itself was written before she was
twenty-one, and no doubt had been frequently lingered
over during those eventful ten years of life in which the
story of youth and romance is generally lived through
one way or other. *Sense and Sensibility* followed immediately, then *Northanger Abbey*. We doubt much whether
three such works, so full of natural insight, and what, for
want of a better title, we call knowledge of human
nature, were ever produced at so early an age by any
other writer, male or female, since the world began.
Jane Austen, the rector of Steventon's daughter, could
not have any knowledge of the world. She must, no
doubt, have paid at least one visit to "the Bath," and
seen with lively bright youthful eyes John Thorpe driving about in his high gig, and sat through a wistful evening by the side of some good-humoured chaperon, who
wished, like Mrs. Allen, that they knew somebody; but

this little experience probably was the extent of outdoor knowledge possessed by the country girl. And who can tell by what witchery it was that she divined the rest?

"She had no separate study to retire to," says her biographer, "and most of her work must have been done in the general sitting-room, subject to all kinds of casual interruptions." Thus it was a very different scene from that of the Irish mansion, full of children and systems of education, where everybody was being trained from morning till night, and where Maria Edgeworth carried the skeleton of her tales to her father to be approved of, or handed the MS. over to him to be pruned and cut down —in which this young Englishwoman let loose her youthful genius. In the Rectory parlour, where Mrs. Austen and Cassandra sat at their needlework, and all the little parties of the neighbourhood would be discussed, and the girls' new bonnets settled upon, Jane, at her "little mahogany writing-desk," at one side of the table, was in the full tide of all the little nothings that make up the gentle tenor of daily life in the country. No doubt, she was the first to see, glancing up in the middle of a sentence, Miss Bates coming up the little avenue with her budget of village news—and would stop and play with her pen, and make her little caustic remark, with glee in her eyes, as the good woman ran on with a hundred breaks and lapses: or pause and come back out of the midst of the Bennets to join in the discussion soon reproduced in her manuscript, as to whether the horses could be spared to take the ladies into the little town, with a full sense of the seriousness of the question. Can any one doubt that Jane had to run away from her desk and leave the half-written page to be fluttered by the sweet-smelling air blowing in from the garden, to do a dozen little errands, that her sister might not be disturbed in the middle of her fine buttonholes, or at the crisis of a piece of fancy-work ?   The girl might have taken to worsted work instead, and probably there would not have been much difference in the two pursuits, so far as any-body knew ; but by and by it would begin to be understood that it was amusing to hear what Jane had been writing, and how far Darcy and Elizabeth had got in their affairs.   She would do a little dressmaking by intervals, and work a bag for a present, with a pretty housewife full of silks and needles in it, and a little copy of verses in the pocket, so neatly written out that it was a pleasure to see.   No doubt the rector's wife was vexed at first that the child should be so idle, scribbling instead of doing her needlework — but always so ready to look up from her writing and nod her pretty curls, and set them laughing with those little merry speeches of hers, and her sweet little laugh at everybody, who could find fault with her ?   Probably when it came to be ascertained that a book was the issue of all these harmless scribblings, this, after the first movement of incredulity, would be the best joke of all.   It seems very likely that a feeling on the part of her parents that publishing a book would be something of a stigma on their young daughter, kept *Pride and Prejudice* in manuscript for ten years.   It is not so stated, but in these days publishing a book was a doubtful advantage to a rector's daughter, and might have been looked upon in the county society with no favourable eye.

The character of these books is too well known to require description.   Of Miss Edgeworth, whose fame in her life was greater, we feel at liberty to indicate several special points in her stories ; but who needs to be told about the Bennets in that wonderful, dingy, old-fashioned country house, with the father in his library, slipshod but caustic, contemptuous of his silly girls and their still more silly mother : and Mrs. Bennet, so ready to espouse the cause of the silliest, too opaque to understand her husband's jeers, but not to feel the grievance of them: and stolid Mary, always ready to oblige the company with another song; and Mr. Collins, who thinks it incumbent upon him, as heir of entail, to marry one of the Miss Bennets, and who understands so well that no elegant female can be expected to say yes at once? The whole little landscape rises before us—the country town where the officers are so constant an object of interest, the girls' delight in watching them from their aunt's window, the muddy country roads, the little entertainments, the new people who laugh at the rustics, and all the flutter and chatter and speculation about young Mr. Bingley and Miss Jane. Miss Bingley and her sister are a trifle vulgar,—the only approach in the book to that danger,—and probably reflect some town intruders, whom the rector's daughter had noted with keen enjoyment in their condescending notice of her friends and herself. Everything is told with the most delightful impartiality and good humour, but with a pleasure in the exhibition of all these follies, which is not perhaps so amiable as the young writer was. Except in Elizabeth, and her favourite sister Jane, the too-sweet and pliable heroine, no ideal figure finds a place in this young woman's work. She takes her fun out of the father and mother without a scrap of hesitation, and laughs at everybody all round, even her hero, who deserves it, though he comes at the end so nobly out of his troubles. One wonders whether there was anywhere about, near Steventon, a Lady Catherine, who permitted the parson to make up her card-table, and insulted him and all his belongings. We are driven back to search for the real originals, who probably never existed, of these characters, out of sheer inability to conceive how the country girl of twenty could have found such varieties of human mind and temper in

her own young imagination. *Sense and Sensibility* is
perhaps not so difficult. The gushing girl is never far to
seek, and though it is almost impossible to imagine anything so utterly rash, and unpractical, and deluded as
Marianne and her mother, yet there is much less that is
wonderful in the production of such a tale of sentimental
complications in the parlour of Steventon Rectory than
in the brilliant and varied picture of character and life
which preceded it.

Northanger Abbey is once more on the higher level.
Such a picture of delightful youth, simplicity, absurdity,
and natural sweetness, it is scarcely possible to parallel.
Catherine Morland, with all her enthusiasm and her
mistakes, her modest tenderness and right feeling, and the
fine instinct which runs through her simplicity, is the
most captivating picture of a very young girl which fiction,
perhaps, has ever furnished. Her biographer informs us
that when Miss Austen was very young she amused herself with writing burlesques, "ridiculing the improbable
events and exaggerated sentiments which she had met
with in sundry silly romances." It is to be hoped that
he did not rank the *Mysteries of Udolpho* among these
silly romances; for certainly it is with no ungenial
criticism that the young author describes the effect upon
her Catherine's ingenuous mind of the mysterious situations and thrilling incidents in the books she loves. It
is, on a small scale, like the raid of Cervantes upon the
books of chivalry which were so dear to him, and which
the simple reader believes, and the heavy critic assures
him, that great romancer wrote *Don Quixote* to overthrow.
Miss Austen makes her laughing assault upon Mrs.
Radcliffe with all the affectionate banter of which she
was mistress — the genial fun and tender ridicule of a
mind which in its day had wondered and worshipped
like Catherine. And she makes that innocent creature

ridiculous, but how lovable all through !—letting us laugh at her indeed, but tenderly, as we do at the follies of our favourite child. All her guileless thoughts are open before us—her half-childish love, her unconscious candour, her simplicity and transparent truth. The gentle fun is of the most exquisite description, fine and keen, yet as soft as the touch of a dove. The machinery of the story is wonderfully bad, and General Tylney an incredible monster ; but all the scenes in Bath—the vulgar Thorpes, the good-humoured Mrs. Allen—are clear and vivid as the daylight, and Catherine herself throughout always the most delightful little gentlewoman, never wrong in instinct and feeling, notwithstanding all her amusing foolishness.

These three works were the productions of Jane Austen's youth. Out of timidity or fastidiousness, or the reluctance of her family to identify her with anything so equivocal as authorship, they were not published for nearly ten years, the first appearing in 1811. Whether they passed through her hands again during this interval there is no information. The wonderful polish and finish of the work would make any amount of revision seem possible ; but we think it very doubtful that there was much revision. It does not accord with what we know of the circumstances that she should have been turning over, refining and re-refining, all in the family parlour with the common life around her at every point and on every side. Indeed, it would seem that the first manuscript was cautiously offered to a publisher so early as 1797, but was declined ; and still worse, that *Northanger Abbey* was sold to a bookseller in Bath for £10 : " But it found so little favour in his eyes that he chose to abide by his first loss rather than risk expense by publishing such a work ! " and kept our beloved Catherine in a drawer till the author, having achieved her first modest success, bought the manuscript back again. Probably it was these discouragements after all which kept the books in her hands for so many years.

After a long pause, however—during which she was more in the world, living in Bath and Southampton, and presumably occupied with positive existence more than with imagination—the publication of her first work, and her settlement once more in the country, seem to have re-awakened the dormant faculty; and between 1811 and 1816 she wrote *Mansfield Park*, the longest, and, we think, least valuable of her books, and the far more admirable *Emma* and *Persuasion*, both masterpieces. *Emma*, perhaps, is the work upon which most suffrages would meet as the most perfect of all her performances. It is again the story of a girl, full of mistakes and foolishness, but of a girl very different from Catherine Morland. That delightful little maiden was very young, very simple, at the age when life is all one sweet wonder and surprise to the novice; but Emma is more mature and her own mistress, used to a certain supremacy, and to know her own importance and feel herself a power in her little world. Perhaps the author has scarcely the same sympathy for her that she had for her younger heroine, for some of Emma's mistakes are sharply punished, and her own movements of self-reproach and self-conviction are very keen; but then her errors are of a graver kind altogether, and involve the comfort of others, as only the actions of an important personage with some responsibility on her shoulders could do. But Emma's wilful womanhood, and her busy schemes and plans for the settlement of other people's fortunes, are scarcely less attractive than the infantine freshness of Catherine: and the group round her are drawn—we would say with greater perfection of experience and knowledge of the world, did we not remember that *Pride and Prejudice*, the first of the series, was as wealthy and varied in character.

But, at least, if *Emma* is little advanced in power of conception from that wonderful work, there are traces of a
maturing mind in the softened medium through which the
author contemplates her *dramatis personœ*. In her earlier
work, excepting and not always excepting her pair of
lovers, she has an impartial and amiable contempt for all,
and laughs at every one of them with a soft cynicism
which sees in the world chiefly an assemblage of delightfully absurd persons, who lay themselves out to ridicule,
turn where you will and from every point of view. Even
Darcy himself, though he imposes upon her by his
grandeur and heroic qualities, is not always safe from
her dart of keen and smiling derision, and nobody but
Elizabeth, who occupies in the book something of her own
position, escapes her amused perception of universal
weakness. But by the time she reaches the length of
Emma, those eyes full of insight have acquired a deeper
view. Amusement is no longer the chief inspiration of
her observant vision. She laughs still, but it is in
another key. Mrs. Bennet was vulgar and heartless,
despicable as well as ridiculous; but Miss Bates, though
we laugh at her, excites none of the feelings of repulsion
which move us for almost all Elizabeth Bennet's family,
except Jane. The broken stream of talk, the jumbled
ideas, and everlasting repetitions of the village busybody,
touch us with an affectionate amusement. We are never
so angry with Emma as when, in her irritation after one
of her failures, she is unkind to Miss Bates This good
woman is managed with such skill and tenderness that
she cannot be too diffuse and wandering, too confused
and tedious, for the kindness we have for her. Her
author laughs too, but softly, with a glimmer of moisture
in those keen eyes which had no sympathy to spare for
the Bennets; and in all Mr. Woodhouse's maunderings
there is the same touch of humorous charity. They are

respectable to her in their weakness, as their predecessors
were not.   It is no longer saucy youth, remorseless,
amused with everything, picking up every human creature
about on the point of its dazzling spear for the ridicule
of the world—but a sweeter, chastened faculty, not less
capable of penetrating and divining, but finding something more to divine and penetrate than is dreamt of in
the philosophy of twenty.   With such a deepening and
ripening of moral perception, what might we not have
had if this wonderful observer of the human comedy had
lived to the full extent of mortal life?   But this is a
vain question, and we may console ourselves with the
belief that the supply of living energy in us is pro-
portioned to the time we have to use it in.

Persuasion stands by itself among the busy chapters of
common existence in which so many of the humours of
life are exhibited to us, as a story with one sustained and
serious interest of a graver kind.   To be sure there are
abundance of amusing characters and sketches, but Anne
Elliot herself, pensive and overcast with the shadow of
disappointment and wistful uncertainty, fixes our regard
from beginning to end with a sentimental interest which
is not to be found in any other of Miss Austen's works.
Nothing can be further from a love-lorn damsel than the
serious and charming young woman whose vicissitudes of
feeling we follow with so much sympathy ; but this is the
only exclusively love-story in the series, far more distinctive as such than the duel between Darcy and Elizabeth,
and intellectual trial of strength which ends in the mutual
subjugation of these two favourite figures.   Anne is introduced to us in her dignified and sweet seriousness, always
very courageous and cheerful, and in full command of herself, but paled out of her first bloom, and with a little
tremor of anticipation and wistful wonder whether all is
over, continually about her in the very air.   And to us

too is transferred that sense of suppressed anxiety and mute fear and hope.   We follow her about always with our ears alive to every sound, amused in passing by the other people's eccentricities, but most occupied with her and with what is going to happen to her.   Miss Austen is not a sentimentalist—love in her books takes no more than its proper place in life.   Never from her lips would that artificial creed " 'Tis woman's whole existence" have come.   One can fancy the glow of lambent laughter with which she would have demonstrated the foolishness of any such melodramatic dogma.   But her little cycle of clearest life-philosophy would not have been complete had she not once given its full importance to this most momentous of human sentiments.   Nobody knew better that Anne Elliot would have lived and made herself a worthy life anyhow, even if Captain Wentworth had not been faithful ; but there would have been a shadow upon that life—the sky would have been overcast, a cloud would have hung between her and the sun : and as step by step we get to see that her lover is faithful, the world cheers and lightens for us, and we recognise the divinity of happiness.   It is the least amusing of Miss Austen's books, but perhaps the most interesting, with its one *motif* distinct and fine, the thread that runs through all.

These works had no dazzling or instant success—but they made their way quietly into the esteem of the public. Oddly enough, of all people in the world, the Prince Regent admired these purest of domestic romances, and there is a semi-ludicrous episode narrated in Miss Austen's biography concerning a certain secretary of the Prince, who showed her over Carlton House, and intimated to her that if she wished to dedicate her forthcoming book to his royal master, the permission to do so would be graciously accorded to her.   Poor Miss Austen ! it was an embarrassing honour, and we may easily imagine that the last patron she would have chosen was precisely this royal admirer. But there were others more worth such a woman's while, who gave her the tribute that was her due. " Read again, and for the third time at least, Miss Austen's very finely written novel of *Pride and Prejudice*," says Sir Walter, always generously open to every excellence. " That young lady had a talent for describing the involvements and feelings and characters of ordinary life, which is to me the most wonderful I ever met with. The Big Bow-wow strain I can do myself like any now going ; but the exquisite touch which renders ordinary commonplace things and characters interesting from the truth of the description and the sentiment is denied to me. What a pity such a gifted creature died so early ! "

She died in 1817 at the age of forty-two—a life long enough, but for the mysterious blank of ten years in it, to have accomplished much more. But what she has left us is perhaps more perfect workmanship in all than the work of any of her contemporaries. The change of manners is great since her day, though it is not so very far off. When we think of the comparatively small incomes with which she endows her rich men, and all that they seem able to do with their money, the difference makes us sigh : but in other points of view there are perhaps improvements to be recorded. Miss Austen, like every other writer of fiction, is fond of the picturesque position of a country clergyman, with which, indeed, she must have been thoroughly acquainted ; but nowhere in High or Low or Broad Church could we find now-a-days the very secular persons who do duty in her pages under that character. That was the time when to obtrude religion upon your neighbours, or indeed any subject of the kind, save in the pulpit, was the worst of bad taste, and you were supposed to keep your views strictly to yourself on this matter though no other. And it cannot be said that, clerical or lay, there is much strain after the ideal in the minds of her various personages. They are generally very well satisfied with the good things that fall to their share, and do not waste their time in any foolish endeavours after the better. The deep vexation of Fanny Price over the vulgarity and shabbiness of her father's house, and her longing after the superior grace and beauty of Mansfield Park, where she was brought up as a dependant and very hardly treated, are almost servile, and give an unpleasant if very likely true impression of the way in which even a fine spirit may be beguiled by external advantages. Miss Austen herself thinks this very natural, and thoroughly justifies Fanny : but it is not an elevated point of view. Actual existence, however, as she sketches it, and all the amusing and delightful human creatures whom she introduces, in the warmth of natural life and humour, are more worth than the finest sentiments or the most skilful machinery : and in these points Miss Austen has no superior, and very few that can be called her peers.

The third representative woman fitly embodying her country by the side of the Irish and the English was Susan Ferrier, a little younger, and a much less voluminous writer : that is to say—for the epithet is as inapplicable to Miss Austen as to Miss Ferrier—where her English contemporary produced six books, she wrote but three, a trifle to Miss Edgeworth, who far exceeded both put together. Needless to say that in our own days none of these really great writers could be so much as named, if quantity were the chief distinction, beside a score of little names which have deluged their age. *Marriage* and *The Inheritance*, indeed, are almost the sole pillars of Miss Ferrier's fame, for her last work, though it has occasional gleams of fine humour, and the group in the chief's house is as good as the best of her productions, is not of great quality as a whole. It is not generally supposed that mirth is characteristic of Scotland, but certainly there is more laughter to be got out of Miss Ferrier's three books than out of the voluminous series produced by Miss Edgeworth. It is on this ground that she is strong : her heroes and heroines are a little too excellent for flesh and blood, while her foolish and fashionable ladies, the butterflies of London society, whom she is fond of introducing to spread confusion and dismay into a primitive Highland society, are almost too foolish, artificial, and heartless for belief. But she has no sooner brought in one of these fine ladies into the house, be it the limited dwelling-place of a small laird, or the castle of a Highland chieftain, than her eye glows with fun, and all the absurdities of the position flash out before us in a light of genial humour, satirical yet kind. Lady Juliana has made a love-match in the most absolute and silliest ignorance of what she is doing, and her handsome soldier carries his bride to the tall gray house among the moors, which he has not himself seen since his childhood, and of which he thinks as a boy thinks of his home—and straightway there opens before us the homely unlovely house, full of fussy homely people, an old laird fresh from his fields, a host of anxious maiden aunts all eager to be of service——Miss Jacky, who is superior and sensible ; Miss Nicky, who is the housekeeper ; Miss Grizzy, the tender-hearted one, who is all kindness through and through. Their little formalisms, their alarm and surprise at the beautiful creature whom all their simple efforts cannot satisfy, their prejudices and simple conviction of the greatness of their castle and their race, all become visible in clearest vivid portraiture, each individual, but all in perfect harmony. Nobody, not Sir Walter himself, has given us a picture of the commonplace of Scottish gentry, the homely family life, the eccentricities of the old, and bashful rusticity of the young, to match

these curious revelations.   Miss Ferrier wrote of what she
knew.   Miss Grizzy was as familiar a figure to her,
evidently, as Miss Bates was to her English contemporary.
And she does not spare us a detail of the shabbiness, the
absence of everything beautiful, the bare and sordid aspect
of life in homes out of which gallant soldiers were issuing
every day, and in which, what we are accustomed to think
of as the most desirable of all classes, the country gentry,
were trained.   The delicate satirist brings in her Lady
Juliana to give the whole force of the picture by contrast.
Not that the fashionable young lady, so terribly astray in
such a house, is made to secure any of our sympathies,
but her horror and astonishment throw a fuller light on
the whole scene, and bring out all the grotesque features
which familiar eyes apprehend dimly.   Though we dislike
the senseless little intruder, we cannot help seeing through
her eyes, when she drops unprepared and incapable of
understanding it, into this characteristic group.   Her
horror at the dreary house, rising gradually into hysterical
dismay, as she reaches the prim, unused drawing-room,
with its newly lighted fire, and meets the troop of grotesque
women who rush to receive her with a babel of unfamiliar
voices, strange accents, and language only half comprehensible, is required to bring out the humour of the scene,
in which, however, the beautiful young heroine is much
more odious than the perplexed and fussy old maidens, so
anxious to be kind, and so bewildered by the reception
given to their advances.   This is a scene in which Miss
Ferrier is even more trenchant than Miss Austen.   She
does not spare one eccentricity, or throw one ray of fictitious illumination upon the narrow minds and contracted
unlovely living of the Scotch gentry whom she loved.   In
the house of the Bennets there were at least Elizabeth
and Jane, with their pretty manners and cultivated minds,
to do credit to the family: but the Scottish novelist is

merciless. She makes no effort to harmonise her modern yet old-fashioned household with the tradition of Highland grace and breeding that ought to hang about an ancient race. Young and old alike are rustical, narrow, and coarse, if not in mind at least in externals. There is neither delicacy nor fine perception among them, nor any prettiness either of manner or person. The girls, indeed, are less interesting than their old aunts. Yet having done this with remorseless truth, it soon becomes apparent to us that there is a secret tenderness beneath, which is not in the touch, fine as a diamond-point, of the English writer. The Bennet ladies care nothing for any one, not even for each other, but Miss Jacky, Miss Nicky, and Miss Grizzy, with all their uncouthness, are overflowing with the milk of human kindness. Miss Grizzy, in particular, goes to the reader's heart. Perhaps it is because she is less wise than her sisters. Her bounty and liberality— with so little as she has to give!—are infinite. When she pays her famous visit to the charitable lady who is a collector of pebbles, her impulse to bestow the brooch which is Nicky's and not her own, and the alarmed struggle in her mind as to whether she has any right to be generous at Nicky's expense, and casuistical self-persuasion that Nicky would certainly do the same were she there—is such a sketch as only that mocking love which we call humour, could give. Miss Bates, who is a kind of English Miss Grizzy, had no leisure for any such self-discussion, neither would a similar impulse of generosity have occurred to her. She is perfectly honest and self-sufficing, but her custom is to receive and not to give; while the instinct of Highland generosity—the impulse of a ruling race—is strong in the ungainly bosom of the Scotch spinster. Miss Bates is far more tenderly drawn than the vulgar group of *Pride and Prejudice*, with its unredeemed pettiness and selfishness; but even that, how much below

in sympathy this picture, so heartfelt, so foolish, so un-
couth, so tender and true! Miss Edgeworth has a kind
of partisan kindness for her Irish peasants, of whom she
is the advocate, holding a kindly brief, ready to explain
away their imperfections; but Miss Ferrier loves her un-
couth old heroine, and takes her to pieces with an affectionate and caressing hand.

The *bourgeois* group in the *Inheritance* is less attractive
though not less amusing. Probably Miss Ferrier, in the
instinctive prejudice of class, was more ready to see un-
mitigated vulgarity in the rich people who had sprung
from a common stock than in the poor and uncultured
gentry; but Uncle Adam, the cynical old bachelor, who
lives the life of a retired shopkeeper in a little roadside
villa of the meanest description, though he possesses a
colossal fortune and a fine house close by, is again an
instance of her tenderer skill; for though he talks like a
peasant and lives like a retired cockney, there is the finest
fund of poetry and romance in the old man's nature. He
saves pennies in his little house, but he thinks the money
dross when his niece wants it, and gives her a cheque for
five hundred pounds as he would have given her a handful
of gooseberries; and his adoration of the memory of the
love of his youth is worthy of a poet. But it is Miss
Pratt whom the reader will most readily associate with
the name of the *Inheritance*—Miss Pratt, who is a larger
and more confident Miss Bates, though without that lady's
delightful incoherence, an endless commentator upon life,
unmalicious and impartial, recording everything great and
small, gathering up all the straws of social intercourse,
and dauntlessly regardless of its prejudices. Here the
author is as impartial as her creation, yielding to no sentiment, leaving us with the mere fact of this active, busy
never-resting intelligence, ceaselessly occupied with other
people's concerns, and shrewdly shooting at their motives

—with great success in the case of the less worthy personages of the drama, if with complete failure when the finer and more ideal natures come in her way. Miss Pratt's superiority to all the common weaknesses is as nobly displayed in her indifference to the stupid grandeur of the noble peer who tortures everybody else, but whose authority she sets at naught with bustling unconsciousness, as in her famous drive in the return hearse, which she takes advantage of in the failure of any other conveyance, with the true readiness of social genius. Nor does she stand upon her blood and breeding, when there is news to be picked up—and there is something to be picked up everywhere by so bold an observer. Whether she appears at the castle, sweeping away Lord Rossville with the torrent of her gossip, or amid the Blacks, finding out everything, universally affable and curious, there is no failure in her, she is perfectly sustained, yet quite natural from beginning to end.

Although the third of these novels is in itself less successful than its predecessors, there is perhaps nothing in either of them so perfect as the sketch of the chief's household in *Destiny* and its permanent members. Glenroy himself, the despotic, unreasoning, overbearing chief, trained to consider himself the greatest man in the district, and exacting a superstitious observance of all his will and ways; with his gentleman-in-waiting, Benbowie, the taciturn and self-contained, whose mute presence is as indispensable as that of a piece of furniture, but not much more remarkable; and the delightful, simple, beaming countenance of Mrs. Macauley, the humble cousin and housekeeper, whose perpetual good humour and satisfaction with all around her diffuse warmth throughout the picture—make a perfect group. Here we are on a very different level from that of the humble Castle of Glenfern. All the luxuries of the plains are under the noble roof, and along with them that fading glory so infinitely pathetic in some aspects, so cruelly ridiculous in others, which is all that is left of an antiquated and outworn supremacy of race. The chieftain's unquestioning sense of his own greatness is like that of a monarch : while, like the faithful courtiers of an exiled king, the Highland gentleman and matron receive as something beyond question the commands, the hard words, the exacting requirements of their head. Some one has said that while Sir Walter depicted the last chapter of real power and greatness, the tragic and splen- did ending of the reign of Highland chiefs and devotion of clans, it was Miss Ferrier's part to show the more melancholy downfall, the contempt of the modern world for what had become a mere romantic fiction, and breaking up of all reality in the obsolete position itself.   There is some truth in the criticism as applied to *Destiny*.   It is the reverse of that more dignified conclusion which made an end of the race of Vich Ian Vohr.   The rest of the book is at once too good and too bad for nature.   Never were such irreproachable instructive good people ; never such reckless, frivolous, despicable bad ones.   The colours of the sentimental portion of the story are far too crude and unmodified.   But Glenroy, Benbowie, and Mrs. Mac- auley are admirable.   Here was an insight in which even Sir Walter himself yields the palm to the " sister shadow " of whom he spoke so kindly.   His genius went back upon ages more picturesque.   Miss Ferrier contented her- self with what lay under her own eye.

This gentle but powerful satirist was born in 1782, the daughter of a lawyer in Edinburgh.   Her father, one of the caste of " Writers to the Signet," so largely recruited from among the poorer gentry of Scotland, and one of the most characteristic in Scotch society, was the agent of the Duke of Argyll, and spent much of his time at Inveraray, where his daughter no doubt saw among the English visitors some types of her Lady Juliana, whom she never afterwards forgot. The details of her life, prefixed to Mr. Bentley's re-issue of her novels, afford us a little information with which the world was not acquainted. Her first efforts seem to have been inspired and encouraged by one of her companions in the noble household, Miss Clavering, a niece of the duke, in concert with whom, it was originally intended, her first book was to have been written; but this arrangement, fortunately, was soon thrown aside. It is said that the story of Mrs. Douglas in *Marriage* was from the pen of this young lady; if so, our gratitude for her withdrawal is all the deeper. It would seem by the letters now published that Miss Ferrier took advantage of the many original figures still existing in the society of the North as models for her pictures, and that a knowledge of the originals quickened the delight with which contemporaries received Miss Grizzy and Miss Jacky. When youth was over, she lived a perfectly retired life, in close attendance upon her aged father, devoting herself entirely to him; and it has been said that the seriousness of the religious views which she adopted in after life made her look with regret upon the novels of her youth as frivolous productions, unworthy her religious profession. This is, however, merely a tradition, and her appearance in the memoir of Sir Walter Scott, towards its melancholy close, is in no respect puritanical, but in every way sweet and satisfactory. She was admitted to his most private circle to help and support his daughters at the terrible moment when sickness had bowed down his noble soul and clouded his perfect temper. She was privileged to share with Anne and Sophia Scott the anxious hours of tendance, when, sick at heart to see the gathering gloom, they sat about him and heard him babble on through a hundred half-forgotten stories, painfully losing the thread of them and conscious that he had lost it. In these cases, Lock-

hart tells us, her kind help was of unspeakable consolation.
" Unthinking friends sometimes gave him the catchword
abruptly. I noticed the delicacy of Miss Ferrier on such
occasions. Her sight was bad, and she took care not to
use her glasses when he was speaking, and she affected
also to be troubled with deafness, and would say : ' Well,
I am getting as dull as a post ; I have not heard a word
since you said so and so,' being sure to mention a circumstance behind that at which he had really halted. He
then took up the thread with his habitual smile of
courtesy, as if forgetting his case entirely in the consideration of the lady's infirmity." He had given to her first
work the warmest meed of cordial praise, as was his wont,
and had cultivated her friendship always. She repaid him
now in tender helpfulness, with such gentle good offices ;
and this is almost all that there is to tell of Susan Ferrier.
The distinguished philosopher Professor Ferrier of St.
Andrews, still so tenderly remembered by all who knew
him, was her nephew : an interesting fact for those who
believe in the oblique communication, rather than direct
descent, of literary genius.

There have been more brilliant novelists, more potent
writers, than these three ladies. None of them come up
to the level of George Sand or George Eliot, in sentiment
or philosophy ; but they were of more importance in their
generation than either George Eliot or George Sand, and
laid open the workings of the common life as no one else
had done in the three countries which they represent so
well. In this point of view Miss Edgeworth, though the
least attractive, is perhaps the most important of the
three, as being the first to make known what manner of
country Ireland was. But the others, if less vital in
point of matter, were more vivid and living in their
power of portraiture and representation of life, not in its
extraordinary accidents, but in the most common phases

of every day.   Miss Austen, who confined herself entirely
to these, seeking no foreign aid of highly wrought story
or dramatic incident, was the most perfect artist of the
three, and has kept her place beyond all competitors.
Yet there are points in which Miss Ferrier is almost
superior to Miss Austen, having a touch more tender and
a deeper poetic insight.   There is no more interesting
group in all the literary combinations of their age.
There was, however, no genial link between them, no tie
of association.   It would not seem that they even knew
each other.   Jane Austen was lost in the mediocrity of
that featureless English life in which the good people,
with a proper pride, hold themselves aloof from all the
doubtful classes.   Her biographer is proud to repeat that
she had no literary connections or acquaintances.   A
Marchioness of Something invited her on one occasion to
meet some distinguished persons of that craft; but Miss
Austen firmly declined the honour, which was at the
same time a derogation, and held fast to the dignity, far
superior to personal distinction, of that nameless gentle-
womanhood in which is the quintessence of pride.   The
others were not so exclusive.   Miss Edgeworth had a
great name in her day, and was received with honour
and admiration everywhere; and Miss Ferrier was famed,
at least in Edinburgh—no insignificant distinction.   Both
of these latter names are connected with the genial glory
of Scott, who gave them his friendship and generous
applause.   He could not do what they did, he says, with
the pleasure of an entirely noble and simple mind,
delighting in excellence wherever he found it.

We have already pointed out how curiously *arriéré*
and of an earlier age was the *Simple Story* of Mrs. Inchbald, though it was a popular and much read book, and
actually produced at the same time with Miss Austen's
earliest and perhaps greatest work : the one all of the old

world, conventional, artificial, with a pretty air, if not of the Dresden shepherdess, at least of the imitations of Chelsea and Bow; the other real, living, of this day and all time, notwithstanding the old-fashioned dress of its heroes and heroines. They were contemporaries, yet the antiquated art of the eighteenth century made its bow, or rather its curtsey, with Miss Milner; and the new reign of fiction came in, in individual womanhood, with Elizabeth Bennet. Miss Edgeworth had no predecessor in her special mission, but, so far as one phase of her work went, followed in the traces of an eccentric educationalist, and formed the transition link between those quaint little gentlemen, Sandford and Merton, Master Tommy the spoilt child, and Harry the son of the soil, and the all-instructive Mr. Barlow—and the nineteenth century schoolboy, who has played so large a place in the world since then. Miss Ferrier, too, had a predecessor, though she produced little, whose essay in fiction is in a somewhat similar vein. *The Cottagers of Glenburnie*, published in 1808 by Elizabeth Hamilton, is full of insight into Scottish character, and humorous treatment of its characteristic shortcomings; but it is perhaps too distinctly a story written with a purpose, and that a very homely one, to take a high place in art.

MARIA EDGEWORTH, born 1767; died 1849.

Published Castle Rackrent, 1801.
Ennui.
Vivian.
The Absentee.
Belinda.
Leonora.
Patronage.
Harrington.
Ormond.

Published Helen.

> With many lesser tales, collected as Moral Tales, Tales of Fashionable Life, etc. A collected edition was published in 1832, and again in 1848.
>
> Rosamond, 1822.
>
> Henry and Lucy.
>
> The Parent's Assistant.

JANE AUSTEN, born 1775 ; died 1817.

Published Sense and Sensibility, 1811.
> Pride and Prejudice, 1813.
> Mansfield Park, 1814.
> Emma, 1816.
> Northanger Abbey, } 1818.
> Persuasion,

SUSAN FERRIER, born 1782 ; died 1854.

Published Marriage, 1818.
> The Inheritance, 1824.
> Destiny, 1831.

CHAPTER VII.

LITERATURE IN IRELAND.

THERE is unfortunately but little necessity to apportion a separate chapter to the literature of Ireland. We have already remarked upon the singular absence of literary production, and of genius at all worthy to be called national, which we find at a period so rich in literary power, in the unfortunate island, which, to the great misfortune both of her neighbours and herself, is so closely connected with Great Britain. What a happy solution would it be of many problems could engineering science, which has done so much, find means to move that uneasy Erin out into the wide Atlantic, far enough off from us to give her full scope for independence and self-development! They move houses and churches in America, why not an island? Such a divorce would be hailed, we should imagine, with delight on both sides—and would afford a full opportunity for the putting forth of national effort, up to this time sadly wasted in internal agitations, and affording us no means of estimating the national genius. Great social unhappiness and political restraint do not, however, seem to furnish a sufficient reason for the absence of worthy utterance, especially in a race so generally pervaded by the lighter gifts, at least, of wit and fancy; and we can scarcely accept the Catholic disabilities and the wrongs of Ireland as enough to account for her silence in the world.   No country could be more bound in chains of iron, in political repression and corruption, than was Scotland in the end of last century. It is true that there was no dominant race holding the mastery, and that in religion the people had their own way; but they had no political power, nor freedom of self-government, and the nation was under the heel of an almost irresponsible minister, and an entirely dominant party.   Yet Burns rose out of the homely fields when political freedom had no existence—and the vivacious army of the Critics at an after period burst forth from the very prison-house and coldest shade of social oppression.   In Ireland a few songs and speeches, a little fiction, but even that not of the highest order, is all that we find to distinguish an age which, in both the other countries of the Union, was nothing less than a new birth. Miss Edgeworth and Thomas Moore, both of whom have already been individually treated, are the only names which we can pick out to take their place in the lists of those which are really of national importance ; and the latter we feel can only be admitted on sufferance to any such classification.   He is a poor creature to stand against Wordsworth, Coleridge, Byron, and Shelley—or even against Burns and Scott, who represent the smaller of the partners in the Union ; but, such as he is, he is the best that Ireland has done.

It is true that Sheridan, then just waning, had been in his day one of the most brilliant figures in society, and in the lighter sphere of literary composition ; but in a national point of view there was no meaning in him, any more than there was any promise of a new literary era in the fine comedies which are his only real standing ground in literature, and which belonged entirely, in spirit and scenery and sentiment, to the eighteenth century. It is scarcely possible indeed, even though Sheridan's bril-

liant wit and disorderly ways were a sort of impersonation
of the conventional character of the Irishman, to record
him as Irish at all, save by birth. He was educated at
Harrow, and was nominally a member of one of the Inns
of Court. The society, of which he was so remarkable a
figure, was in London, not Dublin. His romance of early
love was enacted in Bath. His great triumphs as an
orator were in the British Parliament, and not even
upon subjects in any way connected with Ireland. The
younger but much less important orator and playwriter,
Richard Lalor Sheil, was a better representative of his
country. But his plays are of little or no importance,
and he was absorbed in his mature days by parliamentary
life, in which he never made so brilliant a figure as Sheridan.
This, indeed, is the sphere in which the Irishmen have
showed best, and it is a pity that we cannot find justification
enough in his political pamphlets to take in the grandi-
ose, if never entirely grand, figure of Daniel O'Connell,
the great Liberator, the leader of his people, one of the
best and most satisfactory embodiments of his race. The
very limited niche which is all we could give him in
literary history would afford no fit pedestal for a personage
so important in the history of his country. Who can
doubt that he had his faults? That shade of unreality
which belongs to a character so expansive, so eager for
popular approbation, born to please as well as born to
sway, and the inextinguishable twinkle in the eye of a
man who was never quite unconscious of his own art—
the "blarney" supposed to be native to his race, the too-
persuasive eloquence, the touch of humbug in his utmost
sincerity—sadly detract from his greatness. But when
all is said that can be said, there are few manly critics or
generous lookers-on who would not compound for still
more impefections could Ireland and we have back the
Liberator with all his native bigness and large and genial

life. The contrast between O'Connell, born under circumstances which would have indeed excused any degree of
national rancour and bitterness, yet so full, even in hottest
fight, of the happy humour, the instinctive friendliness, and
easy sentiment, which were once supposed habitual to his
race, and the bitter theorists and revolutionaries produced
by a later generation and in an age entirely awakened to,
and eagerly trying to remedy, everything like injustice to
Ireland, is extraordinary. Surely, in the meantime, that
happy humour and engaging eloquence, the wit, the fancy,
the diffusion of a kind of genial genius over the face of the
country, which we once cordially believed in, as characteristic of Ireland, must have died away. Perhaps, indeed,
O'Connell, among his other influences, possessed the power
of making us take for granted the fine faculties of his
countrymen, and thus was not only the glory but the
g'orifier of his race.

To descend, however, from this great representative of
the nation, who stands, like one of her unique towers, in
the midst of her, with no fit competitor near him, and
whom, unfortunately, we have little pretence for introducing, we are obliged to descend into the ordinary strain of
literature, making a great step downward from Sheridan
to his namesake James Sheridan Knowles, a playwright
of considerable pretensions and some skill, though little
genius, whose plays had an enormous popularity, some of
them still, in a certain degree, holding the stage. The
tragedy of *Virginius* and the picturesque *Hunchback* are
still among those which managers occasionally resort to,
to give a prick of new sensation to jaded playgoers. There
was some link of relationship, whence the name, between
the more famous Sheridan and Knowles, who, however,
was of a humbler strain of life—the son of a schoolmaster,
and for some time exercising the same profession.
" Knowles is a delightful fellow, and a man of true

genius," Wilson says of him in the *Noctes*, in respect to a series of lectures upon Dramatic Poetry which he delivered in various places both in England and Scotland. His life underwent a curious change in his later years, when the successful dramatist turned his back upon his art, such as it was, abjured the wickedness of the theatre, and began with all the violence natural to an Irish Protestant, trained in the keen polemics which close neighbourhood to any hostile system invariably cultivates, to assault Popery and the Church of Rome. He ended his life as a Baptist Minister, bitterly regretting, it is said, the time and labour which he had bestowed on the stage and the world.

A very fair and gentle representative of poetry, Mary Tighe, the daughter of a clergyman, the wife of an Irish M.P., is another of the rare instances of literary production in Ireland. She was the author of a poem called *Psyche*, an extremely sweet and melodious rendering of the classical legend, the external form of which, in a slim and sumptuous quarto, with creamy pages as thick as velvet enshrining in big margins a limpid stream of elaborate verse, gives a very just idea of its merit. It is one of those essays in art which at any time it would be cruel to judge rigorously, all the more as it is the composition of a gentle creature who died young and knew nothing of the world—which, with a humane sense of the claims of weakness, generally does receive such gentle efforts tenderly. This lady lived during all her short life in Ireland, an invalid for a great part of it, sometimes receiving the gay and brilliant Sydney Owenson, the *Wild Irish Girl*, in her sick-chamber, but not capable of much society, if indeed there had been any of the literary kind to resort to. But we find little that is worthy the name in the lively Dublin world, which we see in Lady Morgan's recollections, where she herself stood almost alone as the representative of the lighter arts of literature. The common

reproach to Scotsmen that the first step of their progress
is always to leave their native country, which was ludi-
crously untrue in the age we have been discussing, however much it may have been justified before or after,
was strongly in force in Ireland, whence every aspiring
soul in the ways of literature, except Miss Edgeworth,
fled with the utmost speed, Moore giving the first example,
to the centre of fame in London. The records we have
of society in Dublin are few. Moore and Lady Morgan
show us little but a jovial provincialism illustrated by
sundry little local reputations never heard of elsewhere,
while the curious and incoherent work in which Mr.
Madden gives us the history of Irish Periodical literature
presents little more than a chaotic record of dead quarrels,
libels, and vituperations, as violent as it is uninstructive.
Before the Union Dublin booksellers pirated English
publications as Americans do now. Perhaps this crime
against literature has something to do with the stunting
of the race in literary development.

The name of Maturin has almost died altogether from
the recollection of the reader, and it is with difficulty
that the student can find any of the many works which
he poured forth, and which, indeed, are little worth the
trouble of looking for. His high-flown productions and
romantic theatrical figure might, however, have thrown
at least an amusing tragi-comic light upon his surroundings had any record of them been attainable. He was
a clergyman of the Established Church, and lived in
Dublin, "the humble unknown curate of St. Peter's,"
until the great good fortune happened to him of having
his tragedy of *Bertram; or, The Castle of St. Aldobrand*
produced at Drury Lane; where, by the influence of
Lord Byron, it was played in the year 1816, bringing
him a great deal of momentary reputation, and a substantial profit of a thousand pounds—five hundred of

which is popularly said to have come from Lord Byron
to console the unfortunate dramatist for a fierce review.
But this does not seem a very likely story, for neither
then, nor at any other period, were Byron's pounds so
plentiful as to have permitted such a munificence;
though he says himself that he sent applause "and something more substantial" to the Irish poet. *Bertram* is a
play of the most wildly Satanic character, dealing with
crimes of primitive magnitude, with terrific storms and
equally terrific bloodshed, to appal the terrified reader.
It is difficult to imagine how it could have been put
upon the stage at all. The author's intention was to
introduce the highest diabolical agency. "He had our
old friend Satan," says Sir Walter (by whom he was
introduced to Byron), "brought on the stage bodily. I
believe I have exorcised the foul fiend—for though in
reading he was a most terrible fellow, I feared for his
reception in public." At the same time, Scott, with his
usual kindness, describes the play as possessing merits
which are "marked, deep, and striking," though he con-
fesses that its faults are "of a nature obnoxious to ridicule." Byron, however, and the public approved this
preposterous tragedy: and Coleridge did it the extraordinary honour of devoting a whole chapter in the
Biographia Literaria to its slaughter and dissection.
The next drama of Maturin made, however, an end of
his fictitious reputation. Byron describes it as "as
heavy a nightmare as was ever bestrode by indigestion,"
"Maturin's Bedlam," and other equally uncomplimentary
titles. One of the stage directions he quotes is as follows:
"Staggers among the bodies;" and it is not a bad indication of the style of the whole.

After, and indeed before, these dramatic performances,
Maturin wrote many novels. He had begun at a very
early age with *The Fatal Revenge; or, The Family of*

Montorio, a work bearing some relation to the *Monk* of Lewis, one of a numerous school of tragical romances such as used to be found in the old circulating libraries now an institution of the past, and which had a certain reputation.   This was followed in after years by a number of others, of which *Melmoth* is perhaps the best known.   He was at the same time a popular preacher, and collected, we are told, crowds to hear him, " neither rain nor storm " keeping his admirers back.   Personally he was " something of a coxcomb," with long flowing black hair, and a poet's eyes full of fine frenzy.   A somewhat ludicrous description of his habits is given in Scott's Life.   " Hartstonge told us that Maturin used to compose with a wafer pasted on his forehead, which was the signal that if any of his family entered the *sanctum,* they must not speak to him ;" a curious tale to be told to Scott, whom everybody interrupted.   " He was never bred in a writer's *chaumer,*" said the great novelist.   But Scott was very kind to the theatrical Irishman, and sent him money and good advice and help of every kind.

There was, however, one other poet in the island whose reputation is of a nobler and more lasting kind : Charles Wolfe, who has made an impression not easily to be effaced, upon the memory of the world, by one poem, the famous and affecting *Lines on the Burial of Sir John Moore,* which rank among the most remarkable instances on record of real poetical life, in distinction from the hundred fictitious and ephemeral lives which flutter and die, and leave no trace behind.   How many volumes, nay libraries, have dropped easily into oblivion, while these half dozen stanzas have lived and lasted ! No finer or more picturesque piece of verse exists in our record.   It is just so much rhetorical as to give us a pleasant sense of being able to identify the region from whence it springs—with a thrill of personal emotion in it, as if of an individual voice, proud yet sad in tuneful exultation, which sounds like a national accent : and yet even here the nationality is doubtful.   Wolfe was nothing more than a young curate of the Irish Church, by his very position pronounced to be no Irishman, but one of the dominating Saxons who have no right to national honours at all.   And it is most curious to see how entirely it is this class, and not the native race, which we are all ready to acknowledge as so full of genius, which has produced the little there is to distinguish Ireland in literature.   Miss Edgeworth, too, belonged to it, and had no claim to be a Celt.   Wolfe discharged his humble duties, such as they were, we are told, with devotion, and died at thirty, having done no more.   It would seem that he had received only one inspiration, but that a noble and a true one.

The same, so far as nationality is concerned, must be said of George Croly, another nominal Irishman, who was educated at Trinity College, Dublin, and naturally goes to the credit of that country, though he too belonged to the Anglo-Irish Church, and spent the most important part of his life as a clergyman in London.   His works are numberless ; from sermons to novels, from political pamphlets to romantic poems.   The book by which he is best known is the singular romance of *Salathiel*, embodying one of the legends of the Wandering Jew, and showing occasionally considerable power.   This book made a distinct impression upon the mind of the time, and holds a fantastic place, if not on the same level as *Vathek*, at least in a similar fanciful region ; but it has not, like *Vathek*, kept the reputation which in its day it obtained.

A better-known and more characteristic figure is that of William Maginn, one of the most brilliant of the band of magazine writers to whom *Blackwood* first afforded a medium—younger than the great critics of the reviews, more dashing but less serious, who in one way never reached the level of Jeffrey, but in another surpassed and excelled him. Maginn was born in Cork, and was a schoolmaster there for some part of his early existence. At twenty-six he began to contribute to *Blackwood's Magazine*, which had then (1819) been for about two years in existence, and was in full tide of that reckless youth which permitted itself every literary liberty, and to which, indeed—notwithstanding the fires of resentment it lit everywhere, to the anguish of the victims and amusement of the public—almost every liberty was allowed. Maginn was, if anything, less scrupulous than the original coterie of Edinburgh, the compilers of the *Chaldee Manuscript*: and he had not only an excellent style, but an easy and powerful command of classical subjects, than which nothing is more effective and telling in periodical literature. A bit of brilliant translation, an adaptation from Homer, a scrap of Horace, lightly turned into contemporary use, is everything to the light gallop of a slashing article, and confers on the writer a position which the world immediately appreciates, and the less learned envy. Everybody will remember Captain Shandon, in *Pendennis*, peppering his sentences with learned extracts from old Burton. Maginn, unfortunately, had many features like those of Shandon, and like him lived a distracted life from luxury to misery, through prisons and disreputable hidings, and every vicissitude that poverty and levity and bad habits and an unstable mind produce. He was still young and full of hope, "with genius, wit, learning, life's trophies to win," as Lockhart says of him, when he went to London in 1823—abandoning any security of anchorage that he might have had at home. But his career in town was not prosperous. He was employed on various papers, and in 1830 became one of the chief writers in *Fraser's Magazine*, which then came into being, and which moulded itself perhaps too much on the model of the already famous and firmly established *Blackwood*, of which it was the first rival. Maginn attempted in this new undertaking the part which Christopher North played in the old; but, great as was the popularity of the *Noctes*, a second effort of the same kind was a literary mistake, and the attempt showed an absence of originating power, and was probably a cause of permanent damage to the new magazine, which ought, in order to secure the success of its predecessor, to have struck a new vein. And the brilliant Irishman had not the continuance in him of Wilson. He spent himself like a fortune, and died before he was fifty, poor, suffering, and solitary. Sir Robert Peel, the one Minister of State in recent times whose heart was always open to the distresses of men of letters, and to whom it seemed a duty of the State to care for her servants in this department, was appealed to on behalf of Maginn; but too late. Lockhart's epitaph, with its jingle upon one rhyme, has a levity in it which, though probably very harmonious with the relations between them, and with the poor author's reckless and haphazard ways, must, we should think, have jarred even upon the ear of a man about town when given forth over a grave; but the description is worth quoting:—

" He turned author ere yet there was beard on his chin ;
    And whoever was out, or whoever was in,
    For you Tories his fine Irish brains he would spin—
    Who received prose and rhyme with a promising grin—
' Go ahead, you queer fish, and more power to your fin!'
    But to save from starvation stirred never a pin.
    Light for long was his heart, though his breeches were thin ;
    But at last he was beat—"

Poor Maginn ! It was his own fault, as it has been the fault of so many, that their lives are squandered and their faculties lost; but that does not make the loss less pitiful, rather more.

Francis Mahony—or, as he called himself, O'Mahony, better known as Father Prout—was a kindred spirit, with the same mixture of fun, learning, and fluency which distinguished Maginn.   The fact that he was a priest, with something of an academical aspect even at his wildest, lent a certain piquancy to the strange Bohemian with his fine and delicate countenance, and the touch of sentiment which mellowed his mirth.   He is called by somebody " an Irish potato seasoned with Attic salt," and the comparison has a certain appropriateness.   He, too, was one of that roving band of literary irregulars, hanging on about the Press, generally finding their highest latitude in a monthly magazine, with always some scrap of literature in hand, but more enjoyment of the floating atmosphere of literary life than of the work—of whom there were so many, differing greatly from the earlier development of the Cockney school and the *bourgeois* group of writers whom we have already endeavoured to put before the reader, and indeed overlapping altogether the boundaries of time to which we have been obliged to keep.   But there are so few Irishmen to whom we can give a place in this record, that chronology yields to the desire to make the best we can of our subject.   Neither Father Prout, however, nor Sir Morgan O'Doherty, which was the little literary disguise under which Maginn presented himself to the world, were of a character or kind to do much honour to their native country; nor was their work illustrative of its character, or apt, like Scott's, to make it known to the world.   They wrote upon all other subjects with the wit of their nation and the ready command of words which belong to the race; but they did not illustrate or open up the life of Ireland, or aim at any patriotic end.   They were English writers of Irish birth, and that was all.   We may quote, however, one snatch of characteristic verse, which has something in it of the

visionary home-sickness and tender longing of an exile.
To have heard Mahony sing this, an old man, leaning his
fine old head, like a carving in ivory, against the mantel-
shelf, in a cracked and thready voice which had once been
fine, is a pathetic memory.   Between the melodious commonplace of Moore's melodies and the wild and impassioned
ravings of the Shan Van Voght, this more temperate type
of Irish verse, with its characteristic broken melody, its
touch of mockery, its soul of tender if not profound
remembrance, is wholesome and grateful, though it has
no pretension to be great :—

THE SHANDON BELLS.

" With deep affection
  And recollection
  I often think on
          Those Shandon bells ;
  Whose sounds so wild would,
  In the days of childhood,
  Fling round my cradle
          Their magic spells.
  On thee I ponder
  Where'er I wander,
  And thus grow fonder,
          Sweet Cork, of thee ;
  With thy bells of Shandon
  That sound so grand on
  The pleasant waters
          Of the river Lee.

" I've heard bells tolling
  Old Adrian's Mole in,
  Their thunder rolling
          From the Vatican,
  And cymbals glorious
  Swinging uproarious
  In the gorgeous turrets
          Of Notre Dame ;

But thy sounds were sweeter
Than the dome of Peter
Flings on the Tiber,
                    Pealing solemnly
Oh the bells of Shandon
Sound far more grand on
The pleasant waters
                    Of the river Lee !

" There's a bell in Moscow ;
While on tower and kiosk, O,
In Saint Sophia,
                    The Turkman gets ;
And loud in air
Calls ever to prayer,
From the tapering summit
                    Of tall minarets.
Such empty phantom
I freely grant 'em ;
But there is an anthem
                    More dear to me—
'Tis the bells of Shandon
That sound so grand on
The pleasant waters
                    Of the river Lee."

Lady Morgan has a right to an honourable place among this small band of Irish writers. She was born Sydney Owenson, the daughter of a popular actor, and her youthful life was passed among scenes characteristically Irish, the ups and downs of the theatre—a life made up of perpetual variations between luxury and penury, and that shifty life of expedients which quickens the wits, and out of which perhaps its victims, whose sufferings we lament so much, get a degree of excitement, pleasurable as well as painful, which makes them much less miserable than we imagine. When she grew up and it became necessary for her to provide for herself, the lively and brilliant girl took up at first, as a helpless woman has to do, the life of a governess, in which she continued with

varying fortunes, until she discovered that she possessed
a gift by which a living was much more easily made.
The Wild Irish Girl was, in its way, a surprise and
revelation to the world, not the less amusing in that there
was a good deal of absurdity mingled with its gushing
sentiment and melodramatic situations: and that the
authoress was not disinclined to pose as Glorvina, and to
receive the homage of society as the original of that child
of nature. After some years of a literary career, successful enough yet never without drawbacks, she became
attached, vaguely, as companion or friend, to the household of the Marquis of Abercorn, among several other
genteel dependants, one of whom was Dr. Morgan, who
had the charge of the health of the house. The glimpse
we have in her letters and biography of the queer little
court there, surrounding the great people, is curious and
not very pleasant. Her patrons made up a match between
their two *protégés*—not without difficulty, for though the
doctor fell in love heartily, the lady-in-waiting was fanciful
and fastidious, and had to be brought to the point at last
almost by stratagem. The bridegroom was turned into
Sir Charles by the intervention of the Lord-Lieutenant,
and Lady Morgan acquired a title and was launched into
the world, very thankful to be free of her patrons, and to
regain her independence. After a temporary residence in
Dublin the pair settled in London, where Lady Morgan
enjoyed and sought society, and got through a good deal
of literary production. She wrote a book upon France
and another on Italy, the result of journeys through both
countries. Lord Byron praised the latter performance,
and declared it to be true and just. But other critics
were not so kind. The *Quarterly*, in particular, made
her an object of attack in a way which was beneath the
dignity of a great periodical, describing her style, with
some truth but much uncalled-for virulence, as " slipshod

Irish." A writer of Lady Morgan's calibre might count it promotion indeed, to be taken so much notice of by a great organ of opinion now. It might have been expected that the autobiography and letters of a lively observer, however flippant and egotistical, would have thrown some light upon the Irish life of the period and society in Dublin. But we do not find, so far as Lady Morgan can tell us, that even so much of literary society as one of the coteries of the English country towns, of which we have encountered so many, existed in the Irish capital.

There is, however, a delightful and cordial sketch of this capital in the account of Sir Walter Scott's visit to Dublin in 1825, which gives us a much higher opinion of its capabilities. The distinguished persons who crowded to see him were not distinguished in literature : but the genial enthusiasm of the people for the great Scotsman is pleasant to hear of. The "demonstrations of respect which awaited him wherever he moved at the hands of the less elevated orders of the Dublin population," astonished the party. "If his carriage was recognised at the door of any public establishment, the street was sure to be crowded before he came out again," says Lockhart. "When he entered a street, the word was passed down both sides like lightning, and the shopkeepers and their wives stood bowing and curtseying all the way down ; while the mob and boys huzzaed as at the chariot wheels of a conqueror." So great was the emotion that an excellent bailie of Glasgow, something akin no doubt to Nicol Jarvie, shook his head and declared that "*yon* was ower like worshipping the creature," as he looked on.

There was, at this same period, in existence a learned colony in Trinity College, which has worked more laboriously and diligently than almost any contemporary scholars at the work of collecting and editing the ancient records of Irish history, and thus made very important contributions to the knowledge of the world. But these labours are performed with a disinterestedness of which, in spite of ourselves, we take advantage; for it is not for the unlearned to attempt to estimate the value of these researches, and the names of their workers in this rich and important field, though thoroughly well known and honoured in their own sphere, are almost unknown to the general public.

When the first quarter of the century, to which we have confined our record, was just over, a younger band of novelists had begun to appear on Irish soil. The names of John Banim, Gerald Griffin, William Carleton, and Thomas Crofton Croker cannot, any of them, be placed in the first rank—but their works were more national, more worthy of being considered as elucidations of the life of their country and the character of their race than those of any previous writers, with the exception of Miss Edgeworth. There is a sort of arbitrary connection between the repeal of the Catholic disabilities and the appearance of this little outburst of literary energy; but we feel very doubtful whether we should be justified in attempting to establish any reasonable link of association between the two. Gerald Griffin is perhaps the most noticeable of this band. He began in extreme youth, like so many others of his countrymen, by dramatic writing, and when he went to England to try his fortune like the rest, an unknown and unbefriended youth of twenty, in 1823—placed his hopes upon the tragedy of *Gisippus* which he carried with him, and which he fondly hoped was to open to him at once the glories and rewards of a literary career. But his play was rejected on all hands; and when at length it fell into those of Macready and attained a great name on the stage, the author had already passed beyond all knowledge of his triumph. The struggle of the unfortunate youth without friends or means

in London was a very hard and bitter one; but he lived
through it, and his novels, especially *The Collegians*, established his reputation. This book is perhaps now more
widely known by the popular play of the Colleen Bawn,
which was founded upon it, than by its own attractions.
But the story is the least satisfactory part of it, and the
sketches of life and character to be met with in the book
are infinitely more worth the reader's while than the
melodramatic fate of Eily O'Connor, and the despair and
misery of her lover. Not even Miss Edgeworth's account
of the successive squires of *Castle Rackrent* sets forth the
wild groups of Irish gentry with so trenchant a touch as
that with which Griffin represents his Cregans and Creaghs
in their noisy carouses : and his peasants of all descriptions are full of humour and life—more individual and
displaying a more intimate knowledge than those of Miss
Edgeworth. Whether it is that the country has grown
duller and ruder since then we are unable to judge, but
certainly the atmosphere in these novels is of a more
genial kind than anything we hear of now. The country
folks' simple and gay, with their characteristic songs, their
friendly greetings, their light hearts and ready wit, though
not without the gloom of a tragedy here and there, and
as ready to lend their lively faculties to the work of
baffling justice as to any other exercise, are certainly
devoid of the bitterness and sense of injury which seem
so universal now. We naturally look in a work written
before the repeal of the Catholic disabilities for some deep
rankling of injured feeling, but the reader will find no
trace of it in *The Collegians*. Griffin was a pious Catholic,
and ended his life in a religious brotherhood ; his sympathies* were entirely with his race : but the picture he
puts before us bears little trace either of a persecuted faith
or an oppressed nationality. The tragic elements of his
story are drawn, as they might have been in a tale of the

Scottish Highlands, from the exaggerated and unscrupulous devotion of a faithful servant to what in his warped and gloomy mind he thinks the interests of his master ; and while we have a fine example of the astute and triumphant policy of a couple of the rudest peasants in baffling the united powers of magistrate and counsellors, it is in behalf of no political criminal, nor is any feud between landlord and tenant so much as hinted at. A good deal of this is no doubt due to the mind and tendencies of the writer and his pure and gentle genius— but something too must belong to the atmosphere of the time. We have already spoken of the great and wonderful difference between the Arch-Agitator O'Connell, he who was in reality the nursling of wrong, brought up under the shadow of a galling Protestant ascendency, and with every excuse for national rancour, and the bitter politicians of the present day. The novelist affords us a kindred example. He shows us no gloom upon the skies, no burning at the heart of his country. As we walk with him along the mountain paths every one we meet has a cheerful greeting, a genial jest, a song upon his lips—the country is gay, brighter than our fat English levels, the long-winded peasant-stories are full of a humorous contemplation both of earth and heaven. It is hard to realise that the easy lightheartedness which we meet with everywhere is the atmosphere of a country which not very long before had been rent by armed rebellion, and still more recently convulsed by a political struggle in which every element of national bitterness might have been expected to manifest itself. We have few materials for determining what is the poet's, the romancer's account of the country now—but if the daily records be trustworthy the picture would be a very different one in our own day. The following scene, though somewhat long for quotation, affords so bright a panorama of the country as Griffin saw

it, and is so little known, that we may venture to insert
it here.   The story which is being told by Lowry, and in
which a delightfully Irish ghost does his best to make
the fortune of the clever Dan who is its hero, goes on for
several pages, and is too lengthy for insertion :—

"At this moment a number of smart young fellows, dressed out
in new felt hats, clean shoes and stockings, with ribbons flying at
the knees, passed them on the road.   They touched their hats
respectfully to Mr. Daly, while they recognised his attendant with
a nod, a smile, and a familiar ' Is that the way, Lowry ?'

"'The very way, then, lads,' said Lowry, casting a longing look
after them.   ' Goin' to Garryowen they are now, divartin' for the
night,' he added in a half envious tone, after which he threw the
skirt of his coat from the left to the right arm, looked down at his
feet, struck the ground with the end of his stick, and trotted on,
singing—

"' I'm noted for dancin' a jig in good order,
        A min'et I'd march, an' I'd foot a good reel ;
    In a country dance I'd still be the leading partner,
        I ne'er faultered yet from a crack on the heel.

"'My heart is wid ye, boys, this night.   But I was tellin' you,
Master Kyrle, about Dan Dawley's luck !   Listen, hether.'

"He dried his face, which was glistening with moisture, and
flushed with exercise, in his frieze coat, and commenced his story.

"''Tis not in Castle Chute the family lived always, sir, only in
ould Mr. Chute's time, he built it, an' left the Fort above, an' I'll
tell you for what raison.   The ould man of all, that had the Fort
before him, used to be showing himself there at night, himself an'
his wife, an' his two daughters, an' a son, an' there were the strangest
noises ever you hear, going on above stairs.   The master had six or
seven sarvints, one after another, stopping up to watch him, but
there isn't one of 'em but was killed by the spirit.   Well, he was
forced to quit at last on the 'count of it, an' it is then he built Castle
Chute—the new part of it, where Miss Anne an' the ould lady lives
now.   Well an' good, if he did, he was standin' one mornin' oppozit
his own gate on the road side, out, an' the sun shining, an' the birds
singing for themselves in the bushes, when who should he see only
Dan Dawley, an' he a little gaffer the same time, serenadin' down
the road for the bare life.   "Where to now, lad ?" says Mr. Chute
(he was a mighty pleasant man).   "Looking for a master, then,"
says Dan Dawley.   "Why, then, never go past this gate for him,"

says Mr. Chute, "if you'll do what I bid you," says he. "What's that, sir?" says the boy. So he up an' told him the whole story about the Fort, an' how somethin' used to be showin' itself there, constant, in the dead hour o' the night; "an' have you the courage," says he, "to sit up a night, an' watch it?" "What would I get by it?" says Dan, looking him up in the face. "I'll give you twenty guineas in the mornin', an' a table, an' a chair, an' a pint o' whisky, an' a fire, an' a candle, an' your dinner before you go," says Mr. Chute. "Never say it again," says the gorsoon, "'tis high wages for one night's work, an' I never yet done," says he, "anything that would make me in dread o' the living or the dead, or afraid to trust myself into the hands o' the Almighty." "Very well, away with you," says the gentleman, "an' I'll have your life if you tell me a word of a lie in the mornin'," says he. "I will not, sir," says the boy, "for what?" Well, he went there, an' he drew the table a-near the fire for himself, an' got his candle, an' began readin' his book. 'Tis the lonesomest place you ever seen. Well, that was well an' good, till he heard the greatest racket that ever was going on above stairs, as if all the slates on the roof were fallin'. "I'm in dread," says Dan, "that these people will do me some bad hurt," says he, an' hardly he said the word, when the doore opened, and in they all walked, the ould gentleman with a great big wig on him, an' the wife, an' the two daughters, an' the son. Well, they all put elbows upon themselves, an' stood lookin' at him out in the middle o' the floore. He said nothin' an' they said nothin', an' at last, when they were tired o' lookin' they went out an' walked the whole house, an' went up stairs again. The gentleman came in the mornin' early. "Good morrow, good boy," says he. "Good morrow, sir!" says the boy. "I had a dale o' fine company here, last night," says he, "ladies an' gentlemen." "It's a lie you're tellin' me," says Mr. Chute. "'Tis not a word ot a lie, sir," says Dan; "there was an ould gentleman with a big wig, an' an ould lady, an' two young ones, an' a young gentleman," says he. "True for you," says Mr. Chute, puttin' a hand in his pocket, and reachin' him *twenty* guineas. "Will you stay there another night?" says he. "I will, sir," says Dan. Well, he went walkin' about the fields for himself, and when night comes——'

" 'You may pass over the adventures of the second night, Lowry,' said Kyrle, 'for I suspect that nothing was effected until the third.'

" 'Why, then, you just guessed it, sir. Well, the third night he said to himself, "Escape how I can," says he, "I'll speak to that ould man with the wig, that does be puttin' an elbow on himself an' lookin' at me!" Well, the ould man an' all of 'em came an' stood oppozit him with elbows on 'em as before. Dan got frightened, seeing 'em stop so long in the one place, an' the ould man lookin' so wicked (he was after killin' six or seven, in the same Fort), an' he went down on his two knees, an' he put his hands together, an', says he——'

At this point the animated but long-winded story breaks off, and the novelist presents us with another sketch of rural life, which is as bright as it is simple— full of local colour and natural truth—

"A familiar incident of Irish pastoral life occasioned an interruption in this part of the legend. Two blooming country girls, their hair confined with a simple black ribbon, their cotton gowns pinned up in front, so as to disclose the greater portion of the blue stuff petticoat underneath, and their countenances bright with health and laughter, ran out from a cottage door, and intercepted the progress of the travellers. The prettier of the two skipped across the road, holding between her fingers a worsted thread, while the other retained between her hands the large ball from which it had been unwound. Kyrle paused, too well acquainted with the country customs to break through the slender impediment.

"'Pay your *footing*, now, Master Kyrle Daly, before you go farther,' said one.

"'Don't overlook the wheel, sir,' added the girl who remained next the door.

"'Kyrle searched his pocket for a shilling, while Lowry, with a half-smiling, half-censuring face, murmured—

"'Why, then, heaven send ye sense, as it is it ye want this mornin'.'

"'And you manners, Mr. Looby. Single your freedom, and double your distance, I beg o' you. Sure your purse, if you have one, is safe in your pocket. Long life an' a good wife to you, Master Kyrle, an' I wisht I had a better hould than this o' you. I wisht you were in *looze*, an' that I had the finding of you this mornin'.'

"'So saying, while she smiled merrily on Kyrle, and darting a scornful glance at Lowry Looby, she returned to her woollen wheel, singing, as she twirled it round—

"'I want no lectures from a learned master,
    He may bestow 'em on his silly train—
I'd sooner walk through my blooming garden,
    An' hear the whistle of my jolly swain.'

"To which Lowry, who received the lines, as they were probably intended, in a satirical sense, replied, as he trotted forwards, in the same strain—

> "'Those dressy an' smooth-faced young maidens,
>   Who now looks at present so gay,
> Has borrowed some words o' good English,
>   An' knows not one half what they say.
> No female is fit to be married,
>   Nor fancied by no man at all,
> But those who can sport a drab mantle,
>   An' likewise a cassimere shawl.'"

"'Boop-whishk ! Why, then, she's a clean made little girl for all, isn't she, Master Kyrle ?   But I was tellin' you—where's this I was ?'"

We should have liked to add the powerful and dreadful scene in which the dying musings of the poor huntsman Dalton are interrupted by the drunken shouts and laughter of a riotous party in the dining-room, from which there comes a message to the poor sufferer "to give them one fox-hunting screech before you go." The last shout in which his life goes, in the midst of the tumultuous chorus of the half-drunk gentlemen, and the heartless jests and laughter with which they hear that all is over, furnish a stern picture of a life far less attractive and sympathetic than that of the homelier peasant-folk. We add one of the songs which are scattered through the book, and which is full of the sweet tunefulness of the Irish melodies, with a vein of far higher feeling, and the purest natural sentiment :—

> "*Gillia ma chree*,
>   Sit down by me.
> We now are joined, and ne'er shall sever
>   This hearth's our own,
>   Our hearts are one,
> And peace is ours for ever !
>   When I was poor,
>   Your father's door
> Was closed against your constant lover.

"With care and pain,
I tried in vain
My fortunes to recover.
I said, 'To other lands I'll roam,
Where fate may smile on me, love!'
I said, 'Farewell, my own old home!'
And I said, 'Farewell to thee, love!'
Sing *Gilli ma chree*, etc.

"I might have said,
'My mountain maid,
Come live with me, your own true lover;
I know a spot,
A silent cot,
Your friends can ne'er discover.
Where gently flows the waveless tide,
By one small garden only;
Where the heron waves his wings so wide,
And the linnet sings so lonely.'
Sing *Gilli ma chree*, etc.

"I might have said,
'My mountain maid,
A father's right was never given,
True hearts to curse,
With tyrant force,
That have been blessed in heaven.'
But, then, I said, 'In after years,
When thoughts of home shall find her,
My love may mourn, with secret tears,
Her friends thus left behind her.'
Sing *Gilli ma chree*, etc.

"'Oh no,' I said,
'My own dear maid,
For me, though all forlorn, for ever,
That heart of thine
Shall ne'er repine
O'er slighted duty—never!
From home and thee though wandering far
A dreary fate be mine, love;
I'd rather live in endless war
Than buy my peace with thine, love.'
Sing *Gilli ma chree*, etc.

" Far, far away,
By night and day,
I toiled to win a golden treasure
And golden gains
Repaid my pains
In fair and shining measure.
I sought again my native land ;
Thy father welcomed me, love ;
I poured my gold into his hand,
And my guerdon found in thee, love.
Sing *Gilli ma chree*,
Sit down by me,
We now are joined, and ne'er shall sever ;
This hearth's our own,
Our hearts are one,
And peace is ours for ever."

Griffin died in 1840, in the exercise of his humble duties as a member of the Christian Brotherhood at Cork. His publications were all a little after the period within which we have confined ourselves. Banim, his friend and contemporary, began his work about the same period. Carleton was still farther on in time. We give these names, and the above record of the most remarkable among them, by way of making up in some degree the vacancy in which Ireland unfortunately stands at this period. T. C. Grattan, another name of the period, was also a novelist of respectable reputation : but his scenes were not laid in Ireland, nor can he be called a national writer.

We may add that the one only, and not perhaps very dignified, public acknowledgment which the professors of literature ever receive in England was bestowed in a manner which we may call lavish on most of the members of this Irish school of fiction. Lady Morgan, Banim, and Carleton were all recipients of pensions on the Civil List, so that any advantage to be derived from that national compliment was fully accorded to the country, which nevertheless has in this way contributed so little to the common stock.

JAMES SHERIDAN KNOWLES, born 1784 ; died 1862.

Virginius was his first play, produced in England at Covent
Garden, 1820.
Dramatic Works, collected 1843.

———

MARY TIGHE, born 1773 ; died 1810.
Published Psyche, 1805.

———

CHARLES ROBERT MATURIN, born 1782 ; died 1824.

Published The Fatal Revenge ; or, The Family of Montorio, 1804.
The Wild Irish Boy, 1808.
The Milesian Chief, 1811.
Bertram ; or, The Castle of Aldobrand, 1816.
Manuel, 1817.
Women ; or, Pour et Contra, 1818.
Sermons, 1819.
Fredocyno—a tragedy, 1819.
Melmoth the Wanderer—a novel, 1820.
The Universe—a poem, 1821.
Six Sermons on Popery, 1824.
The Albigenses—a romance, 1824.

———

CHARLES WOLFE, born 1791 ; died 1823.
Poetical Remains, 1825.

———

WILLIAM MAGINN, born 1794 ; died 1842.

Contributions to *Blackwood's Magazine*, beginning 1818.
„   *Fraser's Magazine*   „   1830.
And many other contributions to periodical literature.

———

FRANCIS MAHONY, born 1805 ; died 1865.

Published Facts and Figures from Italy.
Reliques of Father Prout, 1836.
Many contributions to *Fraser* and other magazines and newspapers.

LADY MORGAN, born 1783 ; died 1859.

Published St. Clair, 1804.
Novice of St. Dominick, 1805.
Wild Irish Girl, 1806.
Patriotic Sketches in Ireland, 1807.
The Lay of an Irish Harp and Irish Melodies, 1807.
Ida of Athens, 1809.
The Missionary, an Indian Tale, 1811.
O'Donell, 1812.
Florence MacCarthy, 1816.
France (in conjunction with her husband), 1817.
Italy, 1821.
Life of Salvator Rosa, 1823.
Absenteeism, 1825.
The O'Briens and O'Flahertys, 1827.
Woman and Her Master, 1840.
With several lesser works.

GERALD GRIFFIN, born 1803 ; died 1840.

Published Holland-tide ; or, Munster Popular Tales, 1828.
The Collegians, 1828.
And several other works and tales at later dates.

CHAPTER VIII.

THE HISTORIANS AND PHILOSOPHERS : HENRY HALLAM, JOSEPH
    LINGARD——JEREMY BENTHAM, JAMES MACKINTOSH,
    JAMES MILL.

HISTORY and Philosophy have always had a certain
alliance.   It is little possible to investigate the problems
of one science without some tendency towards the solutions
of the other.   The great and many-coloured panorama of
existence, with all those vicissitudes that seem so capricious, those successions that are so inevitable, leading the
mind from generation to generation in order to catch a
thread of meaning or answer a question, has but little
effect upon the spectator if it does not lead him to seek
some acquaintance with the constitution of human nature,
the origin from which all its laws and its irregularities
come.   The great historians of the past have in most
cases recognised the affinity of the two subjects, and the
advantage of securing a larger and more comprehensive
view of facts and events, by due recognition of their moral
and intellectual relations.   In the age which we have been
discussing it is difficult to know under which heading to
classify some of the most important names, since no one
will deny to Hallam the title of a philosophical historian ;
and of Mackintosh and Mill, it is difficult to say which
sphere claims them most.   We will place in this record
the more formal students of history first, without taking

from the others who were historians as well as philosophers their just importance in this lofty field.

The art of history is one which, like all other arts, has greatly changed in its conditions in modern times. On the face of things it would seem that the nearer a historian was to the events which he records, the more accurate and complete his information was likely to be; but it requires little thought to perceive how much that is temporary and evanescent is involved in every contemporary narrative, and how many deluding lights of individual opinion and general gossip flash about the scene, from which it is the province of the historian to choose those points of real illumination which may be reckoned on. Were the means of judging for ourselves in this very department of literature which has occupied us through these volumes taken from us, and our minds left at the mercy of the critics and historians of the period, what a curiously changed aspect would the history of literature in the beginning of the nineteenth century bear! The monarchs of the age would be dethroned to give place to petty satraps, of whom now-a-days we scarcely know the names; and even if the injustice perpetrated were less in degree, the most curious confusion of levels would remain to mar the conclusions of posterity. As it is, we are nothing but witnesses transmitting each our share of evidence to be judged by those who come after, in whose hands a continually accumulating mass of testimony is being collected. It is impossible to doubt that this has its evils too, and that the existence of the partisan-historian, he who proves his points at his will by a careful selection of so much of the evidence as suits him, is the creation of that all-examining, anxiously-weighing modern science which receives every witness with doubt, cross-examines and throws cold water upon him, and to which the easy conclusions of the past are old-fashioned and contemptible.

The close and persistent search to which we are now
accustomed in all sorts of dusty archives and out-of-the-
way corners was scarcely thought of in the easy days of
Hume, when genius and insight were believed in more
than dusty papers, letters, reports, and account-books, such
as now tell so largely in history. The comfortable
independence of his methods has ceased to be possible.
German historians, with their gift of elaboration and the
enormous patience which is so strong a characteristic of
their minds and work, have made a revolution in the
science. The result in England has not been that of
producing impartiality ; but it has enlarged and enriched
our records with many individual studies, more graphic,
perhaps, than a more colourless medium could have
supplied. In no time could the least genial critic venture
to assert that English historians have either falsified or
withheld evidence, or consciously given themselves to the
attempt to make the worse appear the better cause. But
a man may carry out his own tendencies in his work,
and prove to himself the superior excellence of his own
opinions from all the lessons of the past, without infringing truth or doing intentional injustice. Even without
any subservience to opinion, impartiality and a perfectly
even-handed justice are impaired on all hands by individual incapacities. Nature will have her word in the
most severely balanced of minds, and even the finest
intelligence finds points here and there on which all the
teachings of the age are powerless to enlighten it. Thus
the calm and judicial Hallam, the most important historian
of this period, speaks of Francis of Assisi, one of the most
interesting and touching figures of the old world, as " a
harmless enthusiast scarcely of sane mind," all unconscious
how much he impoverishes history and narrows the sphere
of human interest by this failure to comprehend one side,
and that a most striking one, of life and action. This is

not so much want of impartiality as want of perception
—a natural disability.   Thus to the best some portion of
the records of time must always remain obscure.   We are
not sure whether the cause of historical truth is not better
served by those who set forth honestly the claims of their
own side, without intentional injustice to the other, but
also without any attempt to disguise the way in which
their own sympathies go—than by those who laboriously
endeavour to hold the balance with a steadiness which
does not belong to mortal nerves.   The tendency has
perhaps increased in our own times to an undesirable
extent; and Macaulay's Whiggery, and Froude's antagon-
ism to everything ecclesiastical, are in some cases almost
rabid.   But when Sir James Mackintosh led the way
to the glorification of Revolution principles, the political
tendency was rather for good than evil; and nobody
grudges to the Roman Catholics now-a-days that they have
a historian so honourable, so conscientious, and generally
accurate as Lingard, to say the best that can be said for
them.   Amid the multitude of voices on the other side of
the question, the individuality of the champion who
though conscientiously anxious nothing to extenuate, nor
set down aught in malice, has yet his eyes open to every
good, and his mind to every explanation, on one side of
the question, is sometimes a positive advantage.

Mitford's *History of Greece*, which, beginning in 1784,
continued to be published during our period, scarcely
belongs to it, being a work of the former school of historical writing, and superseded altogether by more recent
studies.   It was the first history of Greece in English,
and a scholarly and gentlemanly performance altogether,
though without those lights of more exact science and
deeper research which have since become available.   The
same may be said of other classical histories of less
importance.   Such books as these, when superseded by

better information, fall naturally into the catalogue of
"*books which are no books*," in which Lamb profanely
includes the works of Hume and Gibbon. It is probable
that this whimsical philosopher would have added to his
list the large and important productions of Hallam, as
well as those of his predecessors, as belonging to the class
of works which are read for profit rather than for pleasure.
And in so far as their adaptation to be treated in a popular history of literature goes, Lamb's humorous classification
is not without justice.   What is to be said about a great
historian like Hallam by a modest writer claiming no
authority on his imperial themes ?   Criticism of the style
which has admirably served its purpose would be in-
appropriate, and criticism of his subjects would involve
the reader in a disquisition upon the greater part of the
history of the modern world.   It is another matter with
the poets, the essayists, and the writers of fiction more
familiar to our bosoms than those great teachers, who sit
like the sages above our comments, throned in the calm
of an authoritative chair, the judges of a tribunal at which
the nations themselves come to be judged.   Few in our
country have attained this place so completely as Hallam.
Gibbon's strong antichristian bias, his attacks, both insidious and direct, upon the religion of Christendom have
made him vulnerable, and opened the way to his assailants;
but at the same time, his brilliancy and energy of style
give him an immediate influence upon his readers which
the measured calm and self-controlled sobriety of Hallam
do not possess.   It is scarcely possible that a Constitutional History should be entertaining reading.   It is, in
Lamb's sense, no reading at all, but work demanding all
the faculties, and the most complete strain of attention.
The picturesque is rejected altogether by this severe art,
and all the lesser devices with which writers of a lighter
strain think no shame to attract the attention of their

readers, are entirely banished. But the value of the works in question is rather enhanced than lessened by this studied absence of the graces. Their learning, their judgment, their importance as standards of opinion, their solidity as a foundation of future researches, is all the more indisputable that no glamour is ever thrown into the eyes of the reader, and no supreme sympathy with the historian's view ever allowed to bias his judgment. There is little in these works to tempt the roving eye of the devourer of literature who reads for simple pleasure, but their style is such as to put no obstacles in the way of those who read for information and improvement. It is throughout good, clear, and lucid, with an occasional rise into something like eloquence. It is, however, very difficult to discuss in detail works of such a kind; and we cannot do better than to adopt the principle which Mr. Hallam himself sets forth as his own guide in a similar case.

"Some departments of literature," he writes in the Preface to his *Literary History*, "are passed over, or partially touched. Among the former are books relating to particular arts, as agriculture or painting; or to subjects of merely local interest, as those of English law. Among the latter is the great and extensive portion of every library, the historical. Unless when history has been written with peculiar beauty of language or philosophical spirit, I have generally omitted all mention of it. In our researches after truth of fact, the number of books that possess some value is exceedingly great, and would occupy a disproportionate space in such a general view of literature as the present."

Hallam was the son of a dignitary of the Church, the Dean of Bristol, and he lived all his life in the atmosphere of letters and classical lore. His first step in literature was made in the *Edinburgh Review*, a few years after its first appearance; but his politics were not of that complexion, though this literary tie, and his friendship with many eminent members of the Liberal party, gave a false

impression on this point, and laid him open to the assaults
of the *Quarterly Review*, the natural enemy not only of its
rival the *Edinburgh*, but of everything that could be supposed to belong to the opposite party, according to the
fashion of the time.   Miss Martineau, in one of the brilliant
little sketches of her contemporaries which she contributed
to the newspapers of the day, affords us some information as
to the personal aspect of the great historian, in which we
can more fully trust to her, than in her discriminations of
character and purpose.

"The reader of his weighty (not heavy) works," she says, "impressed with the judicial character of the style both of thought and
expression, imagined him a solemn pale student, and might almost
expect to see him in a judge's wig ; whereas the stranger would find
in him the most rapid talker in the company, quick in his movements, genial in his feelings, earnest in narrative, rather full of
dissent from what everybody said, innocently surprised when he
found himself agreeing with anybody, and pretty sure to blurt out
something before the day was done, but never giving offence, because
his talk was always the fresh growth of the topic, and, it may be
added, his manners were those of a thorough-bred gentleman."

" Hallam with his mouth full of cabbage and contradiction,"
Sydney Smith said of him when describing a dinner party.
This lively, talkative, argumentative person does not fit
at all into the serious image presented to us in the histories, so grave, so careful, so full of large reading and sober
judgment.   The same authority tells us, as an instance of
the manner in which literature leavened all his thoughts,
that the political enthusiasm about Spain which rose in
England at the time of the heroic resistance made by that
country to Napoleon, turned the mind of the historian to
the study of Spanish literature, the natural result in his
mind of a new interest.

The incidents which have given interest to Hallam's life
have, however, little to do with books or learning, and belong to the closest of domestic sentiments. He had a son in

whom all that a father's wishes could desire seemed embodied
—a young man whom all his contemporaries unite in
describing as of the highest promise, and who, indeed, is
spoken of with a not unnatural inflation and exaggeration
of style by those who loved him, as of one who had
scarcely his equal among men. It was ill-advised, we
think, and shows how uncritical love can be, that Arthur
Hallam's remains should ever have been exposed to the
judgment of critics less enthusiastic : for there is little
in them to justify the lofty estimate of his powers formed
by all his friends. But, at all events, his fate has been a
rare one. Not long after this young man had completed,
amid universal plaudits and approbation, his academical
career, and when he was entering upon life in all the hope
of highly-cultured youth, sharing all his father's tastes and
pleasures, and affording him that satisfaction in his child,
grown a man and a dearest friend, in addition to the
natural tie, which is of all human pleasures perhaps the
most perfect—he went abroad with his father upon a
journey of pleasure. "At a German town he was slightly
unwell with a cold, and Mr. Hallam went out alone for
his afternoon walk, leaving Arthur on the sofa. Finding
him asleep on his return, he took a book and read for an
hour ; and then he became impressed by the extreme stillness of the sleeper. The sleeper was cold, and must have
been dead almost from the moment when he had last
spoken." This was the calamity which produced the
wonderful poem of *In Memoriam*. It places the great
historian, the calm and profound scholar, the man whose
lofty impersonal work was one of the glories of the time,
in the very heart of pity and tender sympathy : for that
must be a cold heart indeed which can hear of such a
catastrophe unmoved. A similar affliction occurred twice
again in the melancholy yet steadfast and courageous life
of the great writer. His wife and his eldest daughter

both died in the same way. His second son, about the same age, was also taken from him. His calm life of letters, undisturbed by any pangs of poverty or agitations of ordinary trouble, full of wealth and prosperity and success, was thus made into a continual tragedy. Many men have held their own in the face of vexing anxieties and disappointments of all kinds, unable to get any satisfaction for their soul out of a hard and bitter existence. But this man had everything that life could bestow, easy success, and all the graces and sweetnesses of life — yet death with them, taking all he loved from him, a strange and terrible example of the vanity of human things. He went on courageously with his life and his work in spite of all.

The *History of the Middle Ages* and the *Constitutional History of England* were produced in the early part of his life. The former is perhaps his greatest work, and it is impossible not to admire the large and noble investigation of universal life into which the writer enters, perceiving in every change of living its after development, and tracing from step to step the bursting of successive husks, the opening out of new channels, the gradual rise and growth of the forces with which we are now familiar in their far distant origin, so much unlike, yet so closely connected with the present issues — and at the same time the dyings-off, the failures, the unproductive attempts of the past. The *Constitutional History* was the natural successor of the earlier work carrying out the narrative of the development of law and government in England from the prefatory sketch which is to be found in the eighth chapter of the *Middle Ages*. No one will seek in these volumes for the picturesque scenes, the breathless excitement of the latest fashion in history, that which, according to Macaulay's prophecy, would be "more in request at all the libraries than the last novel;" but the reader will find in them something more consonant with the old ideal of historic teaching, the guidance of the closest investigation, the lights of boundless research, the decisions of a calm and steady judgment. The *History of Literature in the 15th, 16th, and 17th Centuries* was the occupation of a later period, of the much-tried and tragic years of which we have already told the melancholy story. Perhaps the idea of so huge a piece of work came to his mind as a kind of consolation amid all the surging returns of grief; but it would be vain to claim for this elaborate book the same rank or importance as belong to his other productions. These remain as standards of national instruction. They were of course subjected to the usual amount of criticism at the time of their publication: were considered on one side dangerous, as " dealing with deductions rather than details," and on the other as " strikingly practical;" by Southey as " the production of a decided partisan;" by Macaulay as distinguished by a "calm, steady impartiality." But now that contemporary voices are silenced, they remain standards of historical knowledge indispensable to all students, and setting forth the growth and development of the English constitution and laws on one hand, and of the gradual emergence of modern systems of law and government out of the ruins of the old world on the other: as has been done by no other hand.

And whatever critics might say of him in that brief contemporary scuffle through which every new work has to win its way to fame, the verdict of the world in Hallam's case was never doubtful. His books are not for the careless reader: but their authority and weight are undoubted, and all that honour and high appreciation could do was his, to make his existence more possible for him. And notwithstanding his many bereavements, and the quenching out for him of all the happier lights of life, he lived to be an old man, and never abandoned society

and its delights. There is a passage in his criticism upon
Milton, which throws a touching light upon the chief consolation of his lonely life. He has been reminding the
reader that all the classic suggestions, and even imitations
to be found in Milton's poems, must have come from
recollection.

" Then the remembrance of early reading came on his dark and
lonely path like the moon emerging from the clouds. Then it was
that the Muse was truly his—not only as she poured her native inspiration into his mind, but as the daughter of Memory coming with
fragments of ancient melodies, the voice of Euripides and Homer
and Tasso, sounds that he had loved in youth, and treasured up for
the solace of his age. They who, though not enduring the penalty
of Milton, have known what it is—when afar from books, in solitude, or in travelling, or in the intervals of worldly care—to feed
upon poetical recollections, to murmur over the beautiful lines whose
cadence has long delighted their ear, to recall the sentiments and
images which retain, by association, the charms that early years once
gave them, they will feel the inestimable value of committing to
memory, in the prime of its power, what it easily receives and
indelibly retains. I know not, indeed, whether an education that
deals much with poetry, such as is still usual in England, has any
more solid argument among many in its favour, than that it lays
the foundation of intellectual pleasures at the other extreme of
life."

When we read this we can scarcely fail to think of
the old man, alone in those long yet so swiftly passing
years, that compose the end of life, largely surrounded by
friends, and distractions, and all the lively coming and
going of society, in which he himself was as lively and
busy a figure as any—yet like every old man when
strength began to fail him, and all that were his very own
had gone from him, inevitably alone for many a lingering
hour. A natural sympathy identifies the writer himself
with his subject, and we cannot but feel that he too, withdrawn by age and bereavement into some such hermitage
as that which his blindness made to Milton, must have
consoled himself in his solitude with " the beautiful lines

whose cadence had long delighted his ears," walking softly back as through long silent libraries, through his studies and collections of the past. The thought has in it a fine and dignified repose, a melancholy quiet, which indeed cannot but be sad, but which is better and more seemly than much that is supposed to be happiness.

We are brought back to the recollection of what we have called, without any disrespectful meaning, the Partisan-Historians, by the next name we encounter, that of the Catholic writer whose heart, no doubt, had burned within him to see the calmness of assumption with which Protestant England—then in one of her most Protestant moods—satisfied herself as to the atrocious tendencies of Popery, its monopoly of persecution and bloodshed ; and though she became rabid with terror at the very name, yet plumed herself on the scornful certainty that the Roman Catholic Church was a thing of the past. It is strange, indeed, that the members of such an ever-living and dauntless priesthood, with organisations so powerful and servants so devoted, should have let the other side so long have their way undisturbed. The subdued forces and patient waiting of the entire Catholic community for so long a stretch of time, its consent to be vanquished, and endurance of suffering and scorn, is a very remarkable feature of these times, and shows the stunning effect of its final downfall and disappointment, when the day of the Stuarts came to an end, more emphatically than any-thing else could do : as well as the never-dying hope and certainty of eventual triumph which has always been its inspiration. It is accordingly with a sense of pleasure that we hear the first voice rise from this humiliated com-munity, humiliated in England almost beyond example. How it was possible that they could have endured so long all the Tests and insulting disabilities under which they lay, and that, at least in England, so little of the

bitterness of a grievance should have showed itself in
their minds, is very remarkable in the records of religious
endurance.   John Lingard was one of the Catholic priests
of the old school, trained at Douay in all the lore and
traditions of a class which is universally acknowledged to
have been more refined and cultivated, more liberal and
less polemical, than that with which we have more
recently made acquaintance.   When the troubles of the
Revolution arose in France, and the college was broken
up, Lingard came back, with most of its members, to
England.   In these days there was little hope in Rome
of any reconquest of this country to the old faith ; and
however Catholic disabilities might rankle in the bosoms
of those who had to sacrifice their rights as citizens to
their faith, there had not as yet begun to arise among
them either the indignation which prompts to action, or
the hope of doing any good by it.   It is curious, indeed,
to find so little evidence anywhere, either in England or
Ireland, of the bitterness which political and social disabilities ought, it would seem, to have produced.   It was,
as we have said, a time when Protestantism was rampant
in England.   There was no High Church party ; or if it
existed in tradition, its habits were fox-hunting, and its
religion, according to Scotch nomenclature, " moderate."
All that was living and active was evangelical ; so-called
Ritual was at the lowest ebb; Popery a feeble and hopeless piece of antiquity.   And when the learned and
laborious priest in his Lancashire village began upon his
history of England, nothing could have appeared more
unlikely to any spectator or critic than that there should
come a time when a large section of the Church of England herself should be pleased to contemplate history from
the same point of view.   Lingard held the humble position
of what was in reality a dissenting minister, in the village
of Hornby, far away from the great world, humbly paid

and lodged, though there would be, no doubt, among his congregation some great personage or other attached to the Catholic faith to give him a link of connection with the greater world. Here he remained all his life, unmoved by the honours which were, if he chose, within his reach, and here died, having resisted all efforts to raise his rank or magnify his position. It is said, even, that the Pope offered a cardinal's hat to the humble rural priest who was doing a work so important to the Church ; but this wonderful honour, never, probably, before offered directly to a person so humble, did not tempt him. He is said to have returned the excellent answer and excuse for his refusal, that " it would quite put a stop to the progress of my history." The Papal See has seldom been so observant of humble merit.

His first work was upon the *Antiquities of the Anglo-Saxon Church*, and was received with a violent and alarmed No-Popery article from the pen of Southey in the *Quarterly*, though with some faint praises from other quarters. The *History of England* was published when the author had reached the full maturity of life after years of preparation and laborious research. How far that research extended to original documents was doubted at the time, and it would be impossible to attempt to decide the question now ; but the work, on the whole, outlived all the assaults made upon it, and has always been treated respectfully in the world of letters. At a time when the easier and more graphic style of literary composition had scarcely been allowed to force its way into the solemn methods of the historic muse, Lingard used a natural and graceful diction, which is still readable after Froude and Macaulay. He was one of the first adventurers in the new epoch, pricking over the plain on his own account, instead of marching square and solid like a battalion with the force of a Hume or a Gibbon

undisturbed by other competitors in the field. Though
he lived out of the world, he was no mere bookworm; but
when he was assailed, could defend himself with all the
vigour of a practised fighter. The *Edinburgh Review*, in
the person of Allen, the medical adviser and prime
minister of Holland House, fell upon him with all its
ponderous force; but the poor priest, out of his little
parsonage, held his own gallantly, neither crying out, like
so many victims, nor flinching from the shock of arms.
Not to touch upon the most difficult crisis of all, the age
of Henry VIII. and Elizabeth, it would be vain to say
that his treatment, for instance, of such a figure as that
of Wycliffe is generous or even fair. The reader cannot
fail to see that all the consequences, so unforeseen, of
Wycliffe's early protest against the corruptions of the
Church have got into the eyes of the historian and given
a grudge to all he says. But if he imputes to the Reformer
a certain dissimulation in the explanation of his own
words, he attributes to him no unworthy motive, nor any
political object beyond those which his champions would
gladly allow—the furtherance of liberty, the abolition of
local bondage, and the relief of the commonalty from
taxes beyond their power of paying. The manner of the
treatment is ungracious—the historian disliking the hero:
but not so much as Gibbon disliked Christianity, to take
an example prior to the Roman Catholic historian, or as
Mr. Froude disliked Mary Stuart, to take a later instance.
The student will take these partialities for what they are
worth; the common reader, in all likelihood, will be little
affected by them. It is a necessity of all judicial processes to hear both sides of the question, and the preponderance of testimony was so much on the other side
that this honest and dignified partisan is of advantage to
the decision.

And it makes an agreeable addition to the literary

records of the time to see this obscure priest, with his little flock about him, saying his mass in his village chapel : retiring among his books, interrupted, perhaps, in the middle of a chapter to carry salvation to some sickbed : putting away the cardinal's hat, with perhaps a touch of fine impatience, as an interruption to " the progress of my history :" and, after his long life, dying as he had lived, among the same village community, the director of their simple souls, before anybody had dreamed that a hierarchy could be re-established, and Cardinal Archbishops flourish again in England. There is no telling whether, perhaps, the village priest's Catholic history may not have had some share in bringing that new development about.

The works of Dr. Thomas M'Crie may claim a place on a similar line with those of Lingard—higher, in so far that his impartiality is less severely tested ; not so high in national importance, since the general mind never condemned Knox and the Scotch Reformers as it had condemned the Roman Catholic champions. But it must not be forgotten that the tendency of history and opinion had been to the Royal side in Scotland, and that where Mary Stuart was the favourite heroine, John Knox was scarcely like to have his full rights as the great patriot and wise statesman he proved himself to be. And no more deadly wound could have been aimed at the national prejudices and prepossessions than Sir Walter, the pride of Scotsmen, had aimed at the heroes of the Covenant. We may flatter ourselves that it was easier to show the noble love of freedom and dauntless spirit of these rustic martyrs than to vindicate Mary Tudor and her supporters ; but at least there was in it a kindred inspiration, though so different an aim.

We require to go a long way back into the old century

to pick up the philosopher whose works and thoughts
made a new beginning and a separate theory in mental
and political science, as distinctly as Wordsworth made a
new beginning in poetry.   Jeremy Bentham was twenty-
two, and had just made the first step in his career by the
publication of his *Fragment on Government*, when Wordsworth, the eldest of all the poetic race, was born; but he
lasted out the first quarter of this century in eccentric
vigour, and his system is as much identified with the
age we have been discussing as the poetry itself, which
distinguishes it among all ages.   Bentham, like every originator, has something in him of that absence of natural
lineage which distinguished the old priestly patriarch on
the Chaldean plains.   He is "without father and without
mother" in his rank as a philosopher.   His system,
according to his own account of it, seems to have sprung
from his perception of the necessity of a link of general
principle to bring together the subjects and studies which
interested him most.   It is the custom of philosophy in
the present day to ignore all possibility of that creation
of something out of nothing which once was thought the
prerogative of genius, and to trace every new line of
speculation, every new development of thought, every inspiration even of poetry, to influence and training.   This
idea had not been thought of in Bentham's time; and
though he was not of an imaginative mind or apt to
reject the agency of secondary means, yet his claims as
an inventor are as distinct as if it had been a piece of
machinery he had put together, and not a scheme of
philosophy.   His dormant intelligence was fired by a
suggestion found in one of Priestley's letters, he tells us;
but his system was not Priestley's, nor developed out of
anything that came from that sectarian thinker.   The
contact between the two minds was momentary; the
touch was like that of fire to tinder, or rather like the

firing of the train by an accidental spark; and all that
followed arose from the application of an original mind
to difficulties, which many, no doubt, had felt without
attempting to solve them before. Bentham's system
has had the greatest influence upon the world since his
time. It is sufficiently important to be considered a new
departure in the world of thought; and, as such, it has
received the allegiance of as devoted a band of disciples
as ever surrounded any master in science or morals. The
prophet was one of the oddest that ever moved humanity,
a strange little being full of quips and cranks : in mind
a sort of thinking machine, working up every kind of
harsh material, and rolling out schemes, codes, and legislative suggestions by the mile, with an inexhaustible
fertility; in habits a recluse, though surrounded by an
endless flow of society, and incapable of existing, it would
seem, without a little court of dependants and admirers;
in all studies but his own destitute of so much as the
capacity to understand—like one of those abnormal
beings, the sport of science in the present day, of whom
accident or misadventure has annulled one side of the
brain, and who are incapable of exercising any but one
set of faculties. It is true that our impression of him is
chiefly derived from the descriptions of his old age, with
its shrill gaiety and eldritch affectionateness; his laugh,
which is something between a cricket's chirp and the
cachinnation of a pantaloon; his babble of superannuated
fondness for the naughty or good boys (according as they
pleased him), who bore names so provocative of kindness
and fondling as those of Henry Brougham and Daniel
O'Connell, both of whom were supposed to sit on the
knee, and to be fed with pap by the spoon of the cack-
ling old patriarch. It is difficult, with the picture of this
chuckling and chirping grandfather in his chair, amid all
the oddities of his philosophical workshop, with his band

of adorers about him, all distinguished by titles of jocular
abuse or drivelling fondness, and all, so far as appears,
responding with never a snarl to his requirements, to
remember that Jeremy Bentham was not always an old
man, and that the fashion of him was different in his
youth. But there was nobody in his youth to give us
any record of the dry and industrious student whose
curiously keen faculties, knocking up against the walls of
tradition and legal fiction on one side, and burrowing at
the roots of law and metaphysics on the other, could
not rest till they had offered substitutes for all the antiquated wisdom of the ages, and replaced every time-
honoured expedient with a novelty. His own recollections of the past, carefully collected by Dr. Bowring from
the conversations which, under the tender title of Bo, and
amid much petting and fondness, he held with his master
—are rather gossip about other and chiefly unknown
personages, than revelations of himself. From these,
however, we gather that he began his consciousness of
life as a frightened little boy, cultivated into the propor-
tions of an infant prodigy by a vain father, who was
proud of his babyish proficiencies, and pounced upon
every sign of faculty, even in the way of dancing and
drawing, both pursuits odious to the child, with an eagerness which drove young Jeremy into childish secretive-
ness, and shut his heart (if he had one) against his too
admiring parent. He was educated at Westminster
School and Queen's College, Oxford, where he was
entered, a dwarfish weak-kneed boy, at twelve and a
quarter, carrying with him a high reputation and the
nickname of the little philosopher. He took his degree
at sixteen, and was hurried through his terms at Lincoln's Inn with all possible celerity. But it would seem
that the father's love or vanity was, at first, grievously
disappointed when the results of this rapid training were

looked for. We are able to fish out from a mass of
irrelevant matter the following account of the first step
he made in life. It occurs in a statement of his horror
and dismay at finding that his father had betrayed the
secret of his authorship of the work in question, his complaint on which subject occupies far more space than the
novel little bit of self-disclosure which follows.

"For some time before the publication of the 'Fragment,' I had
been regarded in the light of a lost child ; despair had succeeded to
the fond hopes which something of prematurity in my progress had
inspired. On my being called to the bar I found a case or two at
nurse for me. My first thought was how to put them to death, and
the endeavours were not, I believe, altogether without success.
Not long after, a case was brought to me for my opinion. I ran-
sacked all the codes. My opinion was right according to the codes ;
but it was wrong according to a manuscript unseen by me, and in-
accessible to me—a manuscript containing the report, I know not
of what opinion, said to have been delivered before I was born, and
locked up, as usual, for the purpose of being kept back or produced
according as occasion served. . . . My optics were to such a degree
disturbed, that to my eyes the imperfections of this phantom rule
of action seemed only errors calling for an easy remedy. I had
not learned how far they served as sources of wealth, power, and
factitious dignity. I had contracted—oh, horrible !—that unnatural
and at that time almost unexampled appetite, the love of innovation. . . .

"The reader cannot have gone through the first sentence in the
'Fragment,' without having seen the passion that gave rise to it—
the passion for improvement—I mean in these shapes in particular
in which the lot of mankind is meliorated by it, a passion which
has been rekindled by recent incidents, and is not likely to be ex-
tinguished but with life ; a passion for improvement in every line,
but more particularly in the most important of all lines—the line
of government. At an age a few months before or after seven years,
the first embers of it were kindled by Telemachus. By an early
pamphlet of Priestley's, the date of which has fled from my recollection, light was added to the warmth. In the phrase 'the greatest happiness of the greatest number,' I then saw delineated, for the
first time, a plain as well as a true standard for whatever is right
or wrong, useful, useless, or mischievous in human conduct, whether
in the field of morals or politics. It was, I think, in my twenty-

second year that I saw in it the foundation of what seemed to me the only correct instruction or encyclopædical arrangement—a map or chart of the field of thought and action. It is the same map which stands in the work entitled 'Chrestomathia.' I felt the sensation of Archimedes when I committed the first rough and imperfect outline to one side of a half-sheet of paper, which, not entirely useless, served, I hope, to kindle a more substantial flame.

" No sooner had my farthing candle been taken out of the bushel than I looked for the descent of torches to it from the highest regions ; my imagination presented to my view torches descending in crowds to borrow its fire. Of disposition, in the midst of such excellence with which, as all pens and all voices concurred in assuring me I was so abundantly encompassed, I could not suspect any deficiency ; for clearing away the imperfections which still remained in government, all that was wanting was a few of those lights which, I could not tell how, had happened to take my mind for their first visiting place. "

The astonishment with which he discovered that this was not the case, that nobody wished to be enlightened by him with those new lights which were to banish all darkness, gradually worked further discoveries in Bentham's mind. But, in the meantime, his position outwardly was not a comfortable one. His father, though deriving some satisfaction from the publication of the *Fragment*, which, being brought out anonymously, was attributed to various great personages until his vanity betrayed the secret and stopped the sale—was disappointed and angry, " always out of spirits for my want of success." " Mine was truly a miserable life," Bentham says. " I had been taken notice of by the great when a little boy at Westminster School ; for I was an object of praise from the earliest time of which I have any recollection. *That* filled me with ambition. But I met with all sorts of rebukes and disappointments till I was asked to Bowood."

It was the appearance of the *Fragment* which procured him the notice of Lord Shelburne, afterwards Lord Lansdowne, and this invitation to Bowood which was so great a crisis in the life of the thrifty, industrious, self-occupied, young philosopher. He got rid of his father's constant visits and importunities about his work, which galled him greatly, for the elder Bentham (not unnaturally, some people will think) made frequent investigations as to how the *Policy of Punishment* or the *Observations on the Hard Labour Bill* were going on; and it restored him to that notice of the great for which, philosopher as he was, he seems to have pined. The letters from this place form a curious record of the gossip of the time, and of the place which a man of inferior position, however distinguished, inevitably takes in a great house; and the flatteries and complacencies, the growing conviction that heaven and earth hold nothing so important as this noble family, the pride with which every new privilege is noted, furnish a strange commentary upon the philosopher's higher pretensions and impartial survey of mankind in general. What could the delights of science and learning give that was equal to admittance into Lady Shelburne's dressing-room, and all the talks and pleasantries and music that went on there, the ladies so austere and dignified, very prudes to other people, all sweetness and complaisance to him? Here, it appears, to give the scene its last seduction, Bentham found the only, and entirely hopeless, love of his life. The Miss F——— of his letters is a very easily deciphered hieroglyphic. She was inexorable, it would appear, and still inexorable when after sixteen years' separation they met again, and it became apparent that Bentham had not got over his passion. His biographer informs us that to the very end of his life " I have often heard him speak of that lady with tears in his eyes." One can scarcely help feeling that the hopelessness of the love must have been one of its attractions; for to imagine old Jeremy Bentham with his little train of followers, the queer little antiquated celibate, as

grotesque as anything that ever came out of the fancy of
Dickens, in the position of a married man, the companion
of a fair and fastidious lady, is beyond the power of
mortal imagination.

His friendship with Bowood and all its sirens lasted
some four or five years; and whether it was brought to
an end at last by the presumption of a proposal on the
part of the tame philosopher, whose very privilege of
entrée to my lady's dressing-room no doubt signified that
he was perfectly safe as an inmate, and not sentimentally
dangerous to the most susceptible imagination, cannot be
told—but it seems very possible that it may be so.   He
went to Russia afterwards with my lord's blessing and
strenuous recommendations, and with a fine aim in the
way of carrying with him every kind of possible amelioration and improvement for Russia, " under the auspices of
Prince Potemkin, in whose service his brother was then
engaged."   The improvements came to little, so far as
Russia was concerned; but Bentham, with the aid of his
brother, there worked out a wonderful scheme called
Panopticon, which for several years after his return was
foremost in his thoughts.   It was a design for a model
prison of very peculiar construction, partly the invention
of General, afterwards Sir Samuel Bentham—who had a
great deal of genius in this way, and was also the inventor of a new kind of vessel called the vermicular, which
Bentham was sanguine would work an entire change in
navigation.   The Panopticon was to be an immense cir-
cular building, with a great well in the middle, from
which the gaolers were to superintend the whole range
of convicts in the cells, where each was to work alone,
one side of the cell being entirely open towards the
centre, fully lighted night and day, and exposed to the
continual inspection of the watchers in the middle.
Minute details of the watching and regulations outside,

and of the manner of employing the prisoners within,
were added to the scheme. And some of the details are
curious enough. From the calculations given, it is clear
that Bentham intended to feed his criminals chiefly or
entirely upon potatoes. In point of clothing he considered stockings unnecessary unless on Sundays; shirts
are also rejected as unnecessary, and the shoes were to
be of wood, not leather. The most extraordinary feature
in the plan was the system of continual inspection,—the
unhappy prisoners being understood to be under the eye
of their guardians constantly, sleeping and waking,—
but the other details were likewise novel and startling,
and the principle of providing for and maintaining the
prisoners by contract, instead of by the indiscriminate
use of the public money through public functionaries,
was, to the mind of Bentham, a still more important one.
The curious fact is that he all but carried his scheme,
and was actually entrusted, by an Act of Parliament,
with a thousand convicts to test it, when the king himself, whom Bentham had offended, stepped in and arrested
the proceedings by giving his veto against the scheme.
So far had matters gone that Bentham obtained from a
subsequent Parliament the immense sum of £23,000 as
compensation for the losses he had undergone in connection with it. Bentham himself had undertaken to be the
contractor, the chief gaoler living among his prisonful.
The importance of this plan could not be further proved
than by the great sum thus granted as compensation.
Notwithstanding that the existing system of prison
management has been largely influenced by Bentham's
suggestions, the fundamental idea strikes us as very
extraordinary now, as well as many of the minor details
—such as his hope to make the chapel, which was to be
also in the centre of the building, on Sunday " a sort of
place of public entertainment suitable to the day, like

that afforded by the Magdalen and the Asylum," a place where people could come to stare, like Asmodeus, at all the unhappy wretches whose life, in every detail, was gone through under an inspector's eye.

It must not be forgotten, however, that Howard had but lately opened the whole question of prison management, and given his heroic life to the cleansing and reformation of the dismal dens in which criminals were left to rot and die in body, and to corrupt each other mutually in mind. The light and air and publicity which were thus to be poured upon the place where felons bore their punishment was part of his system, and he had regarded the latter particular as a special safeguard against the evils of the old *régime*. Whether, however, Howard contemplated carrying publicity to such a pitch as to keep his unfortunate clients, night and day, under the inspection of their keepers, we are not informed. Bentham repeatedly asserted that but for George III. he should have had the management of all the convicts of England, and after them, of all the paupers, in his hands.

But this strange scheme came to nothing, as so many other benevolent enterprises of the kind have done. That it should have been so near success seems to us the most wonderful feature in it. It appears to have been one of the chief interests in Bentham's life for a great number of years. The plan was originated in 1788, propounded to Government in 1792, and only finally settled in 1811 by the payment above mentioned. Wilberforce speaks of Bentham's strong feeling on the subject and profound disappointment at its failure—a disappointment which certainly was of a generous kind; for the life he had proposed to himself as chief gaoler of a huge prison, living in his central chamber, in the midst of the most hardened and debased of criminals, is as unlike the scheme of existence which could have proved satisfactory to a philosopher, as can be conceived. But he was very tenacious and slow to relinquish any plan he had formed.

Bentham's attempts at the consolidation of the laws and formation of a penal code, were as unsuccessful, in a practical point of view, as his Panopticon. He neglected no opportunity of pressing his services upon every newly-formed or revolutionised nationality, from France—by which in the palmy days of the National Assembly he had been adopted as a citizen along with half-a-dozen other Englishmen—Russia (of which he had great hopes), and America—to such smaller sections of the world as Venezuela, to which he had a great mind to emigrate under the protection of Miranda, for the purpose of making it into a Utopia of political economy and philosophical legislation. But in the latter as in the former cases difficulties intervened, and the ever ready code, which he was continually retouching and perfecting, was nowhere adopted. At the very end of his life he wrote to one of his foreign correspondents, " I am alive though turned of eighty-two ; still in good health and spirits, *codifying like any dragon.* Thus with a chirrup of obstinate fidelity as dauntless as any trumpet note, the old man stuck to his lifelong occupation, undaunted by the fact that all the world had refused his help in this particular. What he did succeed in was in sowing principles, suggestions, knowledge, broadcast among the classes of which legislation is the natural trade, perhaps as effectual a way of influencing the world as if he had been allowed to codify like a dragon, potentially as well as in his closet. Bentham was not one of the writers who have to wait long and wearily for recognition. His first *Fragment* gained him, as has been said, the happiest influence of his life, the friendship of Lord Lansdowne ; and his reputation as an authority upon questions of law and political philosophy seems to have taken root from that period, and to

have remained unquestioned even by those who agreed the
least with his views.   He was not much over forty when
the French Assembly conferred the honour of French
citizenship upon him, " considering," as the patent sets
forth with characteristic grandiloquence, " that at the
moment when a National Convention is about to fix
the destinies of France, and probably those of the human
race, it belongs to a generous and free people to welcome
all intelligence, and to grant the right of access to this
great work of reason to men rendered worthy of it by
their sentiments, their writings, and their valour !"   What
magnificent sentiments were these ! and what an opportunity for Bentham, had he been able to take advantage
of it !   All that came to him from his offers of enlightenment to France was, however, the appointment of a committee of the Convention to report upon his Panopticon
scheme, which never came to anything.   But that his
name and fame had travelled far is very apparent.

It is curious, however, to note in his case the benefits
of patronage, as conferred by this short episode of Bowood.
It made him acquainted with people whose acquaintance
was in itself a kind of fame.   It gave him his great
disciple and expositor Dumont, a Frenchman who had
been tutor to Lord Lansdowne's sons, and who, when once
made acquainted with the philosopher, attached, like himself, to that noble house, made himself, for a great part
of his life, the interpreter and high priest of Bentham,
merging his own powers in those of his master, and com-
municating to France, with curious self-devotion, a better
and more readable version of Bentham's principles than
Bentham himself was able to give to his own country.
Dumont was the most serviceable of the many retainers
whom Bentham attached to himself; but he had other
disciples to whom his service was as that of a feudal
superior.   Notwithstanding the weird and uncanny aspect

of the old man, as he is revealed to us by Dr. Bowring, in his shrill levity and cheerfulness, there must have been attractive qualities in him. It is evident that he had an instinct like that of the Ancient Mariner, for the men who were born to hear and understand him, and great readiness in adopting into his affections every new notability whom he approved of. Mill, the sternest of thinkers, was for a considerable time his henchman and attendant; and he received an amount of service and devotion, which few of the greatest of mankind have gained from their fellow-creatures. It may be that his own entire detachment from family and natural ties had something to do with it, besides his power of helping in his turn, young men who gave up their time and independence to him; but it requires more than this to induce men of education and ability to undertake even the personal service of their philosophical master, as his young disciples who lived in his house, always two of them on duty, seem to have done —at least it is a return to mediæval fashions of discipleship with which we are little acquainted in the nineteenth century.

The reader will find some account of Bentham's system of philosophy farther on. It involves, directly in one group with him, the gentle and noble figure of James Mackintosh who assailed it, and the stern and harsh one of James Mill, who, with equal vigour and unmannerliness, made himself its champion. They were both Scotsmen, and Bentham did not like Scotsmen. But they were as unlike as it is possible to conceive. Before, however, passing on to these antagonists yet fellow-workmen, we must add a word or two to this record of their master. There is no notable person of his generation who is more open to ridicule. His excessive activity made him thrust into every difficult situation with an absence of that perception of absurdity which saves many men from open folly.　Perhaps there was a touch of chivalry, a remnant of the romantic courage which prompted a knight to offer himself as the champion of his country, as well as a wonderful amount of vanity and misapprehension of magnitudes in the philosopher's mind, when he proposed to Wilberforce (like himself a French citizen by patent of the National Assembly as one of the heroes of humanity) that they two should go to France as ambassadors to re-establish friendly relations between the two countries.　The claims which he puts forth for himself in proof of his eligibility to this office are—1st, The order by the Assembly to print the Panopticon plan; 2d, An invitation from Talleyrand to go to Paris with the idea of setting up a Panopticon; 3d, The "flaming eulogiums of some extracts from my papers on the judicial establishment," printed in periodicals directed by Mirabeau and by Brissot; with other exquisite reasons.　Wilberforce quashed the scheme in a very brief note.　"There is much in what you urge, and I will turn it in my mind; but I doubt if anything can be made of it"—but Lord St. Helens, to whom it was also referred, took the trouble to enter into an elaborate explanation of the impossibilities of the plan.　This was probably a mere bubble of the combative and active mind of the philosopher, but it has a very grotesque aspect among the many restless offers and schemes of his life. The prodigious letter, or rather pamphlet, in the form of a letter (sixty-one pages) which we find in another place addressed to Lord Lansdowne, and taking his patron to task for not putting him into Parliament as Bentham understood him to have promised to do, is another proof that some impulses of ambition, apart from his science and his schemes of public improvement, legislative and otherwise, occasionally crossed his mind.　The following statement, however, of the relative position and importance of his own and the philosophical systems which preceded his, reaches a much higher point, and may be reckoned as the very sublimation of self-applause.

"What Bacon did was to proclaim *Fiat experimentum;* but his own knowledge of natural philosophy was ignorance.

"What Locke did was to destroy the notion of innate ideas ;

"What Newton did was to throw light on one branch of science.

"But I have planted the tree of Utility—I have planted it deep and spread it wide."

Of his opinions on literature in general not much is to be said. "What I read of Socrates is insipid," he says. "I could find in him nothing that distinguished him from other people, except his manner of putting questions." Coming down to an age more near our own, he informs us, "I never read poetry with enjoyment. I read Milton as a duty. Hudibras for the story and the fun ;" so that, presumably, as poetry, Lycidas and Hudibras ranked on about the same level in the philosopher's mind. And his mention of Milton at all was, perhaps, suggested by the fact that it was Milton's house in which he was living, a fact which had induced the old Jeremy, Bentham's father, to buy a portrait of the poet, and put up an inscription in the garden to his memory. When discoursing of his contemporaries, Bentham speaks of the "servile poet and novelist Walter Scott," and the "ultra-servile sack-guzzler Southey." "I shall laugh heartily to see your figure in the neighbourhood of those reptiles Scott and Southey," replies his correspondent the mild-mouthed and modest Parr. Thus the philosophers communed together. On the other hand, we must add a few words of a more genial kind, an old man's summing up of his philosophy, which exhibits him in a very different light. It was written for a lady, who wished for his autograph a few months before his death.

"The way to be comfortable is to make others comfortable.

"The way to make others comfortable is to appear to love them.

" The way to appear to love them is to love them in reality.

"*Probatur ab experientiâ* per Jeremy Bentham, Queen's Square Place, Westminster.   Born 15th February anno 1748 ; written 24th October 1831."

This little matter-of-fact periphrasis of the great Christian rule puts the philosopher in a happier light. But the queer figure of the old man shuffling about his garden, his white hair streaming from under a straw hat, legs and arms muffled up in shapeless woollen : or " vibrating" round the platform upon which his table and chairs and bookcase were placed, indoors, his teapot " Dick" singing over the lamp, his confidential friend in waiting, attended by two young secretaries—" reprobates" in the quaint language of the house—makes one of the strangest of domestic pictures.   It is far more like a picture out of Dickens than a scene of actual life.   While the guests were still present the queer little old man was undressed, by one of the disciples, his nightcap tied on, his old eyes bathed—his old voice running on all the time in a perpetual shrill chatter of elaborate jokes and chirrupings.   Never was a stranger comic-tragic figure, yet nothing solemn in it, more like an ape of genius chattering and tricksy, than one of the great minds that inspire an age.   But such he was, in his strange all-laborious way.

The name of James Mackintosh is one which possesses more of that personal attraction in which, curiously enough, the figures of the past vary as much as do those of our personal acquaintances, than either of the historians and philosophers already noted.   He was one of the men never so successful as they seem to have a right to be, who awaken great expectations, and now and then attain great though evanescent triumphs, but by some failure of fortune, or absence of faculty, never rise to the height which appears their due, or get any consolation of this fluctuating and

never fully accomplished fame. He was the son of a
Highland laird, and himself the heir of a little northern
property, with which, however, he soon parted by that
almost inevitable process of getting rid of what they have,
which young men born to a small fortune so generally go
through. He was full of faculty and genius from his
earliest years—the fact that it must be Jamie Mackintosh
being at once recognised in the countryside, when a learned
stranger told the story of his encounter, on a country
road, with a remarkable boy. He was a "spontaneous
child," some old observer said of him, and there could not
be a more attractive description. And he was a dreamer
as well. "I used to fancy myself Emperor of Constantinople," he says. "I distributed offices and provinces
among my schoolfellows, I loaded my favourites with
dignity and power, and I often made the objects of my
dislike feel the weight of my imperial resentment. I
carried on the series of political events in solitude;"—
and he adds that this habit continued with him all his
life, not in the more common way of imagining success
and triumphs for himself in his proper pursuits, but in
weavings of imagination as far removed from reality as
the crown of Constantinople was from the schoolroom at
Fortrose. "I have no doubt," he adds, "that many a man
surrounded by piles of folios, and apparently engaged in
the most profound researches, is in reality often employed
in distributing the offices and provinces of the empire of
Constantinople." But this dreamer was no inactive boy.
The spontaneous life in him poured forth in all channels.
When he was but thirteen he got up a debating society in
his school, and harangued the Inverness-shire lads "till
his soprano voice failed." "One day he was Fox, another
Burke, or some leading member of the Opposition; and
when no one ventured to reply to his arguments, he
would change sides for the moment, personate North, and

endeavour to combat what he conceived the strongest parts
of his own speech. I was greatly surprised and delighted
with his eloquence in his character of Fox against some
supposed or real measure of the prime minister." Thus
the little actor conned his mimic part, little thinking how
soon he was to find a place among those he imitated.

At fifteen Mackintosh went to Aberdeen to college,
and there fell into a course of reading which helped to
direct many of his after efforts. Warburton's *Divine
Legation,* he thinks, perhaps "tainted my mind with a
fondness for the twilight of historical hypothesis; but
certainly inspired me with that passion for investigating
the history of opinions, which has influenced my reading
through life." Here he met Robert Hall, the future great
preacher, and the two ardent boys, both golden-mouthed
and full of dawning eloquence, living together in the same
bare half-furnished house, walking together on the sands,
in the roar of these northern seas which half drowned
their eager young voices, discussed and reasoned of every
subject on earth and heaven. The young Englishman
was orthodox in the straitest sense of the word, the young
Scot, who at fourteen had been "the boldest heretic in the
county," a daring speculator and questioner: and the
subjects upon which they differed were much more numerous than those on which they agreed. During one
winter they met at five o'clock every morning in the cold
and dark "to read Greek"—a third youth, no doubt one
of those devoted and admiring retainers who are always to
be found on the path of the young heroes of the universities, getting up to make coffee for them: and this early
meeting: the two youthful faces over their books, most
likely by the light of one poor candle, the friendly minis-
trant coaxing his fire into brightness, the fumes of the
boyish cookery—and, no doubt, the little interval of jest
that would come into the midst of Plato or Herodotus. as

the three youths warmed themselves with the smoking coffee, furnishes us with a pleasant scene. The future statesman and the future preacher struggled and wrangled and were never still, loving and confuting each other with all the warmth of fervid youth. To Hall, Mackintosh always appeared to have " an intellect more analogous to that of Bacon than any person of modern times;" while to Mackintosh, a somewhat careless youth, with a warm love of pleasure and no very straitened creed, " the transparency of his friend's conduct and the purity of his principles " inspired a respect which he describes as awe. Altogether there could not have been a more interesting conjunction.

Mackintosh left college at nineteen, having taken his degree — a course more rational surely than the long extended preliminary training of the present time : and though he would have preferred the bar or to be a bookseller (an idea which filled his advisers with consternation), he became neither, but began his studies for the medical profession. It was in this capacity that he went to London, a lively young man of twenty-three, more distinguished in all the debating societies than in the schools, although there, too, his comprehensive genius held its own. It was not, however, as a physician but as a speaker, in the ferment of the political societies which were universal at the time, that Mackintosh made his first success in London. It is clear that nothing attracted him so much as that art of oratory which, in his then circumstances, he could practise only as a relaxation. This kind of relaxation, however, combined with others less legitimate, swallowed up altogether the life of the young man, who, though a Scotsman, was as prodigal, lavish, and incautious as most of the young Scotsmen whom we have previously encountered in these volumes have been. At the moment when he was thus afloat in London, with no settled pros-

pects, his little Highland estate, newly come into his hand
on the death of his father, already beginning to melt away
in his careless keeping, Mackintosh took a step which to
most wise people would seem the most imprudent of all,
but which immediately replaced him in the way of salvation.   He married and returned to the hopes and possibilities of more practical life.   It was not very long after
this event that he won his spurs in literature, suddenly
leaping into the midst of the fray and striking upon the
shield of no neophyte like himself, but of the most distinguished of warriors, the great Burke, the most eloquent
and potent champion against whom young assailant ever
tried his powers—as if a young Lovaine with maiden
arms had defied Lancelot himself.   The occasion was that
centre of all the excitement and commotion of the time,—
the French Revolution : against which Burke had arisen at
once to denounce with half-prophetic force, and at the
cost both of friendships and traditions, its dangerous tendencies.   So strong was the feeling, and so many were the
sympathisers in favour of the new outburst of freedom
and popular rights, that answers came forth on all sides
to this attack.   Among these was the well-known *Rights
of Man* by Thomas Paine.   Neither the great Burke nor
his violent adversary belongs to our period : but when
James Mackintosh, young, unsettled, and not knowing
what to do with himself, full of the ardent hopes and
strong political feeling of his generation, seeing in the
great events on the other side of the Channel the self-
emancipation of a heroic nation and the beginning of a
new era of freedom and life, came forth before the world
with his *Vindiciæ Gallicæ*, his apology and justification of
he Revolution, which as yet had not dipped its garments
in blood, he was as true an embodiment as could have
been found of the new age, full of hope and warm idealism
and that certainty of being able to better the world, and

turn evil into good, which is one of the finest characteristics of noble youth.

The *Vindiciæ* was an eloquent and glowing defence of
the French nation and its leaders, and of the spirit, as yet
all undeveloped and apparently containing in it the germ
of every heroic quality, of the new revolution.   Its arguments are not without suspicion of sophism and special
pleading, but its generous inspiration and hot and eager
championship, made up of the natural English desire to
see fair play, and the warm enthusiasm for liberty of the
young England of the moment, are very potent and
attractive.   The impression made by it was great.   The
first edition was published in April 1791, and by August
of the same year the third had been called for.   It was
from the obscurity of a cottage at Little Ealing, where the
young medical man, who certainly had not been successful, nor perhaps had much tried to be successful, in that
profession, had retired for economy and quiet, and very
likely with the intention of weaning himself from the
temptations of town—that this generous plea for France
and freedom, and the hopes of a new world, came forth.
His young wife, no doubt with many an anxiety in her
mind, not only for the bread of the children who began
to gather about the rash pair, but for the vindication to
the world of those powers which had as yet been little
more than wasted upon political societies and fruitless
debates—sat by him silent as a mouse, not permitted
even the resource of that endless needlework which a
young mother, in those days, had more completely upon
her hands than now, scarcely turning the pages of her
book lest she should disturb him as he worked.   One can
scarcely help feeling that her presence meant a certain
moral compulsion and guardianship to keep him to his
work, which, it is allowed, he needed in those days.

But this was an end of the obscurity and unsuccess of

the young Scotsman.   His book was received with applause everywhere.   Fox, who had separated himself from
his brother-in-arms in consequence of the *Reflections*, to
which it was an answer, and Burke himself, who was
magnanimous enough to appreciate the writer's admiration
and respect even through the fervour of his attack, both
praised his performance ; and young Mackintosh stepped at
once out of his obscurity into the acquaintance of the
world.   Perhaps it was the new vigour given by success
which prompted him more definitely to abandon the profession of medicine, for which it is evident he never felt
any enthusiasm, and to adopt that of the law, which was
much more congenial to his mind.   He was called to the
bar in 1795, and by that time had fully entered upon the
craft of literature as well.   The nature of the man is well
exemplified in the fact that within four or five years after
the production of the *Vindiciæ Gallicæ*, his frank and reasonable soul, unfettered by those artificial bonds of consistency which a young man is so often afraid to break, had
owned the rashness of his own plea, and abandoned the
uncompromising defence of France, which, possible in
1791, was no longer possible after the Terror.   His reviews
of Burke's subsequent publications on the same subject,
brought him to the personal knowledge of the great writer
and statesman, to whom he made haste to express his profound regard and veneration.   " From the earliest moment
of reflection your writings have been my chief study and
delight," he says.   " For a time, indeed, seduced by the
love of what I thought liberty, I ventured to oppose,
without ever ceasing to venerate, that writer who had
nourished my understanding with the most wholesome
principles of political wisdom. . . . Since that time a
melancholy experience has undeceived me on many subjects in which I was then the dupe of my own enthusiasm.
I cannot say (and you would despise me if I dissembled)

that I can even now assent to all your opinions on the present politics of Europe. But I can with truth affirm that I subscribe to your general principles." This is deeply interesting as affording us an example, very rare in the literature of the time, of the effect produced upon candid and generous minds by the downfall into blood and outrage of the first fair hopes of the Revolution. But Mackintosh carried a peculiarly sensitive mental thermometer, and was always ready to admit those modifications of opinion which life, whether we admit them or not, is sure to bring.

He had not long been called to the bar when he appeared before the world in a series of *Lectures on the Law of Nature and Nations*, delivered, after some demur on the part of the benchers, in the Great Hall of Lincoln's Inn, of which he was a member. It is not to be wondered at that a serious and conservative body should have hesitated before permitting the defender of revolution and of that nation which, for at least one terrible moment, had abrogated law altogether, to discourse upon such a subject under its sanction and authority. But the result justified the confidence which, not without trembling, they had put in him; and his lectures were received with large approval and admiration. His setting forth of the two great institutions of property and marriage as the foundation of relative duties afforded a contrast which men who had lately risen from the first exciting perusal of the *Political Justice* of Godwin would feel in its fullest extent; and his definition of Liberty must have solaced many troubled imaginations, blown up and down by the wild philosophies and still wilder events of the age. " Men are more free," he wrote, " under any government, even the most imperfect, than they would be if it were possible for them to exist without any government at all. They are more secure from wrong, more undisturbed in the exercise of

their natural powers, and therefore more free, even in the
most obvious and grossest sense of the word, than if they
were altogether unprotected against injury from each
other." But this was a wonderful departure from the
ideas and hopes of the dawning of Freedom. His disgust
with the further developments of contemporary history
has all the warmth of disappointment in its strong expression.

"There is nothing in public matters to speak of," he writes in
1800, when the Consulate had just been established, "except the
last extraordinary revolution in France, which has rooted up every
principle of democracy in that country, and banished the people
from all concern in the government, not for a season, as former
usurpers pretended, but for ever, if this accursed revolution is
destined to be permanent. . . . It is my intention, in this winter's
lectures, to profess publicly and unequivocally that I abhor, abjure,
and for ever renounce the French Revolution with all its sanguinary
history, its abominable principles, and for ever execrable leaders.
I hope I shall be able to wipe off the disgrace of having once been
betrayed into an approbation of that conspiracy against God and
man, the greatest scourge of the world, and the chief stain upon
human annals. But I feel," he adds, "that I am transported by
my subject to the borders of rant."

The warmth of this revulsion, however, again troubled
him when, looking back from a distance and from comparative tranquillity upon all the agitations of this period,
he confides to a friend the final form of his matured ideas,
"As a political philosopher," he says, "I will not say that
I now entirely approve the very shades and tones of political doctrine which distinguished these lectures. I can
easily see that I rebounded from my original opinions too
far towards the opposite extreme; I was carried too far
by anxiety to atone for my former errors." These changes
of a sensitive soul, disturbed out of all the traditions of
well-balanced thought by the extraordinary events hap-
pening around him, are more interesting and instructive
to the distant spectator than all the dogmas of consistency;

though at the same time we cannot but admit that such candour has its dangers too, and that the position of a man always conscious that there is much to be said on the other side, has an element of insecurity in it. There were people, of course, who said that James Mackintosh's recantation was brought about by interested motives; it is one of our greatest advantages in the present day that such imputations are rare, and that writers of honourable feeling are slow to suggest a dishonourable motive. The variations of his sensitive mind, as he was thus driven from one side to the other, take an altogether different aspect when we read how they appeared to Bentham looking on with cynical, yet not unkind spectatorship:—

"When I saw you," says the elder philosopher, "enlisted in the defence of a castle of straw, which I had turned my back upon as fit for nothing but the fire, I beheld with regret what appeared to me a waste of talents so unprofitably employed. When I heard of you being occupied in teaching the anatomy and physiology of two chimeras, the same sensation was again repeated. A crowd of admiring auditors of all ranks—and what was it they wished or expected? Each of them some addition to the stock of sophisms which most of them had been able to mount by his own genius, or pick up by his own industry, in readiness to be employed in the service of right or wrong, whichever happened to be the first to present the retaining fee."

After the lectures, which had attracted a great deal of attention, Mackintosh made his way into the more usual honours of his profession. He tells his wife in a letter, of a great speech he had made, which he felt to be full of commonplaces, but which filled "the whole county of Norfolk," assembled at Norwich, with rapture. "Half the court was drowned in tears," and the attorneys, deeply impressed, rushed round him with briefs. Some time after he made a still greater and more important appearance in London, where he defended a certain M. Peltier, an *emigré*, and the editor of a furious little paper called the *Ambigu,* in which the First Consul had been fiercely attacked. The great Erskine wrote to compliment the comparatively unknown young barrister upon his "most powerful and eloquent speech;" and the counsel for the prosecution began his own address with the expression of a fear that "after the attention of the jury had been so long riveted to one of the most splendid displays of eloquence he ever had occasion to hear," his speech would have but little chance. Immediately after, while the firmament was still ringing with these plaudits, Mackintosh accepted an appointment as Recorder of Bombay, which seems to have been a rather rash and unwary proceeding——a sort of sacrifice of the birds in the bush to the one in hand, which poverty and impatience combined, so often force a man into. It would have been natural to expect that such brilliant appearances would have instantly increased his profits at the bar, and opened a career to him in his profession at home ; but, whatever his motives were, the decision was made, and in 1804, with the usual knighthood which distinguishes a judge, but not without misgiving, he banished himself from the scene of all his triumphs to the never congenial sphere of India. " I am waiting," he says, in his last letter written from England, "in hourly expectation of the ship which is to convey me far from those scenes of civilisation and literature in which I once, in the fond ambition of youth, dreamt that I might perhaps have acted a considerable part. Experience has refused my ambition . . . and reason informs me that there is no country in which I may not discharge a part of the debt which I owe to mankind. I do not, however, affect to leave my country without pain." So engaging is Mackintosh's character, and so easy seems the impulse that might have turned him to a better and more glorious path, that vain as is the reflection, it is scarcely possible for the reader not to feel a pang of regret at his rash abandonment of the field, and a pained and impatient sense of what might have been had he not taken so fatal a step.   He was in India seven years, which was so much time lost in respect to his career, a period full of possibilities never to be recovered.   He seems to have felt, through all his time of banishment, a sense of the mistake he had made, and there is a kind of sigh in the following note, made on his voyage home, which is more touching than many louder lamentations :—

"It has happened by the merest accident that the *Trial of Peltier* is among the books in the cabin.   But when I recollect the way in which you saw me opposed to Percival on the 21st of February 1803 (the day of the trial), and when I compare his present situation, whether at the head of an administration or an opposition, with mine, scanty as is my stock of fortune, health, or spirits, in a cabin nine feet square on the Indian Ocean, I think it enough that I am free from the sourness of disappointment, and I need not conceal from my other self that I feel some surprise."

It was little wonder that he should feel surprise at such a contrast.   To be a statesman at the head of imperial affairs instead of a superannuated Indian judge, many men would have accepted the sad and sudden end which put so startling a conclusion to the happier rival's career.   Mackintosh came back with a pension of £1200 a year, broken health, and a general separation from all the ways of advancement.   A faint possibility, however, that something worthy of his powers might yet open upon him, existed at first.   He was offered by Percival, immediately on his arrival in England, a seat in Parliament (the words read curiously nowadays), with a prospect of further promotion afterwards.   But he declined to come into the House as a Government nominee on account of his opinion on the Catholic Disabilities.   Percival's murder occurred at the very moment when his reply to this offer was written, and none of the political leaders who followed took any trouble about Mackintosh.   He found

an independent seat in the House of Commons some time
after; and at a later period was made a privy councillor.
But this empty honour and the privilege of having right
honourable to his name was all he ever came to. Vague
intentions of service and much general admiration and
well-wishing attended him, beside the appreciation of
society for one of the most brilliant and entertaining of
its members; but this was all. In 1818 he became
Professor of Law and Politics in the Indian college at
Haileybury. After his brilliant beginning, and the place
which he always occupied in public life, it is strange to
see the fine pleader, the experienced politician, the admired
conversationalist, a name continually recurring in all the
highest records of the national life, drop into such an
appointment at last as would not have been too much for
him to expect when he started from Edinburgh thirty-
five years before, in all the brilliant faculty and hope of
youth.

We cannot pass over without notice the friendship
which existed between Mackintosh and Madame de Staël,
and which associated him constantly for a time with that
remarkable woman, whose appearance wherever she went
alarmed and excited the men of letters of her day in the
most curious way, with a whimsical mixture of panic and
dislike. Mackintosh, it is evident, felt nothing of this
amusing terror: and the lady proved her discrimination
by a warm preference for his society. "She treats me,"
he says, "as the person she most delights to honour. I
am generally ordered with her to dinner, as one orders
beans with bacon." She, on her part, made no secret of
her regard: "*C'est très ennuyeux de dîner sans vous, et la
société ne va pas quand vous n'êtes pas là*," she writes, and
even in Paris finds no one equal to him. It is evident,
however, that Madame de Staël had fathomed his character
as well as she appreciated it. We find her writing to

Lady Mackintosh of a favourite plan she had, which was to induce Sir James to settle, like Gibbon, on the Lake of Geneva to finish his history. "Que pensez-vous de ce projet?" she says. "Sir James est un peu incertain de sa nature, et je ne crois point à son histoire si vous n'êtes pas le pouvoir exécutif de cette enterprise." When we read this we cannot but remember the young wife who sat by Mackintosh's side, not venturing to turn the leaf lest she should disturb him while he wrote his *Vindiciæ Gallicæ*. It was a second Lady Mackintosh to whom the brilliant Frenchwoman wrote, and she, though evidently a most congenial and faithful companion, does not seem to have had the strength or patience to be thus the "pouvoir exécutif."

Between the early blaze of eloquence and enthusiasm which dazzled the world in the *Vindiciæ Gallicæ*, and the later works which retain a more permanent place in the literature of the country, there is a long, and we can scarcely help thinking, a painful interval. The *Dissertation on Ethical Philosophy* was not completed till 1830, two years before his death. His history, of which he had begun to compose stray pages during his voyage from India in 1812, changed in form and scope, and, shorn of much of its intended importance, did not begin to appear till the same year. And his most important historical work, that in which his whole powers were put forth, and where he had full opportunity for the development of the philosophy of history, his favourite study, was one which he did not live to complete, and which, so much as was completed of it, was given to the world after his death, without the revision or correction which he would certainly have given, and by hands altogether destitute of his skill and genius. The Revolution of 1688, which was the beginning of a new era in the national life, had thus occupied in turn two of the greatest minds among English politicians and statesmen at the very end of their career, a curious and touching coincidence. The subject, which had dropped from Fox's dying fingers, fell also from those of the successor whom Fox applauded in his youth, and who, after the struggles and disappointments of a lifetime, took up the half-executed task, only to leave it in his turn a noble fragment, a preparation for greater things. It is hardly possible to think of this but as the filling up of that measure of disappointment, of unfulfilment, which was the lot of James Mackintosh. Had he been able to accomplish this, a certain compensation for wasted life and fruitless hopes might have been his; he would have done what it had been the ambition of the noblest of his party to do, and set forth with all the force of a philosophical inquirer those principles which had changed the face of England and established a new rule, the rule of modern civilisation and reason, through many drawbacks and the absence of all poetic grace, over all the romantic traditions, sentiments, and attractions of the old. It would have been, one might have thought, a way of making up for so many things which had failed in his life and to his hopes. But it was not so. This last and greatest work came imperfect, with burial wreaths about it, maimed and incomplete, to the world: and thus the last word of unaccomplished hope, of a success never so great as it should have been, of efforts balked and labours unfulfilled, was said.

For the sake of the succession and inheritance which followed, we may quote what Macaulay says of his great predecessor.

"We have no hesitation in pronouncing (in the *Edinburgh Review*, July 1835) this fragment decidedly the best history now extant of the reign of James II. It contains much new and curious information, of which excellent use has been made. . . . We expected to find, and we have found, many just delineations of character and many digressions full of interest, such as the account of the order of Jesuits, and of the state of prison discipline in England a hundred and fifty years ago. We expected to find, and we have found, many reflections breathing the spirit of a calm and benignant philosophy. But we did not, we own, expect to find that Sir James could tell a story as well as Voltaire or Hume. . . . The most superficial reader must be charmed, we think, by the liveliness of the narrative. But no person who is not acquainted with that vast mass of intractable materials of which the valuable and interesting part has been extracted and condensed, can fully appreciate the skill of the writer. Here, and throughout the work, we find many harsh and careless expressions, which the author would probably have removed if he had lived to complete his work. But, in spite of these blemishes, we must say that we should find it difficult to point out in any modern history any passage of equal length, and, at the same time, of equal merit. We find in it the diligence, the accuracy, and the judgment of Hallam, united to the vivacity and colouring of Southey. A history of England written throughout in this manner would be the most fascinating book in the language. *It would be more in request at the circulating libraries than the last novel."*

As the utterance of the writer who, taking up Mackintosh's subject, exactly fulfilled the prophecy of the last sentence, there is an amusing appropriateness in the quotation. Macaulay, though he belongs to a younger generation, with which at present we have nothing to do, was in this, as in some other respects, the reverse of all that has been said of Mackintosh, a man born to success as the latter was to disappointment.

We began by remarking upon the curious personal attraction which even through the medium of a somewhat dull biography, one figure out of the past, among many who touch us not at all save intellectually and historically, will exercise upon the reader. In this way a tender radiance glows about the name of a man who was not one of those magicians who have a natural spell over our hearts, who was no poet but a philosopher, lawyer, and politician, and who has been set before us by no skilful hand, such as that of those biographers who have made a distinct revelation of their subject, from great Plato to little Bozzy. Mackintosh had not even this advantage. He shows forth dimly through the opaque medium of his memoirs, or in the merest momentary gleam in the recollections of his contemporaries, but never without the attraction—perhaps of that same quality, first of all, which the keen-sighted old Scotswoman noted, who called him a "spontaneous child." He is always natural, unaffected, answering to the influences of his time, without *parti pris* or thought of his consistency, or of himself at all. We may add from the same critic whom we have already quoted, a few lines full of feeling and affectionate regard, written after Mackintosh's death.

"All the lines of that venerable countenance are before us, all the little peculiar cadences of that voice from which scholars and statesmen loved to receive the lessons of a serene and benevolent wisdom, are in our ears. . . . In his most familiar talk there was no wildness, no inconsistency, no dreaming nonsense, no exaggeration for the sake of momentary effect. His mind was a vast magazine admirably arranged ; everything was there. . . . It would have been strange indeed if you had asked for anything that was to be found in that immense storehouse. The article which you required was not only there ; it was ready. . . . He was singularly mild, calm, and impartial in his judgments of men and of parties."

James Mill was of the same country as Mackintosh —a Northern Scot, though not of Celtic race. This latter circumstance may partly account for the difference between them, which was as great as if half a world had lain between their places of birth. To come suddenly out of the genial presence of the one into the gloomy companionship of the other involves a greater shock of difference than could we pass in a moment from Italy to Iceland. Mill was one of the sternest and most rigid representatives of that northern race which, notwithstanding the very different qualities of the names which make it illustrious, has so continued to retain its con-

ventional character for harshness and coldness that we
are almost forced to believe there must be some truth in
the imputation.   There would be so if the Devil's advocate could produce many such men as James Mill to
counterbalance Scott and Mackintosh as specimens of the
character of their countrymen.   He was the son of a
humble family in the district of Angus ; and, as many
other promising lads have done, attracted the attention of
those about him by his early abilities, and was sent to
college to be trained for the ministry of the Scotch Church
—the one outlet in which rustic genius was sure of
finding an opening.   The peculiarity in his case was,
that it was not his own family who pinched and scraped
to procure him an education, as so many have done, but
that he owed his training to a gentleman of the neighbourhood, Sir John Stuart, who divined his powers.
When his education was completed, he found himself
unable " to believe the doctrines of that or any other
church," his son informs us ; and though " licensed as a
preacher," this grim and formidable intellectual agent
never in any way carried out the purpose of his education.
After a few years which he spent in the work of a tutor,
he boldly launched himself upon London.   In one of
Bentham's rambling recollections, he describes himself as
having " taken up Mill when he was in great distress,
and on the point of migrating to Caen " (of all places in
the world !).   He is said by the same authority to have
had an annuity from the nobleman to whom he had been
tutor.   For some years after their first meeting, his con-·
nection with Bentham was very close.   " He and his
family lived with me a half of every year from 1808 to
1817," the philosopher says.   They were in the habit of
accompanying Bentham to his summer residence, whatever it might be—to Ford Abbey especially, a beautiful
old house which he rented for a number of years, where

the younger man came with " his wife and family and a
servant," a large addition to the bachelor household.   It
was no small proof of the natural amiability of old
Jeremy, by this time between sixty and seventy, that he
should have tolerated the presence of a brood of youngsters,
even when one of them was the wonderful boy, afterwards fully revealed to the world which had previously
known only the outside of him, in the autobiography of
John Stuart Mill.   Many other advantages evidently
came to the family from the friendship of Bentham.
" I brought him and his family hither from Pentonville,"
the old philosopher goes on ; " I put them into Milton's
house (afterwards his own dwelling-place), where his
family were all at ease.   Afterwards I gave him the lease
of the house he holds, and put it in repair for him."
This house was next door to his own in Queen's Square
Place, and thus Mill was established under his master's
wing.   John Stuart Mill, very likely unaware of the
great obligations of his father to his benefactor, or seeing
them from a different point of view, yet adds, in his
curious account of his own extraordinary education, his
sense that his sojourn at Ford Abbey as a boy was " an
important circumstance" in it.   "The middle-age archi-
tecture, the baronial hall, and the spacious and lofty rooms
of this fine old place, so unlike the mean and cramped
externals of English middle-class life, gave the sentiment
of a larger and freer existence, and were to me a sort
of poetic cultivation," he says.   The account of the intercourse as reported on both sides is very characteristic.
Bentham's is given with a kind of careless liberality, a
good-natured half contempt for the circumstances of the
poor man, to whom he evidently felt he had been a kind
of providence.   But the son of that poor man has no idea
of any such relationship.   " I do not know how soon
after my father's arrival in England they became ac-

quainted," John Stuart Mill says with dignity ; " but my
father was the earliest Englishman of any great mark
who thoroughly understood, and in the main adopted,
Bentham's general views of ethics, government, and law."
A cynic would smile at the difference between the point
of view of the conscious benefactor and that of the family
he served ; a contrast of feeling so common, almost in-
variable, so long as such relations last, with perhaps a
little too much claimed on the one side, and too little
given on the other.

Notwithstanding these potential services and kindnesses, however, Bentham was under no delusion as to
the amiability of his disciple and companion. " He will
never willingly enter into discourse with me," he says.
" When he differs, he is silent. He is a character ; he
expects to subdue everybody by his domineering tone,
to convince everybody by his positiveness. His manner
of speaking is oppressive and overbearing ; he comes
to me as if he wore a mask on his face." And there
were occasional breaches between them, as is apparent
from a strange letter written by Mill to Bentham in Ford
Abbey, when they were living under the same roof, proposing that they should separate at the end of the summer,
in consequence of some real or supposed coldness on
Bentham's part, but that this separation should be effected
without a word said, either between themselves or to
others — a characteristic way of conducting a quarrel.
During the time of this close intercourse " he was writing
his *British India*, while I was writing all manner of
things," Bentham adds. The *History of India* was Mill's
first work, and the foundation of his fortunes. It was the
first important work on the subject, and was of the most
bold and trenchant character, entering fundamentally
into the history of Eastern society and civilisation, and
discussing freely, not only the means by which the East

India Company could justly regulate so great an empire, but also the failures and mistakes it had made. " His interests," says Bentham again, " he deems to be closely connected with mine, as he has a prospect of introducing a better system of judicial procedure in British India." That his son should describe the book, in the fulness of years and judgment, as " one of the most instructive histories ever written," is perhaps natural in any case ; but it is still, notwithstanding so many new lights, a standard work, and one which no student of the affairs of that wonderful country could pass by. There could be no better testimony to the sense and judgment of the directors of the East India Company than the fact that the daring critic and historian, who had not certainly aimed at pleasing them in any way, received very shortly after the publication of this book an appointment in their service of the most responsible description, as one of the " Assistants of the Examiners of Indian Correspondence, —officers whose duty it was to prepare drafts of despatches for India, for consideration by the Directors." Thus uncompromising honesty and courage received their reward in a way by which rewards are but seldom attained.

After this Mill's career was prosperous, and his future assured. He had leisure for a considerable deal of miscellaneous literary work on the *Edinburgh*, and afterwards, when that was established under Bentham's auspices, on the *Westminster Review*, and replied in a hot and vigorous " Fragment on Mackintosh," to the strictures made upon Bentham's utilitarian system in Sir James Mackintosh's Dissertation. His *History of India* and *Analysis of the Human Mind* are his chief works, and would have been about all we should have known of James Mill but that he produced—a thing more rare than any history—one of the strangest compounds of human qualities and paradoxes which the world has known, a son, John Stuart

Mill, already quoted, faithfully named after his ancient patron, and the object of the most astounding training to which any unfortunate soul was ever subjected. The character of the man shines through the beginning of his son's autobiography as a light through a lantern. The picture thus afforded to us of a wondering half-scared child, whose keen uncommon intellect was able to respond like a machine to the guiding touch, with little sense of what was being accomplished in it—and of the father, alarming, serious, almost awful, a strange demi-god, un-relenting, but not unkind, enduring with a kind of stern patience the boy's appeals and mistakes, and bearing him up with the compulsion of a strong will and untiring soul into regions far beyond the commerce of a child, is very curious and interesting. With the same indomit-able perseverance and patience which were necessary to enable him in ten years' time, besides the constant necessities of pot-boiling for a large family, to write the *History of India*, this extraordinary Scotsman set himself to re-create a human soul, and did it triumphantly, making of a susceptible and sensitive nature, full of attractive weakness, credulity, and sentiment, an infant freethinker, a baby philosopher, a scholar in petticoats—a man, when he grew up, who knew almost everything except him-self, and whose rigidity of second nature, the art and influence of his father, never ceased to jar against, yet never overcame, the docility and softness of the first. In the strange household thus revealed to us, there is no shadow of any woman, no sound of domestic chat, no genial companionship of brothers and sisters, but only a prolonged encounter of two wits, the one teaching, the other listening and obeying; the man without ruth or thought for the flesh and blood he is straining, the other with innocent child's eyes fixed upon that prominent figure, ready to follow till he dies. The only thing it reminds us of is the painful training of a young acrobat, where the child obeying a lifted finger goes sheer on to risk any fall or mutilation, or death itself, nothing being worse to its scared faculties than the beating or vituperation which a mistake would occasion. Mill did not either whip or vituperate so far as appears, but his son, we can see even in the record, has his eye nervously, constantly, upon him from beginning to end : and a more extraordinary exhibition of the mental force which one nature can exercise upon another never was.

There are few things more curious than the revelation of such a mind and story, and it is a testimony to what we may call the universal imagination, the rudely symbolic faculty by which human nature classifies character, that this perfectly sincere and honest individual, in mind so much above the common level, in character so unusual, is the very embodiment of what we call the conventional, the popularly invented and received type—at once of a philosophical tyrant, a severe father, and a Scotsman. His tyranny was entirely well meant, his severity adapted to what he considered the loftiest ends, and his nationality swamped by convictions very different from those which belong generally to his race. Yet had it been given to any imaginative writer on a commonplace level to invent an intellectual Scot, it would have been a vulgarer Mill whom he would infallibly have set before the world. In his son's record, James Mill attains, as is not unnatural, an importance not elsewhere given to him, and, indeed, figures as almost more the inventor of Benthamism than Bentham himself. He was, at all events, one of the strongest and most able upholders and exponents of the Utilitarian philosophy. The master and the disciple diverged in later days from each other, in sympathy at least. Mill became independent of Bentham's help, and naturally his time was no longer his own when he entered

the India House and finally attained that independence :
and other disciples arose who, perhaps, did not please the
stern and exacting temper of one who felt himself the
chief expositor of the veiled prophet; but the master
never ceased to interest himself in the schemes of the
disciple, nor the disciple to explain and reiterate the
dogmas of the master.   Bentham would seem to have
shared even, to some extent, in what we have called the
greatest production of Mill, the creation of the mind of
his son.   The following letter, written evidently in the
view of some generous arrangement on the part of Bentham to promote the boy's interests in case of his father's
death, has something touching in it.   It was written
before Mill had begun to see land, while he was yet in
the midst of his difficulties, living with Bentham half the
year and struggling through the remainder as he could.
The child in question—strange little subject of so many
philosophical experiments—was but six years old.

" I am not going to die, notwithstanding your zeal to come in
for a legacy.   However, if I were to die any time before this poor
boy is a man, one of the things that would pinch me most sorely
would be, the being obliged to leave his mind unmade to the degree
of excellence of which I hope to make it.   But another thing is
that the only prospect which would lessen the pain would be leaving him in your hands.   I therefore take your offer quite seriously
. . . and then we may perhaps leave him a successor worthy of
both of us."

Many a parent has entertained similar hopes, and has
been woefully disappointed.   Mill was one of those happy
enough to see all his hopes carried out.   The result has
been a spectacle to all the world, regarded by few with approval, by all with astonishment; but from his own point
of view there can be no doubt that the philosopher-father
secured a success far sweeter and more complete in this
particular, than by his works either of philosophy or history,
a success not made in pen and ink but in flesh and blood

The names of Malthus and Ricardo have a right to a place in any record of philosophy, though scarcely in literature. They are little more entitled to be called writers than those who avail themselves of the arts of design, for the purpose of making mathematical diagrams, are to be known as artists. Literature is with them simply a vehicle for the conveyance of their theories to the world. Malthus was a well-born Englishman of the class of country gentry, and was educated at Cambridge, where he became a Fellow of Jesus College. He was a clergyman and held a cure in the Church for some time, but ended as a professor at Haileybury, where Mackintosh found him, and found in him a congenial soul when he accepted a similar appointment there. It is difficult to understand what caused the violent prejudice and obloquy with which his book upon population was received. A sort of madness seems to have affected his generation on this subject, as if it had been immoral to discountenance imprudent marriages, or to recommend to his countrymen the thought of ascertaining their own capacity to support a family before venturing upon the cares of one. Such sentiments are universally applauded in private, and why the public statement of them should have been attended by odium it is impossible to divine. Whether his calculations were altogether trustworthy is, of course, a totally different question. The works of Ricardo were entirely on Political Economy, works of the greatest importance in that science, but scarcely coming within our range as literature at all.

THE UTILITARIAN THEORY.[1]

The history of philosophy, in this age, is prominently that of one system only. Apart from the echoes of the

[1] By C. F. Oliphant.

Scotch school, in which Dugald Stewart, by his lectures, attracted listeners from far and near, its principal interest centres in one theory and, to a great extent, in one man. Stewart, in all probability the greatest philosopher of the age, did not, in spite of his ability, attain to the important position that was yielded, without opposition, to Jeremy Bentham. This man, contradicting everybody, arrogating to himself a higher place in the philosophical world than Aristotle or Bacon, attracted the attention of his time not more by the startling originality of his doctrines than by the imperious self-assertion with which he laid them down. Even so strong a mind as James Mill's came entirely under the mysterious subjugation, which seems to have been one of the chief powers of Bentham's intellect, and he treats the assaults made upon his master by Sir J. Mackintosh much in the same tone in which an earnest theologian would comment upon the published opinions of an avowed atheist upon matters of religion. The political controversies of the time are chiefly concerned with Bentham's new system; it forms the basis upon which Malthus built up his much discussed theories on population, and it is not too much to say that the history of the philosophy of the age is the history of Bentham and of utility. It is as the champion, or rather the inventor, of the utilitarian theory that Bentham claims for himself the highest place in the history of philosophy; it is in the same character that Mackintosh devotes all his powers to his annihilation, and it is again on the same ground that Mill takes up his defence against Mackintosh. The theory of utility is the only original philosophy of the period; the really more important school of the Scotch professors belongs properly to an earlier date, and Dugald Stewart, conspicuous as he was as an exponent and historian of philosophy, shone little as an original theorist, the doctrines which he laid before his delighted

classes being those which had been introduced by his
master and predecessor in the chair which he occupied,
Reid.   Teaching no new truths, he was still unrivalled
as an expositor of doctrines already set forward, and
Mackintosh goes so far as to say of him that "without
derogation from his writings, it might be said that *his
disciples were among his best works.*"   But, even granting
Stewart's supremacy as a teacher, as a theorist Bentham
is undoubtedly the centre round which the philosophical
activity of the period before us groups itself.   The circumstances of the time were all in favour of the success
of a new school: a state of affairs familiar enough to the
ancients, but never satisfactorily treated, or even really
appreciated by modern philosophers up to this time,
now called for a return, more or less complete, to the
tenets of the ancient masters.   The impossibility of
distinctly separating from each other the principles of
moral and political science was one of the truths most
apparent to the ancient philosophers.   It was their favourite theory that there could be little difference between
the principles upon which an individual ought to order
his own life, and those upon which a legislator ought to
order the affairs of the state or nation subject to him.
Hence the two researches could be carried on side by
side, and when we had once found out the highest rule of
living, we might be fairly certain that we possessed also
the guide to perfect legislation.   But at the time when
Bentham arose this principle had fallen into comparative
neglect, and though for some time past the problems of
legislative science had been brought prominently before
the eyes of all thinking men by the events of a troubled
period of history, and had been solved in ways more or
less concordant with the generally received maxims of
political philosophy, yet such problems still remained as
isolated difficulties overcome by exceptional means, with-

out there being any clear perception of a general principle, applicable in every case, and showing the way out of all difficulties. Adam Smith, who preceded Bentham in the field of Political Economy, had confined his attention almost entirely to the sphere of that science, devoting himself to the practical difficulties connected with national wealth, but making no attempt to arrive at a general principle of political philosophy as a whole, legislative as well as economic. It was this general principle that Jeremy Bentham attempted to produce, and to find it he had to go back to the old connection between moral and political science. But though the idea with which he begins is an old one, he makes it his own at once by beginning, as it were, at the other end of the system. To Aristotle Ethics were a part of Politics, because a man could only be properly considered as a member of a community, and his happiness was a consequence of the happiness of the community to which he belonged. To Bentham, on the contrary, the individual is the chief consideration; to him "the community is a fictitious *body*, composed of the individual persons who are considered as constituting as it were its *members*. The interest of the community then is what?—the sum of the interests of the several members who compose it." In short, to the ancient philosopher the individual was nothing more than a member of the community; to the modern the community was nothing more than an assembly of individuals.

It was in this conception of the community and of its true interests that Bentham found the theory which made him so conspicuous a figure in his own age, and has raised him to such prominence in the general history of philosophy. If the community is to be considered as nothing more than a mass of individuals, then naturally the happiness of the greatest number of those individuals must occur to every one as the obvious synonym for the happi-

ness of the community, and the ultimate end to which all
the actions of its members should tend.   And with still
stronger force it is apparent that if all moral actions
should proceed from a desire to promote the happiness of
the greatest number, legislation, which places the interests
of the community in the first rank, should always be
governed by the same principles of utility, and that no
laws are good which do not tend directly or indirectly to
produce the same effect.   As an example we may instance
the laws on usury which have been universal in all
countries, by way of limiting the power of the rich lender
over the poor borrower, and preventing what had been
found to be one of the cruellest of individual wrongs.
Bentham entirely disapproves of these laws, on the ground
that every artificial means of controlling the operations of
money and trammelling its circulation, is against the
interests of the mass, always benefited by that circulation,
however individuals may suffer.   In this, as in every
similar question, individual interests are to give way and
individual wrongs to be accepted as a necessity, unpleasant
indeed, but not sufficiently important to arrest the career
of " Utility," the greatest happiness of the greatest number.   Here, as in most of the purely theoretical parts of
his system, it is difficult to deny that, as a principle of
legislation, this sounds eminently reasonable.

In questions of moral science, however, his theory is
open to opposition on one or two of those principal and
ever open points of esoteric philosophy, the examination
of which hardly comes within our present scope.   It will
be enough to state briefly that Bentham strongly espouses
one side in the great controversy as to whether our actions
are inspired by our reason or by something else ; or, in
the usual terms, whether the ultimate motive of moral
action is something within ourselves or something external
to ourselves.   The theory of morals which he wishes to

establish fixes the ultimate motive as something which he calls pleasure, which determines our actions from without, while our reason only plays the ancillary part of elaborating the steps by which this end may be attained, without being any real authority upon the question of the desirability of its being attained. The two motives for moral actions laid down by this particular theory are the ideas of pleasures and pains; that is, the ultimate motive of action is the realisation of a pleasure or the avoidance of a pain. "Take away *pleasures* and *pains*," says Mr. Bentham, "and not only *happiness*, but *justice* and *duty*, and *obligation* and *virtue*, all which have been elaborately held up to view as independent of them, are so many empty sounds." A little later on, to prevent all doubt as to the thorough exclusion of reason in constituting these ends our motives for action, we have the further explanation, "It is no otherwise than through the *imagination* that any pleasure or any pain is capable of operating in the character of a *motive*." (In both the passages quoted, the italics are Bentham's.) This theory, which makes the motive an idea conceived by the imagination, to which the reason guides our actions, has been called the Determinist theory, as determining our acts from without, and to this Bentham appears clearly to have given his adherence.

The word pleasure, too, brings Bentham again into the region of ethical controversy. Like all moral philosophers from Plato and Aristotle downwards, our modern theorist gets entangled in the attempt to make "pleasure" a chief point in his system of morality. His vague and speculative idea of pleasure, to be conceived apparently in the abstract, entirely apart from any conditions, can convey very little practical idea to the mind. It is a phantom as impossible to grasp as the most indefinite of the Platonic ideals.

In political philosophy the points which he thinks of essential importance, are, to a great extent, identical with those subsequently demanded by the Charter. Universal suffrage he regards as indispensable, with the concomitant points of secret voting, annual parliaments, and the payment of members of the House of Commons. So far, these are the mere commonplaces of political philosophy; plans brought forward from time to time by theorists, and likely to be so brought forward again and again, until either they are accorded, or a decisive proof is given that their attainment is hopeless. But, save in one particular, these principles have not as yet gained favour in this country, notwithstanding the gradual enlargement of the franchise to an ever wider and farther-reaching sphere; the ballot, the sole particular in which his plan has been realised, is still on its trial, and does not seem to have carried out the hopes founded on it.

The real objection to Bentham's political philosophy is its universality; the theory of utility is essentially one which, if true anywhere, must be true everywhere, a characteristic useful, and even necessary to a sound theory of morals, but an important if not a fatal objection to a theory of political government. Every great problem that has yet arisen in this sphere has tended still further to enforce the truth that no universal theory of government can be laid down which will not have, in all its practical workings, to be modified according to the different customs and circumstances of different nations. These special circumstances may affect a theory in so many ways, as to the ease with which it can be introduced, the practical utility of its introduction, and the difficulties in the way of its execution, whether from already existing adverse prejudices, or a general want of respect for its provisions, as to make it impossible for any man to lay down an absolute rule for the government of a nation with anything like the certainty which may be claimed for a similarly universal rule for the regulation of individual characters or actions.

Bentham's first published work, entitled *A Fragment on Government*, was nominally an examination of a passage in Blackstone's *Commentaries*, but the germs of all his subsequent theories are to be found in it. In this he first announces his zeal " for improvement in those shapes in which the lot of mankind is meliorated by it," and declares his indebtedness to a pamphlet of Priestley's, then recently published, for the phrase which had struck his mind so much, " the greatest happiness of the greatest number," the sentence which he afterwards made his motto. His subsequent publications include many pamphlets on the special political questions of the day, including the celebrated *Defence of Usury*, but the principal works by which his distinctive theory is illustrated are the *Introduction to the Principles of Morals and Politics*, and the *Discourses on Civil and Penal Legislation*, published respectively in 1789 and in 1802.

Sir James Mackintosh has gained the name, enviable or unenviable, of the man who *should* have been the most important figure of the time, just as Bentham has the reputation of *being* the central figure. James Mill is perhaps the only philosophical writer who has failed, purposely perhaps as a disciple of Bentham, to acknowledge his pre-eminent merit. As a historian of the philosophy of the period immediately preceding his own, and that of which he formed a part, he has gained by his *Dissertation on the Progress of Ethical Philosophy* a reputation second to none. His general qualifications as a historian of philosophy may be well illustrated by the opinion of Sydney Smith, who says that " he had looked into every moral and metaphysical question from Plato to Paley." And it is less as an original theorist in either morals or

metaphysics than as a critic that he claims our attention.
His own theory of the motive of moral action he derives
to a great extent from the philosophers who preceded
him; in fact he says himself that Dr. Butler's three first
sermons are the real source of all his moral philosophy.
The importance of the moral sentiments is the chief
ground upon which he works, though his sympathy with
Hartley's principles of association makes him develop them
into the ultimate motive power which he calls conscience.
The point about him, however, that we have most to
regard at present is that he was one of the few men of
his time who emphatically declined to accept Bentham's
estimate of his own importance in the sphere of philosophy, and declared to the world which he had enslaved
that his theories were based upon unsound foundations,
expounded in unintelligible terms, and capable of no sort
of practical application.   The phraseology in which Bentham has chosen to set his theories before the world must
have struck everyone who has even dipped into his writings.   Not only does his wish to take in strict order all
the notions contingent upon the idea which he may chance
to be enunciating lead him into the confusion of endless
parenthetical sentences, but his dissatisfaction with the
usual phrases of moral philosophy then familiar to the
popular mind tends to make his utterances difficult of
comprehension.   To take one instance among many, there
is probably no phrase more familiar to everybody than
that we do a thing because we *ought* to do it: to this
mode of expression Bentham has an insuperable objection,
and suggests that whenever the word "ought" is used we
should retort "why?"   The answer to this last question
would, of course, from his point of view, be because it
tends to the general happiness, but it is difficult to think
that this sort of phraseology can be as intelligible, and
consequently as useful in practical crises as that which is

more familiar to us.   Mackintosh's vehement objections
to Bentham's theories are chiefly founded upon one great
charge, well enough known to all who have gone at all
seriously into the abstruse discussions of the different
modern theorists in the realms of moral philosophy.   He
accuses Bentham of having made the inexcusable mistake
of confounding the *Theory of Actions* with the *Theory of
Sentiments*, or, in other words, of making no distinction
between the mental process which precedes and originates
moral actions, and the standard or criterion by reference
to which we approve or condemn such actions.   There is
no doubt that in most of the systems of moral philosophy
with which we are acquainted these two points are invariably kept distinct and separate ; in fact, there is perhaps
no principle, save that of Utility as understood by Bentham,
which could combine the two in the way that he does.
But it seems to be a mistake to charge Bentham with
making a blunder in this.   The explanation which suggests itself is that Mackintosh did not perceive that this
confusion of two distinct ideas was not the blunder that
he considers it, but was intentional on the part of Bentham,
and that the theory originally designed to bring under one
head the problems of moral and political philosophy, was
equally framed with a view to simplify the difficulties of
the former by bringing to one main test those of both its
branches, and making the origin of our moral actions itself
the criterion by which our approbation of them is to be
regulated.   Sir James's objections, in short, may fairly be
deemed arguments, and to our mind most cogent arguments, against Bentham's system ; but we cannot for a
moment conceive that Bentham made the confusion
alluded to otherwise than purposely.   It is from its effect,
intended or accomplished as it may be, in unifying or
bringing under one head a vast number of different questions that the principle of Utility derives its chief import-

ance.   That its tendency to increase the general happiness
is an element, and a considerable element, in the goodness
of an action, no one could venture to deny, but Sir James
Mackintosh, with the bulk of modern philosophers, while
acknowledging this, yet made the distinction that, while
the idea is inseparable from our notion of moral approbation, it is entirely and easily to be distinguished from the
sources of our moral action.   To Mackintosh the supreme
sanction, which with him comes to the same thing as the
ultimate general motive of our actions, is the authority
and influence of conscience, which he separates from
reason.   The chief opposition that he seems to fear is that
of the school who term all appetites and all affections the
result of "self-love," and, taking this term as his text, he
proves that self-love can be, and probably is, absent from
the state of mind from which benevolent actions emanate,
and that even the appetites which might fairly be deemed
selfish may be entirely independent of the supposed
supremacy of "self-love."   Mackintosh's theory is really
more akin to the old, and even then exploded, theory of
sympathy than to any other system before him, but his
adoption of the ultimate sanction of conscience keeps us
still in the difficult position of having nothing tangible,
nothing about the meaning of which all men are agreed,
to go by.   The indefiniteness (practically) of his own
system is not much less than that of the ideas against
which he is striving.

So strenuous an opponent of Bentham's theories could
not but find a severe antagonist in James Mill.   Himself
a moral philosopher of no mean eminence, he can scarcely
find any heavier charge against Mackintosh than that
he condemned and even scoffed at Bentham.   His first
remark upon the connection sufficiently illustrates the
tone of his subsequent observations : " Sir James has made
the most perfect exhibition of himself in the article on

Mr. Bentham." He goes on, in the same spirit, to remark that Mackintosh's language proves him "to have been a man who, in speaking of others, to serve a purpose, little minded whether he was speaking correctly or incorrectly." Not even the most ardent admirer of Bentham's theories could call this a fair way of commencing a review of any criticism of any philosophical system. Mill's remarks on Mackintosh are throughout rather unfair, but the *Fragment* cannot be fairly estimated unless we attempt, which is not our task at present, a thorough review of the works of the man whom it condemns. Why Mr. Mill should have chosen for refutation the statements that Bentham and his followers "braved vulgar prejudices," and that in their phraseology and otherwise they "sought distinction by singularity," it is difficult to guess, unless it means, that, as a horse-dealer is always most eloquent in praise of the worst points of the animal which he is selling, so Mill lends his support to Bentham against the accusations which he knows to be truest.

James Mill's chief work is the *Analysis of the Human Mind,* in which he does his best to make an enlargement and illustration of Bentham's theories into an original work. His first step is the division of our states of consciousness into *sensations, i.e.* the class of feeling "which exists when the object of sense is present," and *ideas, i.e.* "that which exists after the object of sense has ceased to be present." After careful analysis of these two heads, and a dissertation upon language and nomenclature, in which we find most probably the source of the stress laid by his son upon the importance of thoroughly appreciating the exact signification of words in the study of Logic, Mill proceeds to condemn the ideas previously held about consciousness and conception, which had been called "powers of the mind," an expression which, after the perusal of all Mill's arguments, still appears more expressive than the

phrase of "states of the mind" which he wishes to substitute for it.   The only point in which Mill goes a little
beyond his master is in his extended use of the principle
of association ; like Bentham, he separates sensations into
pleasurable and painful sensations, but the theory of the
association which forms many individual ideas, first into
one complex idea, and subsequently into a generality, goes
rather further than Bentham chose to venture.   But this
generality it is hard to realise, for "when an idea becomes
to a certain degree complex, from the multiplicity of ideas
it comprehends, it is of necessity indistinct."   General
ideas, such as, for instance, the idea of "man," which Mill
himself selects, are, according to his theory, only to be
acquired by the association, or, so far as we can gather,
the agglomeration of individual ideas, and even then must
be to a certain extent vague and indefinite.

Besides the *Analysis of the Human Mind,* and the
Fragment on Mackintosh, which, though we have treated
it first, was the last of Mill's philosophical works, he
published nothing in philosophical literature worthy of
notice except the *Elements of Political Economy,* which
is no more than Bentham without his cumbrous phraseology.

The mention of Political Economy in this age, brings
before us the name of a much-abused man, Mr. Malthus.
In the one branch of the science to which he devoted
himself, he may be said almost to have created a new
school, and *Malthus on Population* will be quoted as an
authority, whether with favour or disfavour, so long as
this particular branch of Political Economy continues to
occupy the minds of theorists.   On general points, though
a great deal of his attention is devoted to details, the
subject of his work may be described as the ratio of the
population of a country to the food which the land can
produce for their support.   It must be remembered that

Malthus wrote in an age of Protection, and that the prevailing idea of the time was that the population of a country was to be fed by the produce of that country; and, things being as they were, it was a somewhat alarming revelation when he proved that, whereas the population tended to increase in a geometrical ratio as 1, 2, 4, 8, etc., the food-producing capabilities of the land could only be made to increase in an arithmetical ratio, as 1, 2, 3, 4, etc. This being so, the writer's attention was naturally directed to the possible checks on the increase of the population, and it is for this that his name has been held up by pseudo-philanthropists to the abuse of the easily-led portion of mankind, as a man devoid of sympathy towards the poorer classes, a cold-blooded statistician with an utter disregard of the feelings of the people about whom he writes. As well might a doctor, who prescribes unpleasant medicines, be called hard-hearted; all that Malthus does is to point out the fact that an evil exists, and that there are remedies, some always present and always working, and some which, in contradiction of those which do exist and should not, should exist, and might exist, but as a rule, do not. Some of the checks to population may perhaps be taken as being between these two extremes, such as utter destitution, compulsory military service, the prevalence of epidemic disease or any similar cause; but apart from such more or less exceptional checks, Malthus divides his remedies into these two classes—firstly, preventive, meaning such as are instituted by the action of reason and prudence, such as the avoidance of marriage without the prospect of being able to sustain a family; and secondly, positive, by which he implies such checks as rise unavoidably from the laws of nature, and which he classes as misery, under which head comes the utter destitution mentioned above, with the addition of severe labour, unwholesome occupations, bad nursing, or undue exposure to the weather. All forms of vice too are positive checks, but these are of the kind which have to be taken into consideration only because they exist, and the continuance of which the most ardent opponent of the excessive increase of population cannot wish. If, upon these principles, Malthus is to be criticised in such terms as everyone must have heard used about him, it is difficult to know what social system can be so framed as to escape censure.

Malthus published one essay upon the *Principles of Population* before he gave to the world the work upon which his reputation is founded. Among many treatises upon the different points of Political Economy raised in his time, an *Inquiry into the Nature and Progress of Rent, and the Principles by which it is Regulated,* published in 1815, is perhaps the most important.

HENRY HALLAM, born 1798 ; died 1859.

Published View of the State of Europe during the Middle Ages, 1818.
Constitutional History of England, 1827.
Introduction to the Literature of Europe in the 15th, 16th, and 17th Centuries, 1837-39.

JOHN LINGARD, born 1771 ; died 1851

Published Catholic Loyalty Vindicated, 1805.
Antiquities of the Anglo-Saxon Church, 1809.
History of England from the first Roman Invasion to the Accession of William and Mary, 1819-1830.
And many polemical pamphlets.

THOMAS M'CRIE, born 1772 ; died 1835.

Published Life of John Knox, 1812.
Life of Andrew Melville, 1819.
Suppression of the Reformation in Spain, 1829.

JEREMY BENTHAM, born 1747 ; died 1832.

Published A Fragment on Government, 1776.
                View of the Hard Labour Bill, 1778.
                Principles of Morals and Legislation, 1780.
                Defence of Usury, 1787.
                A Plea for the Constitution, 1803.
                Scotch Reform Considered, 1808.
                Elements of the Art of Packing, 1810.
With many other works on political and economical science.
His chief works were reproduced in French by Dumont.
                Traités de Législation Civile et Pénale, 1802.
                Théorie des Peines et des Recompences, 1802.

Sir JAMES MACKINTOSH, born 1765 ; died 1832.

Published *Vindiciæ Gallicæ*, 1791.
                Introductory Discourse to Lectures on Law, 1799.
                Dissertation on Ethical Philosophy, 1831.
                    (in *Encyclopædia Britannica*) separately, 1836.
                History of England, 1830-31.
                Fragment on Causes of Revolution of 1688, 1834.
                Life of Sir Thomas More.

JAMES MILL, born 1773 ; died 1836.

Published History of India, 1818.
                Elements of Political Economy, 1821.
                Analysis of the Human Mind, 1829.
                Fragment on Mackintosh, 1835.
With many lesser works on political subjects, and contributions
                to reviews and other periodicals.

Rev. THOMAS ROBERT MALTHUS, born 1766 ; died 1834.

Published An Essay on the Principle of Population, 1798.
       „   „   enlarged in 2d edition, 1803.
                An Inquiry into the Nature and Progress of Rent,
                1815.
                Principles of Political Economy, 1820.
With smaller works on Political Questions, the Corn Laws,
                Poor Laws, etc.

CHAPTER IX.

THEOLOGIANS.

IT is hardly possible to reckon so important a name as
that of Paley as belonging to the period within which we
are limited.   It is true that his last publication, and one
of his most important, came before the world only in
1802, but neither in his life nor his work was there any
variety from the moderate religiousness and scientific
dignified apologetics of the eighteenth century, to which
he belonged.   His first publication on Moral Philosophy
appeared to some of Bentham's friends to be likely to
"take the wind out of the sails" of the Utilitarian system,
and alarmed them momentarily, eliciting from the philosopher himself a half cry of panic.   But this alarm
seems to have been without foundation.   Paley's works,
whether judiciously or not we need not pause to inquire,
are still text-books at the universities, but the scepticism
against which he sets his forces in array was not of the
kind to which we are now accustomed, which takes much
of the force from his defence.   They are still however
eminently readable in a merely literary point of view, and
extracts might be made, in which the reader would find
much happiness of expression and force of illustration,
without any of the disadvantages of antiquated polemics.
Dr. Watson, the Bishop of Llandaff, who lived for some
time, almost a neighbour of the poets, on the edge of the

Lake country, and in his day too defended Christianity,
without perhaps any very warm enthusiasm for it, requires
mention at least.   Godwin dedicated to him a volume of
the sermons which he had preached in the earlier part
of his career, which was, perhaps, but a doubtful compliment to his orthodoxy.   Dr. Horsley Bishop of St.
Asaph, Dr. Beilby Porteous Bishop of London, and Dr.
Marsh Bishop of Peterborough, can scarcely be said to exist
save to students of the most dusty shelves in theological
libraries.   Dr. Hartwell Horne, the author of the *Introduction to the Study of the Scriptures,* is better known and holds
a more living place : but even he still lingered in the eighteenth century, and cannot be called a man of his time.

It is not, however, in detached names or treatises that
we find the special religious interest of the age, but in the
predominating Evangelical party then in full zenith of its
power in England, first in all great and good works, and
attaching to itself not only the most devout but the most
benevolent and philanthropic spirits of the age.   The
men who with the hard labour of twenty years won from
England the abolition of slavery—a step which cost so
much in actual expenditure, and by which the nation
ventured nobly upon a great sacrifice and effort for abstract right with doubtful results—belonged, without
exception, to this straitest of religious communities.
These men can scarcely be said to belong to the history
of literature, but they all dabbled in composition more or
less, pouring forth pamphlets, speeches, pleas of every
kind, masses of evidence, and appeals full of the eloquence
at least of sincerity, and glowing earnestness and zeal.
Among these guides and leaders, however, were some
whose gift of speech was indisputable, and who have left
behind them volumes of sermons and essays and church
histories which have supplied reading for thousands of
devout persons, and have been considered by their readers

as something almost divine——as far superior to the less
sacred array of books, as heaven is to earth : for the finest
poetry, the highest philosophy, is not read by half so
extended an audience, or regarded with half the admiration which a popular book of sermons will call forth.   To
a great mass of our countrymen, even now, such productions embody all that is known of literature.

Still more was this the case in the beginning of the
century, when books were neither so cheap nor so plentiful as now; and when the Evangelicals were at the
height of their power.   We doubt much whether any
extended religious movement can ever exist, especially
among the millions, which is not strongly leavened with
those views which are identified with the Low Church
party.   The claims of Church and priesthood do not
touch the heart of the populace, and we doubt greatly
whether all the splendour of a restored ritual would ever
have the same effect upon the English crowd as the
homely excitement of a prayer-meeting, or the emotional
preaching of one who acknowledges himself to have been
the greatest of sinners.   In the time of which we treat,
the zeal of Evangelical religiousness was penetrating
among the wealthy, as it had already become supreme in
the lower classes.   It was the time when the " Clapham
Sect" was at its height, when Simeon at Cambridge was
proselytising with all his might, and sending forth, in all
the warmth of a propaganda, the young men whom he
converted ; when Isaac Milner, Dean of Carlisle, a large
and jovial figure full of genial force and breadth of life,
recommended the self-denying doctrines of modern Puri-
tanism by the warmth of his *bonhommie* and enjoyment
of that existence which he fervently believed to be a
perpetual struggle against the world and sin ; when Wilberforce wrote his *Practical View,* and prayed and fought,
and talked and jested, with the same mixture of oppressive

doctrine and gay spirits; when brilliant parties ended
with exposition and prayer, and society itself was almost
persuaded in the midst of corruption and license to be
converted too. Religious life has rarely gone through a
more remarkable phase. It was to break up after a
time, and give way to the germ of reawakening Catholi-
cism and the attractions of tradition in the Church of
England: and in a less important, yet scarcely less
interesting way to find an outlet, bursting its husks, and
pressing into a higher air of enthusiasm, in the movement
of new zeal and high-toned spiritual life, which has been
connected with the name of Edward Irving. But, in the
meantime, the Evangelical party was supreme, doing all
the good that was being done, aiming at every benevolent
enterprise and effort of salvation that came within its
reach, seeking freedom for men's bodies and for their
souls, and believing that it had found a way by prayer
and preaching, and the glow of social piety, to reconcile
the Church and the world.

The incongruous point which has always cast a certain
air of unreality upon a society so truly pious and full of
good deeds and great effort, is the contrast between the
ascetic side of Christianity—the self-denial which was the
chief of virtues, the injunctions to come out of the world
and be separate, the denunciation of worldly pleasures
and gaieties which were its dogmatic utterance—and the
extremely prosperous, luxurious, and enjoyable life of the
leaders of this religious party. When such doctrines are
preached by apostles who go out scripless and shoeless, with
their lives in their hands: when they are put forth by
ascetics worn with toil and fasting, by men whose self-
abnegation is evident, whose life has no solace but God's
service, of whom we can even feel, with a high sense of
fitness, that they have served God for naught and depart to
their recompense in another world, having had none in this

—there is nothing that jars upon our feeling of harmony and appropriateness. But when the same sentiments are preached by the happy and wealthy, men with all the enjoyments of life about them, sitting at luxurious tables, surrounded by happy families, successful in everything, moving in a circle of admiration and love and praise, yet bidding us all the time to come out of Babylon, to love not the world, to regard life as a struggle and this earth as a vale of tears, there is at the best an inappropriateness in the preaching, which, certain as we are of the sincerity of the preachers, perplexes the sympathetic and brings a laugh from the cynic. The picture of the Clapham Sect living in those luxurious villas, with everything that wealth could command, in a pleasant commotion of congenial society, hushed and sanctified by the prayer-meeting, but still full of amusing talk, of delicate flattery, of the very atmosphere of pleasure, is as bright as any picture of society could be, but it does not harmonise well with the tenets of world-renunciation and self-denial. There is no reason why they should not have been happy and enjoyed themselves,—neither was there any reason why Henry Martyn, the devoted missionary, should not have had twelve hundred a year from the Indian government. Nothing can take away from the certainty of his real devotion, his almost martyrdom, " yet the ideal would be better without" that comfortable income, as Sir James Stephen says. And so we feel that the ideal of a Church militant, of a band who in the world are to have tribulation, and who were eager in claiming for themselves all the characteristics of those who were desired in their utter humiliation and poverty to take no thought for the morrow, would have been better had they been less rich, less happily off, less safe from all the assaults of fate.

This, however, though it explains the secret sentiment, not strong enough to be called suspicion, with which this party has always been regarded, the imagination being instinctively displeased by their luxurious wellbeing, is at the best a fanciful objection. And it is better to indicate who they were and what their connection with literature, than to discuss the curious intricacies of nature which make it possible to combine the precepts of asceticism with all the comforts of life, and yet be perfectly sincere both in the profession of the one and the enjoyment of the other. Of William Wilberforce, and of his work and character, everybody knows something. He was the most remarkable and distinguished of the four indefatigable champions whose untiring exertions procured the abolition of slavery—which is fame enough for a man. For twenty years, in season and out of season, he urged upon the country and upon Parliament the horrors of slavery, the shame and sin to a free and Christian people of holding slaves. It has happened on several occasions since then, and notably in our own day, that England has done a thing which cost her a great deal both in purse and feeling, and of the advantage of which nobody was quite convinced, because it was right. The abolition of slavery was one of these. It ruined one of our wealthiest dependencies, it took a great deal of money out of the national pocket, it has not turned out all that hope suggested it might; but, nevertheless, it is a thing which it is impossible to regret, as it was a thing impossible to refuse : and to Wilberforce and his associates, Thomas Clarkson, Zachary Macaulay, and Grenville Sharp, belongs the immortal credit of having convinced and persuaded the national mind that it was impossible. Before he had entered upon this warfare, however, when a young man just leaving college, gay, witty, wealthy, with all the world before him, and no disinclination towards its pleasures, Wilberforce had become a member of the party with which all his life was henceforward associated. The religious teachings which had guided his childhood had been thrown off in the freedom and turmoil of youth, but he was still a young man at the opening of his career when these severe and absorbing doctrines became the deliberate choice of his excellent intellect and fervent heart. The piety of his early home had been inspired by Whitfield, and the wave of religious revival of which he was one of the chief agents; but the fervent religious feeling of Wilberforce was of a different type from that which went out into the highways and hedgerows to compel the poor and neglected to come in. His was not the fashion of mind which naturally seeks the brotherhood of the poor, or yearns over the ignorant masses. There was another work to be done in England, a work which should supplement and complete the work of Whitfield and Wesley. It had been the common people who had heard them gladly, as their prototypes in Judea heard a greater than they. But the other half of the world—the educated, the well-off, the people to whom no missionary or evangelist got access, whom the wandering preacher at the street corner moved only to contempt or resentment, by what means were they to be reached?

Wilberforce's sympathies were all among this higher class. He was as fond of society as he had been before his conversion. An active member of Parliament, a man in full intercourse with the world, and amid all the excitements of public life, street-preaching or personal effort among the miners or the cotton-spinners would have been entirely out of his way; but he could speak to the people about him with at once a warm brotherly sympathy and the authority of one who had made religion his chief object, without relinquishing anything that was really good in life. His ardent mind was full of the desire to do something, to say his say for the sacred cause which he had espoused with all his faculties; and it was this desire and not any literary impulse which produced the *Practical View*, which is his only connection with literature, and the sole permanent utterance of his life. It had been " for several years the earnest wish of the writer of the following pages to address his countrymen on the important subject of religion," he says in his preface to his book. The form it took was that of a contrast between the prevailing " Religious System of Professed Christians in the Higher and Middle Classes in this country," and " Real Christianity;" and the persons he addressed were men such as those whom St. Paul addressed on Mars' Hill, but whom few preachers were bold enough to summon to the bar, with the same unhesitating plainness with which they arraigned their humbler neighbours. Wilberforce did not appeal to infidels or unbelievers. He made no assault upon scepticism. His object was to show the respectable and intelligent how far their calm and easy ignoring of religion, even while professing it, was unlike the spirit of Christianity. There is no special charm of style to redeem his treatise from the respectful oblivion into which—after a popularity greater in degree than that which almost any other kind of literary production enjoys in its day—religious books are apt to fall. And nothing can be more unlike the works which have gained something of a similar influence in our own time. It is to be feared that to Wilberforce that broad and conciliatory treatment which translates the time-worn language of Christianity into the phraseology of its philosophical opponents, by way of betraying these latter tenderly into something like faith, or approval at least— would have appeared flat blasphemy. He would have had no understanding of the process which turns the love of Christ into the Enthusiasm of Humanity. The society which he addressed was not one which required such methods. It was as much Christian as orthodoxy re-

quired, and could be made to demonstrate its zeal for
religion " by mentioning the name of some acknowledged
heretic." What made the heart of the good man burn within
him was to see how completely it could ignore the creed
it held, and how the truths, that were to him vital, had
got mossed over and practically obliterated by spiritual
apathy and the calm of habit. The insidious idea that it
did not much matter what a man believed, so long as he
did believe sincerely, and lived a life in accordance with
his principles, was to him a poison terrible to contemplate.
" With such transcendent means of knowing the way which
leads to life, what plea can we have to urge in our defence
if we remain willingly and obstinately ignorant ?" he asks.
No doubt as to the certainty of the means of acquiring
that knowledge had entered his mind, nor was it necessary
to take into consideration such doubts in his audience.
That they suffered the light to grow dim, or preferred to
enjoy a distant glimmer from its general illumination,
rather than to rejoice in the particular glory of a radiance
which pervaded and revealed every corner of the soul,
was his complaint. It is the universal complaint of the
preacher in all generations, even in the very bosom of the
Church itself; but it is not on religious indifference only,
or neglect of the " transcendent means of knowing," that
a religious writer of the importance of Wilberforce would
be likely to address society now.

He had, however, the fullest hearing in his own day.
The public, to whom his book was addressed, received and
read it with devotion. In six months almost as many
editions were called for, and 7500 copies sold; and from
the time of its publication in the end of last century—
1797—until quite recent days, it has gone on in periodical
reproduction, commending itself still, it is to be supposed,
to devout souls, though no longer perhaps to the higher
classes, the educated part of the community, to whom it